RAISING
SONS
and LOVING IT!

RAISING
SONS
and LOVING IT!

> Helping Your Boys
> Become Godly Men

GARY *and* CARRIE OLIVER

ZondervanPublishingHouse
Grand Rapids, Michigan

A Division of HarperCollins*Publishers*

WITH DEEP AFFECTION and eternal gratitude, we are honored to dedicate this book to the life and ministry of Rev. Dr. Clyde McDowell, loving husband, faithful father, loyal friend, compassionate pastor, and visionary president of Denver Seminary.

Clyde was a model of what it means to love the Lord with all your heart, all your soul, and all your might. He had an especially significant impact on our sons.

Clyde was one of the few people we have known of whom it could be said, in the words of Hebrews 11:38, that he was a man of whom "the world was not worthy." He ran a great race and he finished as strong as he ran. All of us are richer for having known him.

Clyde, we love you, we miss you, and we are looking forward to hearing your hearty laugh and seeing your big smile on the other side.

ACKNOWLEDGMENTS

WE OWE AN ENORMOUS DEBT of gratitude to our sons Nathan, Matt, and Andrew. It's not easy being the sons of parents who teach and travel and write books on raising sons. Thanks for giving us permission to share some of your stories. Know that you've been some of our best teachers and our most patient critics and eager learners. You've given us a deeper understanding of what it means to love, you've helped us develop greater patience, and you've been the source of inexpressible delight and joy. Never forget that next to our relationship to our Lord Jesus Christ and to each other you have been God's greatest gift to us. We love you, we treasure your uniqueness, and we're honored to be a part of your family.

Norm Wright and I had enjoyed a great morning of fishing on the Snake River in the Grand Tetons when, almost out of the blue, he remarked, "You and Carrie need to write a book on raising sons." I don't remember my exact response, but it was something to the effect that I wasn't going to write a book about raising sons until ours were successfully raised and out of the house. The fact that you are reading the words on this page is testimony to Norm's encouragement to not "play it safe," but to share what God has taught us thus far in our adventure of raising sons.

Chapter 3 was written with the help of our good friend Nancy Schmer Hoffmann, R.N., M.S. Nancy had worked as a pediatric nurse for over ten years when God led her to pursue a graduate degree in counseling at Denver Seminary, with a specialty in working with children and adolescents. Nancy works with us as a counselor with the PeopleCARE Clinic, which is part of The Center for Marriage and Family Studies at John Brown University.

Chapters 14 and 15 were written with the help of our good friends Steve and Twyla Lee. Steve and Twyla have been married for twenty-five years and have raised two terrific boys, Trevor and Ryan. Over the years we have communicated, commiserated, and celebrated together, and together have prayed for wisdom in dealing with the challenges (and opportunities) of raising sons. Steve is the coauthor of *Boys to Men* and currently serves as professor of psychology at Huntington College, and Twyla serves as director of the social work program at Taylor University.

We're grateful for the creativity and encouragement of our literary agent, Greg Johnson. We also want to thank Sandy Vander Zicht at Zondervan for the personal interest she has shown in this project, as well as Tim McLaughlin and Dirk Buursma, who helped with the editing.

The support and encouragement of the staff at The Center for Marriage and Family Studies at John Brown University, and especially the exceptional work of Jan Phillips, have been invaluable. A final word of appreciation goes to the donors who have made The Center for Marriage and Family Studies a reality.

Our prayer for our sons and for you our readers is "that Christ may dwell in your hearts through faith . . . that you, being rooted and established in love, may have power, together with all the saints, to grasp how wide and long and high and deep is the love of Christ, and to know this love that surpasses knowledge—that you may be filled to the measure of all the fullness of God" (Ephesians 3:17-19).

CONTENTS

INTRODUCTION
The Masculine Crisis

Out OF THE COUNTRY and enjoying a much-needed vacation, we were in the checkout line in a grocery store and happened to glance at a television monitor displaying a CNN newscast. Suddenly the picture switched from a report on the Kosovo crisis to a BREAKING NEWS! screen. Early into the story we noticed the small print at the bottom of the screen: COLUMBINE HIGH SCHOOL, LITTLETON, COLORADO. Littleton had been our home for a dozen years before moving within the last year to John Brown University in Arkansas, so we were especially concerned about what was happening back in our former hometown.

Even the reporters weren't sure what was happening but mentioned at least a couple of gunmen. Witnesses said they had heard numerous gunshots and seen dead and wounded students. In the hours that followed we saw anguished parents waiting for hours as police teams sealed off the area; student survivors who were either in tears or trying to look cool while reporting bodies lying dead in a school library; and photos of teenage killers who had that morning departed for school with guns, bombs, and booby traps—bent on a fatal mission.

The killers, we learned in the days to come, had hung out with a small group who called themselves the *Trench Coat Mafia*. Rain or shine, they wore black trench coats, sported swastikas on their clothing, advocated white supremacy, played war games, threatened friends and neighbors with death and destruction, and made a video they showed in one of their classes that hinted at the lethal spree they eventually acted out. Most of their classmates thought they were harmless. They apparently chose Hitler's birthday to prove otherwise.

On April 20, 1999, the time bomb of hatred, bitterness, resentment, and repressed anger exploded at Columbine High School and was heard around the world. Targeting kids they knew to be Christians . . . targeting the popular jocks who had made fun of them . . . targeting at least one black boy . . . the two Columbine seniors gunned their way through a well-planned and bloody rampage that left one teacher and twelve students dead, and a score wounded. Then, according to police, Eric Harris and Dylan Klebold took their own lives.

In the days following the massacre, the media scrambled to explain its cause: A diet of violent movies? Video games, whose aim was to see how many cyber-characters you can "kill"? Uninvolved, out-of-touch, ill-informed parents? Schools with too few metal detectors and security guards? The easy availability of guns? Or was it, as one commentator observed, the logical conclusion of a postmodern society that has refused to believe in absolutes, in basic morals, in the existence of right and wrong, in the importance of character and discipline?

Tragically, the Columbine shooting is singular only by virtue of its magnitude. On February 2, 1996, a fourteen-year-old walked into algebra class at a junior high school in Moses Lake, Washington, killing the teacher and two students. On October 1, 1997, a sixteen-year-old in Pearl, Mississippi, killed his mother—then went to school and shot nine students, two fatally. On December 1, 1997, a fourteen-year-old went to his West Paducah, Kentucky, school and killed three students who were praying in a school hallway and wounded five others. On March 24, 1998, two boys in Jonesboro, Arkansas, aged eleven and thirteen, tripped a fire alarm, then shot into the lines of students as they evacuated the building, killing four classmates and a teacher. On April 24, 1998, a fourteen-year-old in Pennsylvania (nicknamed Satan) took his father's pistol and went to his middle school prom, killed the faculty sponsor, and wounded several others. On May 19, 1998, in Fayetteville, Tennessee, an eighteen-year-old student allegedly shot to death a classmate in the school parking lot. Two days later in Springfield, Oregon, a fifteen-year-old entered Thurston High School with three guns, killing two teenagers and wounding more than twenty. The police later found that his parents had been shot to death at home.

Confused by society's mixed messages about what's expected of them as boys, about what it means to be a man; feeling out of touch with emotions they don't understand and don't know how to deal with; raised in a culture that glorifies violence and declares that there are no absolutes—with weights like these, many young men feel a sadness and disconnection they cannot even name. Even if they understood it, most of them don't have the skills or the words to talk about it—or the people they would feel comfortable talking to.

As staggering as these stories are, a common thread running through them all makes them even more distressing. In every one of these shootings the murderer was a boy. At the time of this writing, there are sixty-some adolescents on death row— and all are boys.

The travesties of which Littleton is only the latest are just one indicator that these are difficult and challenging days to *be* a boy and to *raise* a boy. In this book you will read about new research showing that boys are doing worse in school than they did in the past ... that, compared to girls, many seemingly strong boys have remarkably fragile self-esteem ... that the rates of both depression and suicide in boys are frighteningly on the rise.

It is no exaggeration to say that today there is a crisis of masculinity. In the process of raising three boys, we have experienced the pressures of parents raising sons. The media, and especially television, seem to sucker boys into equating masculinity with sexual experience. We live in a culture that is increasingly violent, a culture that provides opportunity—especially in video games—for even young boys to express violence.

One more book is not going to solve a problem this big. Yet, as a result of our research and an ongoing desire to learn more about males, we submit this book in the hopes of making at least a small contribution to the welfare of sons—yours and ours.

"Books in a way are sacraments that make the communion between an author and a reader possible," Ken Gire writes in *The Reflective Life.* He goes on to say the following:

> The white paper and black ink are the means through which one heart is revealed to another. But the paper and the words are merely the elements of the sacrament. What is sacred is the heart that writes the book and the heart that sits in silent communion to take and read what has been written. The words that are read are small, wafer-like things. But sometimes, on some page, God humbles Himself to come through some of those words and touch the reader's heart. It is not the words that are sacred but God who is sacred . . . and the person to whom He comes.[1]

So we offer readers only our hearts, our research, our experience with our three sons. In preparation for this book we have surveyed thousands of other parents of boys for their input and stories. We have read avidly in the marriage/family field throughout our nineteen years of marriage. Both of our professions are in the counseling field. We are relationship pursuers in that we have tried to make relationships primary in our lives, beginning with our intimate relationship with the Lord Jesus Christ.

You'll read a lot about our own children in this book. Nathan is seventeen years old, with a strong will we first recognized when he was a toddler. After years of taming his will, we've seen him arrive nearly to adulthood with an inner strength that is the source of a strong identity. And yes—we still thank God for Nathan's strong will, even when it continues to challenge us. Matt is fifteen, full of life and fun and playfulness. True to his spontaneous and impulsive nature, he makes his share of poor decisions along with the good decisions he makes. So Matt's the son who has needed our help particularly in this area. Andrew, ten years of age, is a people-person. He loves his friends. He amazes us with his maturity and wisdom, even at his young age.

Our children have made mistakes, have been bratty, and have had their times of being disrespectful, disobedient, and downright intolerable. By writing about them here and there within the pages of this book, we don't intend to disclose their every weakness and failure, but only desire to be candid about our weaknesses and failures as parents. We're all still growing and learning—we all have faced difficult days, and surely will again.

In fact, it is those difficult days that made us hesitant to write any book about parenting, at least until our sons leave home. Because all three of our boys are still at home, it's likely that they will still make mistakes. Maybe some big mistakes—at the least, sad ones, at the worst, heartbreaking ones. We certainly know that *we* will keep on making mistakes. There are still plenty of things that could happen that could discredit what we have written here.

We have tried to craft this book in such a way that it does not contain merely our opinion. We don't always assume that what has worked for us will work for you. In fact, we stress the opposite: that every boy is made in the image of God, that God has chosen to make every one of our sons unique. Your son is unique, his brothers and sisters are unique, and his mom and dad are unique. That's why we've aimed to give you a map, some practical tools, and a strategy to understand the uniqueness of your son—some ways to raise him up in the way he should go, consistent with who God designed him to be and become.

Writing a parenting book is a humbling experience. With every page we write we are reminded again and again of our own mistakes. We have so much more to learn about raising sons. We are all in the same boat in our failure to consistently be the right kind of parent, in our confusion over how to raise very different sons, in our sleepless nights agonizing over the welfare of the boys we love, and in the joy our boys bring us.

Yet, however much we love our sons, caring is not enough. Many parents have told us that before they had children of their own they had the idea that if you loved your kids enough, if you prayed for them enough, if you modeled Christ for them enough . . . then you were almost guaranteed to grow healthy kids with a heart for Jesus Christ. Unfortunately, being good parents does *not* guarantee that you will have healthy kids.

Somehow, taking what we've learned from God's Word, developmental research, popular literature, and surveys and interviews with thousands of parents—and after systematically studying these sources—we've identified principles, characteristics, concerns, and strategies for raising boys.

It's said that raising boys is walking a line between feelings of futility and feelings of fulfillment. It seems like you just get to know and understand your son, only for him to change on you. It doesn't seem fair, but that's the way it is. So we pray hard, we ask others to pray hard for us and for our sons, and we ask God to bring good and godly influences into their lives.

So enjoy this book and use whatever is helpful—in order that the relationship between you and your son might be nurtured by insight, by love, and by God's grace.

At the beginning of each chapter we've listed the chapter's key points, so you can see what's coming and so you can decide to digest, skim, or skip that chapter for the time being. We've also included a section at the conclusion of each chapter called *Small Beginnings*, which suggests some simple, practical ways you can apply what you've read. These suggestions have proven helpful not only with our own sons, but also in the lives of hundreds of other parents.

Chapter One

THE UNIQUE CHALLENGE OF RAISING BOYS

UP FRONT *In this chapter...*

- ✦ Now is a difficult time to be a boy and to raise boys—who are experiencing increasing rates of violence, depression, and suicide, as well as decreasing school performance and self-esteem.
- ✦ Society's rules for being a man have changed. No longer marked by clear roles of provider, protector, and procreator, manhood today suffers from contradictory messages about just what it is that makes a man.
- ✦ Boys are often raised to be thinkers, not feelers. Success is defined for boys as strength and silence. Girls, on the other hand, are raised to focus on emotions and relationships.
- ✦ Research underlines the hazards of growing up male—less nurturing by parents, more birth defects and learning disabilities and genetic diseases. Yet there have never been more tools and resources to foster healthy male development and fathering.
- ✦ Although many fathers were taught to shape their life by the expectations of adult figures—and especially father figures—they can learn what it means to be made in the image of God and teach a better way to their sons.

1964 WAS A GOOD year. The Beatles came out with "I Want to Hold Your Hand" and "She Loves You." Manfred Mann was singing "Do Wah Diddy Diddy," and, believe it or not, Louis Armstrong was at number one with "Hello, Dolly."

In the fall of 1964 the Beach Boys released another of their hits, "When I Grow Up to Be a Man," in which they asked what—for boys during the sixties—were normal questions: When I grow up to be a man, will I still have fun? Will I have regrets? Will I still have a sense of humor, will I settle down or travel around? Will I want in a woman what I like in a girl, will I get married, will I stay married, will my kids be proud of me?

During virtually all eras of recorded history, men knew what it meant to be a man. They knew what their roles were and what was expected of them. They were to provide, protect, and pro-create. Even as recently as a generation ago, society was a lot clearer than it is now about what it meant to be a man. The roles were much more clearly defined, the questions much simpler. Men did men things, and women did women things. A man's identity lay in what he did—a pattern the Beach Boys followed when they asked, "What will I be when I grow up to be a man?" For, you see, their uncertainty was about what they would *do*, not what they would be. Would they be drafted? Would they get a good education? Would they have a good job? Would they get married and stay married?

The primary role of the '60s man was *breadwinner.* This man's man was someone who could cuss, chew, spit, swear, fight, fuss, feud, and fornicate. Relationships? They took a backseat. If you are a dad now, research tells us that you probably grew up in a home with a father who didn't know a lot about nurturing, didn't talk much, and wasn't available for you.

Needless to say, today is a whole different story. The social climate has changed, the questions have changed, and the rules have changed. When boys look around at the social landscape for directions on what makes a healthy man, they obtain an abundance of inconsistent, contradictory, and confusing information and attitudes about what is supposed to define masculinity.

As you look at your son and visualize him as a man, what do you see? What do you think it means to be a man? What characteristics come to your mind when you hear expressions such as "He took it like a man . . . Act like the man of the house . . . Are you a man or a mouse?" Where did you learn these characteristics? What are they based on—the standards of our society, or the clear teaching of Scripture? Both? Are these characteristics as valid today as they were twenty years ago?

What it means to be a man is a confusing and largely unresolved issue for many men. Raised with fathers who were often unavailable, uncommunicative, or uncaring, they learned that success meant to be strong, silent, stable, and a good provider. While their sisters received encouragement and training in nurturing and being sensitive to others' needs, the boys received training in logical thinking, problem solving, risk taking, assertiveness, competition, and aggression—and were discouraged from expressing vulnerable and tender emotions.

Most men have been taught how to pursue excellence as breadwinners, human machines, and performers. Meanwhile, everything else has suffered. In fact, it's become clear during the past few decades that growing up male can be hazardous to your health. The following list of male-specific inequities, inferiorities, and wounds describes the male world in which we are raising our boys:

- Infant boys receive fewer demonstrative acts of affection from their mothers and are touched less than infant girls.
- Boys are talked to less often and for shorter durations than girls.
- Infant boys are more likely to be held facing outward, toward the world and other people. Girls are held inward, toward the security, warmth, and comfort of the parent.

- Infant boys crawl, sit, and speak later and tend to cry more, yet girl toddlers are more likely to get a positive response when crying for help than boys.
- When a child complains of a minor injury, parents are quicker to comfort girls than boys.
- Because boys are considered by most people to be emotionally tougher than girls, they are more often reprimanded in front of the whole class for misbehavior, whereas girls are more likely to be taken aside and spoken to more softly.
- Young boys are admitted to mental hospitals and juvenile institutions about seven times more frequently than girls of similar age and socioeconomic background.
- Boys are much more likely to suffer from a variety of birth defects. Boys are more prone to schizophrenia and suffer a higher incidence of mental retardation. In fact, about two hundred genetic diseases affect only boys, including the most severe forms of muscular dystrophy and hemophilia.
- Boys are twice as likely as girls to suffer from autism and six times as likely to be diagnosed as having hyperkinesis.
- Boys stutter more and have significantly more learning and speech disabilities than girls. Some research suggests that dyslexia is found in up to nine times as many boys as girls.
- When boys become teenagers, they are told they must be prepared to be mutilated or die in order to protect women and children and the ideologies of their country.
- In Vietnam over 58,000 American men died, compared to eight women.
- Men have a six hundred percent higher incidence of work-related accidents, and men die from work-related injuries approximately 20 to 1 over women.
- While the government compiles many statistics on the needs of working mothers, few statistics are kept on behalf of fathers, including the special needs of the over three million men who are single parents.

- Suicide rates are about four times higher for men than women.
- Men make up about eighty percent of all homicide victims, are victims of about seventy percent of all robberies, and constitute seventy percent of all other victims of aggravated assaults.
- Men's life expectancy is as much as nine years less than women's.
- Ninety-nine percent of the prisoners on death row are males.[1]

Masculinity is in crisis. These are difficult and even dangerous times to raise boys.

That's the bad news. The good news is that this is also a *great* time to raise a son. These are times of tremendous opportunities to help nurture young men with a love for the Lord, with a passion for truth, and with a commitment to character and integrity.

It's a great time because effective and valuable resources are finally emerging from the Christian and secular communities to help us better understand and more proficiently parent our boys. As late as the mid-1980s, my review of both academic and popular literature on male development and fathering didn't take long at all. I was astonished at the scarcity of information and resources.

On the other hand, there were mountains of literature on women, entire university departments devoted to women's issues, numerous longitudinal studies on the developmental issues unique to women. At one of the largest bookstores in the country, I found a "Women's Issues" section of *sixteen* shelves; with the help of a sales associate I finally found two shelves of books on "Men's Issues"—most written by women disenchanted with men.

In *Knights Without Armor,* a groundbreaking book on the interior lives of men, gender relations expert Aaron Kipnis observed that today "we have *Smart Women, Foolish Choices* and *Women Who*

Love Too Much. There are *Wild Women with Passive Men* and women with *The Cinderella Complex,* who find *No Good Men* while facing the *Don Juan Dilemma* in relationships with men who have *The Peter Pan Complex* or *The Casanova Complex.* They wonder *Should Women Stay with Men Who Stray, Men Who Can't Love,* or *Men Who Cannot Be Faithful?* There are also *Men Who Hate Women and the Women Who Love Them* and *Men Who Hate Women and the Women Who Marry Them,* who have given rise to the *Men Who Hate Themselves and the Women Who Agree with Them.*"[2]

The dearth of men's books in comparison to women's books seemed too blatant a disparity to be a mere oversight. The cover story of the May 11, 1998, *Newsweek* magazine acknowledged how for years the academic community had virtually ignored the needs and concerns of males. "Until recently, girls got all the attention," wrote Barbara Kantrowitz and Claudia Kalb. "But boys need help too."[3]

The good news is that this disregard for male concerns is in the process of being corrected. Researchers are looking at every aspect of the developing male and creating a new field of inquiry: the study of boys. Excellent books have been published recently, containing startling new research on boys—among them, *A Fine Young Man* and *The Wonder of Boys* by Michael Gurian, *Real Boys* by William Pollack, and *Boys to Men* by Steve Lee and Chap Clark.

It's also a great time to raise boys, because in the past decade God has initiated a movement in the hearts of men unparalleled in recent generations. In 1991 a new organization got off the ground with a men's meeting in Boulder, Colorado. The first Promise Keepers conference drew 4,200 men—a number that quickly jumped to 22,000 in 1992 and to over 50,000 in 1993. Today well over a million men have attended a Promise Keepers event. What's even more important is that this work of God in the hearts of men is spreading to churches and denominations around the world.

Yet how, some ask, is the men's movement different from the feminist movement? There is, in our observation, a significant difference. The feminist movement, at least from our perspective, has been primarily a sociopolitical movement that encompassed, among other things, a healthy and legitimate response to the repression, inequality, and abuse of women. It sought equality, increased power, and greater political influence.

What God is doing in men is not a sociopolitical movement, but a personal and relational one. It's not about gaining power, privilege, and prestige, but about how to feel, how to love, and how to be better husbands, fathers, and friends—admittedly a scary proposition for some men. There has even been criticism of Promise Keepers because of an alleged international plot to "feminize" men. Nothing could be further from the truth. The bulk of the men's movement (and certainly the Christian men's movement) is not about the feminization of men, but about their *humanization*. It's about helping men become all that God intended them to be.

Yet change is difficult—and the longer a habit has been held, the harder it is to change. Given that truth, the best time to implement change is before boys become men. We've worked with many men who felt that they were too old or that their habits were too ingrained for any transformation to take place. But through the grace of God, change can—and does—happen.

One way to observe the powerful results of such a change is to look through the eyes of a real man as we worked through some of the issues of his childhood, and how his experiences affected him as a husband, father, friend, and pastor.

A BOY NAMED PAUL

I first became acquainted with Paul through a note he handed me. Earlier that day, as part of a workshop for pastors on effective counseling, I had had the attendees complete a self-test. Paul had attached a copy of the test to the note he gave me.

"As you will see in the test," he wrote, "I have some serious problems with my self-image. I've known this for a long time, and the testing pointed out to me that the problem is more severe than I had realized. I know it is handicapping my ministry and my effectiveness as a witness for Jesus Christ. I'm praying that with God's help and your counsel, these matters can be corrected."

Then came a phone call from Paul early the next week. "This is one of the most difficult things I've ever done," he told me, "but I know my problems aren't going to magically disappear. I need help." Raised in a Christian home, Paul had attended Christian schools, had graduated from a theologically conservative seminary, and was the pastor of a growing evangelical church.

"When I first entered the ministry, I expected conflicts with elders, deacons, and members of the congregation," he continued. "I knew there'd be financial problems. I knew I wouldn't have answers to all these problems, and that I'd need to consult other leaders for advice.

"In short, I felt I had realistic expectations and was well trained to handle the problems of church life."

He paused and took a deep breath. "What I didn't expect, what I wasn't ready for, what seminary hadn't prepared me for, were the struggles *within myself*." These were problems, he went on to explain, of worry, self-doubt, feelings of inadequacy and insecurity, fear of failure.

"In seminary I learned eschatology, ecclesiology, and soteriology—but not what it means to be a man. I never learned to understand and deal with my emotions." So Paul had dealt with these secret, unspoken problems by overworking (he averaged sixty hours a week in the office) and overeating (he was about sixty pounds overweight).

With all his heart Paul wanted to be a good son, husband, father, friend, and pastor. He had exerted enormous amounts of physical and emotional energy striving for his lofty goals. But what I saw before me was a broken, confused, discouraged, and exhausted middle-aged man.

"I feel lost," he confessed. "I'm no longer sure what it means to be a real man. I'm not sure where to start. And I'm not sure I care."

I told him that he wouldn't have made an appointment to see me if he hadn't cared—and that his willingness to be vulnerable with me was another big step on the road to healing.

In a later session we talked about how boys become men. Much of how we see ourselves, I observed to him, is influenced by the way significant people in our lives see us. We discussed how he perceived the ways in which his mother and father viewed him. I asked him to think more about it before we talked again at our next session.

The next week he didn't wait for me to start the session. "You know, as I thought about it, I was amazed at the power of the labels I received from my parents and others," Paul said. "My folks have always stamped me with the label *lazy*, and I always feel that I'm lazy. It doesn't matter if I've already put in twelve hours of work—if I watch TV for just one hour, I see myself as lazy. My father used to say: 'You're so lazy you stink.' That still haunts me. Even when I worked hard as a child, I was never praised or rewarded. I was continually compared to my father, who 'when *I* was a boy' worked harder than Superman himself."

Paul's father was a good and honest man, an elder in his church, a hard worker. Unfortunately, when Paul was young, his father worked so hard that he wasn't home much. Consequently, the majority of Paul's parenting came from his mother.

"I know my dad loved me," Paul remembered, "but when I think of my dad, I think of someone I could never please— someone who was always encouraging me to do more, do better, work harder."

It was several weeks later when Paul dropped off a handwritten note at my office. It read, "In our last session when you talked about how many people do things in order to be loved, and they try to read parents and others to sense what they want from us—that truly describes me. I have spent most of my life trying to please teachers, friends, and parents—and trying to shape my life by their expectations. I went through all of my schooling, including seminary, harboring these underlying motivations, trying to find a deep sense of security and love."

Within nine months Paul had lost nearly forty pounds, was working between forty and fifty hours per week, was spending quantity and quality time with his wife and three young children, and said he was "experiencing the abundant life that Jesus talks about and that for many years I had spoken about. I am learning," Paul told me, "what it means to be a man."

Paul's case is really no different from those of hundreds of men I've worked with. And it could be similar to your own story, or it could become the story of your son. Paul's experience illustrates the importance of understanding what it means to be made in God's image—with a mind, a will, and emotions.

It is not difficult to relate to Paul, for as young boys most of us were taught the rules:

- Work long and hard.
- Ignore your emotions.
- Seek achievement and status.
- Be self-reliant.
- Don't let anyone push you around.
- Don't have close male friends.
- Avoid anything that could even come close to looking like or being mistaken for femininity.
- Maintain an emotionally distant and nonrelational attitude toward sexuality.

Most of us learned these rules too well.

The good news is that it is never too late to change, to grow, to take another step in the process of becoming "conformed to the likeness of his Son" (Romans 8:29). Yet many men simply don't make the attempt to change, to take that step of growth. For every Paul there are hundreds of other men who lack the courage or the opportunity to change—which is why our roles as parents of boys is so critical; it's why we thoroughly reviewed the popular literature and academic research about raising boys, and why we surveyed or interviewed several thousand married and single parents of boys. It is, finally, why we wrote this book.

SMALL BEGINNINGS

1. Take a few minutes to complete this *Report Card for Parents*. It will help you identify some of your strengths as well as some of your areas of need, and it will assist you in applying what you've just read. When you've completed it, if you're in an exceptionally gutsy mood, ask your son to fill it out with you in mind, and then discuss the results.

A REPORT CARD FOR PARENTS[4]

A B C D F   1. Do I praise my son at least once a day?

A B C D F   2. Do I treat my son as a worthwhile member of our family?

A B C D F   3. Am I available when my son wishes to talk to me?

A B C D F   4. Do I include my son in family plans and decisions?

A B C D F   5. Do I set reasonable guidelines and insist that my son follow them?

A B C D F   6. Do I treat my son the way I treat my best friends?

A B C D F   7. Do I treat my children equally?

A B C D F   8. If I tell my son to do something, do I frequently take the time to help him understand why instead of saying, "Because I said so!"?

A B C D F   9. Do I set a good example for my son?

A B C D F   10. Do I think positive thoughts about my son and encourage achievements?

A B C D F   11. Do I take an interest in my son's education and attend PTA meetings?

A B C D F   12. Do I occasionally give my son a hug or friendly pat on the back?

A B C D F   13. Do I encourage attendance at weekly religious services?

A B C D F   14. Do I spend time each day looking over my son's schoolwork with him?

A B C D F   15. Do I send my son off to school each day with a kind word of encouragement?

A B C D F   16. Does my son see me pray?

A B C D F   17. Does my son see me reading the Bible?

A B C D F   18. Does my son hear me take responsibility for my mistakes and apologize when I am wrong?

A B C D F   19. Do I talk to my son about my emotions?

A B C D F   20. Do I intentionally honor my son as much as I think he should honor me?

A B C D F   21. Do I understand my son's culture?

A B C D F   22. Have I listened to some of the music my son listens to?

A B C D F   23. Am I aware of who my son's "heroes" are?

A B C D F   24. Do I understand the basic male and female differences?

A B C D F   25. Do I understand the impact of testosterone on my son's development?

2. What are three of the greatest joys you've experienced as the parent of a boy?

3. What are three of the greatest challenges you face as the parent of a boy?

4. In prayer thank God for the joys and commit your challenges to him. This would be a great time to

recommit yourself to a new beginning in your relationship with your son.

5. If you really want to take your commitment to excellence in parenting your son to the next level, find three friends who will agree to pray for you and your role as a parent every day. For nearly ten years we have had several couples praying for us in our role as parents and for our sons. It has been a great source of encouragement and of accountability.

Chapter Two

WHY BOYS ACT THE WAY THEY DO

UP FRONT *In this chapter ...*

- ✦ The cultural atmosphere of today's world—including substance abuse, teen pregnancy, suicide, rape, robbery, assault—produces physical, emotional, and spiritual anxiety in children. Parents need to be aware of the stressors their sons are facing so they can help them learn appropriate coping skills.
- ✦ The fast-paced life many families lead and the ever-increasing speed of technological and informational change has gravely reduced time for building relationships. Society will not encourage parents to make their children a priority; parents must choose to take responsibility for how they spend time.
- ✦ Teenagers are being bombarded with freedoms formerly reserved for adults—yet their seeming sophistication is characterized by a profound irresponsibility in the use of those freedoms.
- ✦ Conscious and unconscious myths of masculinity influence a boy's development into manhood: Real men are big, brave, and strong ... men can't express emotions or affection ... crying is for sissies ... all men are experts on sex ... work defines a man's existence.

> ✦ In Jesus Christ, God has provided hope and healing for our
> damaged culture. Parents can model the ability to feel and
> to be a whole person for their sons, and they can shine
> Jesus' light into a lost and broken world.

Bullets. BOMBS. THREATS OF violence. The evening
news brought Vietnam and a half century of cold war with
Russia into the homes of baby boomers. It was a scary world, but
somehow through it all we weren't afraid to leave our homes—
probably because the dangers were "over there."

But the war has moved home during the last few years, and
the new killing fields now include our children's schoolyards.
Boys as young as twelve are arrested for crimes as sordid and serious as murder, and guns and other lethal weapons are found at
their homes and in their school lockers. Surveys tell us that many
of our children believe they could be the victim of a violent crime
before graduating from high school. Teens today clearly live in a
cultural climate that takes a physical, emotional, and spiritual toll
on them—and it is critical for parents to be aware of this climate
in order to help their teenage sons cope with it.

THE ADOLESCENT LANDSCAPE

The good news is that most young boys move through adolescence and into adulthood in healthy ways. It would be a mistake to paint a developmental picture of our boys as frustrated,
angry young men only a breath away from lashing out. At the
same time, however, they face significant threats and deal with
a myriad of fears that their parents never knew when they were
their children's age.

"Today's children face challenges, pressures, and worries
that Norman Rockwell never imagined when he painted his

quintessential pictures of Main Street, America," said Donna Shalala, United States Secretary of Health and Human Services. "For too many children, the future looks more like the nightmare on Elm Street than the American dream."[1]

There are plenty of hard facts to support her statement. Consider the fact that in the next twenty-four hours:

- 1,000 unwed teenage girls will become mothers.
- 1,106 teenage girls will get an abortion.
- 4,219 teenagers will contract a sexually transmitted disease.
- 500 adolescents will begin using drugs.
- 1,000 adolescents will begin drinking alcohol.
- 135,000 kids will bring a gun or other weapon to school.
- 3,610 teens will be assaulted; 80 will be raped.
- 2,200 teens will drop out of high school.
- 2,750 kids will watch their parents separate or divorce.
- 90 kids will be taken from their parents' custody and placed in foster care, a group home, or institutional care.
- 7 kids (ages 10–19) will be murdered.
- 7 juveniles who are under the age of eighteen will be arrested for murder.
- 6 teens will commit suicide.[2]

The sobering reality is that homicides are the second-leading cause of death among fifteen- to twenty-four-year-olds. In fact, the Center for Disease Control recently reported that the rate of youth killings in the United States is ten times higher than in Canada, fifteen times higher than in Australia, and twenty-eight times higher than in Germany or France.

Life has always been challenging for adolescents, yet the current consequences of teen behavior are leaving wounds that cut deep into the heart of societal health and morale. Adolescents have always had problems, but seldom like today's problems. You may have seen this comparison:

Typical Adolescent Problems During the 1940s	Typical Adolescent Problems During the 1990s
Talking	Drug abuse
Chewing gum	Alcohol abuse
Making noise	Pregnancy
Running in halls	Suicide
Cutting in line	Rape
Dress code	Robbery
Littering	Assault

These changes are reflected in the media as well. *Roseanne* writer and coproducer Betsy Borns has compared some of the leading characters from the most highly rated television family of the 1990s—the Conners—with their 1950s counterparts, the Cleavers from the *Leave It to Beaver* show.[3]

June Cleaver	Roseanne Conner
Full-time homemaker	Full-time waitress
Tidy house, perfect hair, punctual meals	House is a war zone, hair is a rat's nest, and meals come from a box
Loves baking, washes pots	Loves bakeries, smoked pot
Memorable romantic moment: goes to the door and kisses her husband	*Memorable romantic moment:* goes to a gay bar and kisses a lesbian
What she's proudest of: lives for her husband and children	*What she's proudest of:* allows her husband and children to live

Ward Cleaver	Dan Conner
Steady, white-collar job	Fixes trucks. Has ring-around-the-collar
Often called *sir* by sons Wally and the Beav	Was once called *The Führer* by daughter Darlene
Enjoys taking in news via the paper	Enjoys taking in beer via the can
Children are punished when he comes home	Children are punished when Roseanne feels like it
Sage advice to sons: "Always follow the golden rule"	*Sage advice to son:* "Stop peeing behind the garage—you're killing the tomatoes"

The Beaver	D. J.
Shy, adorable	Sly, incorrigible
Once hid money in sock drawer to save up for a bike	Once hid women's magazines in bedroom to read them, uh, "intimately"
Memorable childhood moment: smashed Ward's car window with a baseball	*Memorable childhood moment:* went to a school party and touched a boob
Charming boyish prank: Got stuck trying to see if there was real soup in a billboard soup bowl	*Charming boyish prank:* stole the family car and drove it into a ditch

Wally	Darlene
Shocking teen confession: admitted he lied to impress a girl; later apologized	*Shocking teen confession:* admitted she tried cocaine; later tried it again
Dream date: quiet evening in a well-lit soda shop	*Dream date:* loud night in a cheap motel
Taste in friends: brought his oily pal, Eddie Haskell, home after school	*Taste in friends:* brought her abused boyfriend, David, home to live
Phase he went through: wore his hair in a ducktail, reprimanded by June	*Phase she went through:* dyed her hair black; sunk into a two-year depression

Times have changed, priorities have changed, and values have changed—and few of these changes have been good for marriages, for families, or for our sons.

THE FAST TRACK—AND ITS EFFECTS

The increasing pace of life can be as perilous for our sons as the changes that have taken place over the past few decades. Julia Ward Howe—who penned the *Battle Hymn of the Republic*—once asked Senator Charles Sumner to help a certain struggling family.

"Julia," the senator said with a sigh, "I've become so busy that I can no longer concern myself with individuals."

"Charles, I find that quite remarkable," the woman replied. "Even God isn't that busy."[4]

Many of us have been seduced into chasing after everything but quality relationships—and too often that excludes relationships with our children as well. Gone are the days of stress-free relaxation and peace of mind. Anxiety and stress abound, and even our vacations are scheduled, pressured, and frantic.

Our kids are growing up in a world that doesn't know how to take a break and feel good about it. "We must have some room to breathe," says physician Richard Swenson. "We need freedom to think and permission to heal. Our relationships are being starved to death by velocity. No one has the time to listen, let alone love. Our children lay wounded on the ground, run over by our high-speed good intentions."[5]

So we are overextended, and there are few prospects for relief in the future. The rate of change in our society is staggering, and that's on a *slow* day. Information is multiplying at exponential speed, and life is becoming more complex each day. The top-of-the-line technology of last year is the has-been of today, but we keep chasing to try to keep up. Dr. Swenson makes this observation: "No one in the history of humankind has ever had to live with the stressors we have acting upon us today. They are unprecedented. Our stress levels are unprecedented for many reasons. . . . Exponential change is one stressor we dare not underestimate. . . . Complexity and overload remain hidden to most people's understanding but are crushing stressors."[6]

The busyness of our everyday lives has crowded out quality relationships. Many parents are so busy working that they have little time for their children. A national survey recently found that the average mom and dad spend twenty-two fewer hours per week with the family than they did only a generation ago. Consequently, we create the illusion of success while sacrificing the richness of relationships and the well-being of our teens. When experts talk about *success* and *progress*, they are not referring to an improvement in the quality of our relationships. Invariably, they speak of progress in terms of money, technology, and material goods. The time and attention our sons desperately need is missing from the standard measurements of success.

Such an inadequate definition of success is recognized by the Carnegie Council on Adolescent Development, which noted that "the social and technological changes of this century, and especially of recent decades, have provided many young people with remarkable material benefits and opportunities to master technical skills; they have also introduced new stresses and risks into the adolescent experience."[7]

It's time that we give back our time, attention, and guidance to our sons. We need to face the fact that society will not help us do so. It will continue to grow more complex, racing faster and faster like a hamster running on a wheel. If our sons are to have the best of our parenting touch, we will need to make a decision to give it to them. As gifts entrusted to us by God, our sons deserve the best parents possible—which means we need to slow down, step back, reevaluate our priorities, and become students of our sons and their generation.

GROWING UP TOO QUICKLY OR TOO SLOWLY?

In the wake of recent violence in our schools, we've been listening carefully to the many voices who argue that our children are growing up too fast. But as we've talked with other parents, we've wondered if the problem really is that kids are growing up too fast—or not fast enough.

Renowned psychologist David Elkind argues that our children are growing up too fast. "Society no longer seems to regard children as innocent or to see childhood innocence as a positive characteristic," he writes. "Children are exposed to every nuance of human vice and depravity under the mistaken assumption that this will somehow inure them to evil and prepare them to live successful, if not virtuous and honorable, lives. This assumption rests on the mistaken belief that a bad experience is the best preparation for a bad experience."[8] Earlier in his book Elkind made the pivotal observation that teenagers have had a premature adulthood thrust upon them:

> Teenagers now are expected to confront life and its challenges with the maturity once expected only of the middle-aged. . . . In today's society we seem unable to accept the fact of adolescence, that there are young people in transition from childhood to adulthood who need adult guidance and direction. Rather, we assume the teenager is a kind of adult.[9]

Psychologist Ronald Koteskey sees the issue in a different light:

> The idea that adolescents should act like children is a part of our invention of adolescence. This began about 150 years ago when educators concluded that it was harmful to mature too early. . . . Today we just accept the "fact" that adolescents are to act like children rather than like adults and it becomes a self-fulfilling prophecy. We do not want them to grow up too fast, so they do not. . . . If you expect your teenagers to act like irresponsible children, they will. On the other hand, if you expect them to act like responsible adults, as people did for thousands of years, they will.[10]

Indeed, developmental research has confirmed that adolescence is now being extended well into one's twenties. On average, men now marry in their late twenties, while women tend to marry in their mid–twenties. Even more striking is the significant number of young adults who continue to live at home, dependent on their parents, delaying adulthood rather than embracing it.

So who's right, Elkind or Koteskey? Are our boys growing up too fast, or not fast enough? Perhaps both, in a way. When it comes to what have been traditionally considered adult freedoms, our boys are clearly growing up too fast. At younger and younger ages they are being handed adult options, particularly violent and sexual options. They simply don't spend a lot of time as innocent children anymore.

Yet it's also true that teenage boys are generally growing up *too slow*. They may walk into adult situations at younger and younger ages, but generally shun the responsibilities, disciplines, and self-restraint that have typically accompanied those adult options. The challenging task of godly parents is to work with their sons prayerfully in ways to make a connection between the much-desired freedom and the much-needed responsibility. For it is the union of this freedom and this responsibility that defines maturity.

MYTHS OF MASCULINITY

In our efforts to make this connection, however, and help our sons grow into maturity, we bump into myths about what it means to be a man. Just as every boy has a conscious and unconscious map, or model, of masculinity by which he measures himself, so each parent has a conscious and unconscious map of masculinity by which they measure their sons. Unfortunately, many of the early lessons young boys learn about manhood often become the sword on which, later as adults, their identity and self-respect are impaled.

So what does it mean to be a "real man"? What do you picture when you hear the word *masculine?* What images come to mind? When you hear, "He's a real man" or "He's a man's man," what kind of man are they talking about? Does anyone in particular come to mind?

Although our society puts a lot of pressure on men to be masculine, society isn't always clear about what it means. This was true when middle-aged folks were kids, and it's even more true today. Psychiatrist and family therapist Frank Pittman makes the following comment:

As a guy develops and practices his masculinity, he is accompanied and critiqued by an invisible male chorus of all the other guys who hiss or cheer as he attempts to approximate the masculine ideal, who push him to sacrifice more and more of his humanity for the sake of his masculinity, and who ridicule him when he holds back. The chorus is made up of all the guy's comrades and rivals, all his buddies and bosses, his male ancestors and his male cultural heroes, his models of masculinity—and above all, his father, who may have been a real person in the boy's life, or may have existed for him only as the myth of the man who got away.[11]

All these social pressures lead to the perpetuation of stereotypes, or myths, of what it means to be a man. Our boys grow up in a world dominated by such myths, handed down from the significant men in their lives and embellished by cultural stereotypes. During the past several years we've worked with hundreds of men who have shared their stories, and from these conversations we've collected a list of stereotypes or myths of masculinity these men felt governed their development—or at least greatly influenced it. If we're not aware of these myths, they can be dangerous, squeezing our boys into a mold that restricts their growth and development.

As we explore several myths of masculinity, ask yourself if your view of masculinity has been influenced by any of them. If so, how? Is it possible that some of these myths still influence how you understand manhood? Could any of these myths be influencing how you parent your son?

Myth: A Man's Man Is Big, Brave, and Strong

Muscles, says this myth, are equated with masculinity—size and strength equal superiority. If you're over the age of forty, you may remember the Charles Atlas advertisements in comic books and magazines—at beach, skinny guy loses girlfriend to muscled guy ... skinny guy buys bodybuilding program and gets buff himself ... former skinny guy goes back to beach and retrieves girlfriend, who oohs and ahhs over his new *Body by Atlas*.

This particular myth was encouraged by many of the stories we heard as children—the man is the big, strong, competent, conquering hero. In the classic myth, the hero, almost always a big, strong man, ventures forth to conquer supernatural and seemingly overwhelming forces. He returns, weary but victorious, and he is richly rewarded.

So what effect have these stories had on our view of males and females?

Even the scriptwriters of the Disney movie *Beauty and the Beast* understood the bankruptcy of this myth. Gaston, the narcissistic and mightily muscled specimen of masculinity, is clearly meant to be the oaf, the bully, and an inferior match for Belle compared to the gentle, sensitive, and protective Beast.

It is true that physical strength and aggressiveness are the male traits that have traditionally set men apart for two activities: livelihood (hunting and gathering) and combat. For millennia men have carried out these activities with enthusiasm, fortitude, and skill. But thanks to a host of changes during the past century, physical strength has become relatively obsolete as a male role requirement.[12] How many jobs are there anymore—at least, how many jobs associated with money, power, and status—that require exceptional physical strength?

We've worked with males who were paragons of physical strength, but who were relational and emotional preadolescents. While they spent hours every week pumping iron, their mental, emotional, and relational muscles had atrophied. However healthy bodybuilding can be, neither size nor strength determines manliness.

Myth: A Man's Man Isn't Emotional and Doesn't Express Affection

When boys are little, they have both the ability and the freedom to express a wide range of emotions. But somewhere along the line they learn it's not okay to express such emotions, natural though they may be. This nonexpression of emotions becomes detrimental in adult relationships, and in marriage it often becomes a source of frustration for wives.

Up until recently, men were often portrayed as calm, cool, and rational, even in the face of great danger. Their emotional displays were limited to righteous anger or an uncomfortable gollygosh-gee-shucks tongue-tied expression of love. On the other hand, women would swoon with emotions at the slightest provocation—they'd even cry over television commercials! Emotions of all different qualities and quantities have been in many cases a woman's trademark rather than a man's.

Yet, to say a man isn't emotional is blatantly false. (In chapter 4 we'll look at what Scripture and developmental literature on boys say about males having emotions.) The corresponding reality, however, is that many males don't understand their emotions and have never learned healthy and appropriate ways to express them. Their emotions *may* be in remission, but they're there nonetheless.

Granted, many males act as though they've graduated from the Marcel Marceau School of Verbal and Emotional Expression, as if to only emphasize how they differ from women in the verbal expressions of emotions. While some of these differences are biological, others are cultural. Women are expected, allowed, encouraged, and even in some sense required to reveal certain emotions—while men are often expected and culturally encouraged to deny or suppress them.

Yet there are numerous exceptions to the stereotypical emotionally bound male—which suggest that rather than being something inherent in all males, the difficulty in emotional awareness and expressiveness is as much a function of social conditioning as biological determinism. After all, even some women find it difficult to reveal their feelings.

To see a powerful example of how to deal with emotions, we need only to look to Jesus, who experienced and expressed deep emotions. Surely we as parents would do well to help our sons cultivate that same ability as we teach them to become a man's man.

Myth: A Man's Man Isn't Weak and Shouldn't Cry

Several years ago Mike Ditka was fired as head coach of the National Football League's Chicago Bears. At his press conference he expressed genuine emotion and shed a few tears. No one laughed at him or called him a "girly-man." In fact most of the men I talked with could relate to his pain and respected his appropriate expression of emotion.

It's not that men need to run around crying all of the time, or that true men should always weep at television commercials. The point is this: Real men have the ability to express vulnerability and shed tears at appropriate times. We should help our sons grow to the place where they are secure enough and aware enough of their emotions that they can shed tears in tragic, painful, or devastating situations. We should help our sons learn, as Paul wrote, that Christ's power is made perfect in our weakness (see 2 Corinthians 12:9).

Myth: A Man's Man Is an Expert on Sex

"I remember my first week in junior high as if it was yesterday."

It was during our second counseling session that Eric told me about his passage into adolescence. "The kids were bigger, the ninth grade boys seemed like men, and the ninth grade girls looked a whole lot different than the girls in sixth grade did.

"I remember like it was yesterday my first day in gym," Eric said in a reflective tone. "I wasn't very big for my age, had no body hair yet, and before that day I had never realized how important the size of my penis was until a big kid with hair all over his body pointed at me and told his friends to look at the little guy with the 'teeny-weenie peeny.' I'll never forget the fear, humiliation, and shame I felt." It was clear to me that even twenty-five years later he still felt some of the humiliation and shame. Eric had bumped into one of the many myths of masculinity that consciously and unconsciously affect the passage into manhood.

We once asked a women's church school class for a list of three things they could do that would communicate love to their husbands. Their list? (1) Sex. (2) Sex. (3) Sex.

Yet just beneath the surface of the women's laughter in response to the reading of the list lay some uneasiness with its reality.

This myth has devastating consequences that are especially powerful as boys move through junior high and high school. These are years of massive changes in their bodies—and years where they can grow in understanding what it means to become a man and to develop healthy relationships with girls. The myth distorts God's design, leads boys to equate sexuality with sexual intercourse, and urges them to view women as objects to be conquered rather than as daughters of God who complement and complete. This myth subjects men to—and causes boys to place each other under—completely unrealistic expectations no one can live up to.

Sure, men tend to value sex in thoroughly different ways than women do—especially in frequency of perceived need for sex. Yet the vast majority of men we have surveyed and worked with do not claim to be great lovers, nor do they have an insatiable sexual appetite (although a few older men *wished* they did). The myth of the man as sexual expert puts enormous pressure on normal men like these and can create a performance anxiety that will cripple a man's ability to function sexually.

This myth also diverts men from developing healthy attitudes about sex. When sex becomes reduced to performance, it's easy to lose sight of the *person;* often all hope for intimacy is abandoned—which leads in turn to misunderstandings about what it means to be a sexual man and makes men much more vulnerable to pornography and sexual addictions.

Myth: A Man's Value Is Determined by What He Does and How Much He Earns

Let's face it—work is necessary for survival. In the best of cases, work also gives a man some degree of pleasure. A third purpose of work for men is more insidious: Work too easily defines a man's masculinity. Work becomes the yardstick by which a man measures his success or failure. We've worked with many men who gauge their self-worth by their professional or occupational status.

Few things are more important to a man's pride, his identity, his sense of value and worth, and his manhood than the work he does. That's why many men become workaholics. There's a difference between loving what you do and becoming addicted to it, between having a passion for your work and being a workaholic. If you can set your work down, let it go at the end of the day, not go through withdrawal, not ruminate about it throughout the evening or weekend—if you can do most of these things, you probably aren't addicted to work.

What do our boys see when they look at their father? A man who plays as hard as he works? A man who works as though Jesus was his boss, or as though the satisfaction of his need for significance is all-important? A man who is financially responsible, or one whose money is his master? A man whose greatest desire is to become more like God, or to get more and have more?

Any addiction, even to something like work, only separates men from other people and from themselves and limits their ability to hear God's voice. The problem isn't the work. Work is necessary; it is important and valuable. The problem is that many males have allowed what they do to define their significance and to be the basis for their security. And on both those counts, work is woefully inadequate.

These myths have produced a generation of men who are perilously out of touch with what it means to have been created in the image of an infinite, yet personal, God. As a result, too many men have little idea of how to take care of themselves. They generally don't understand how to express their emotions; they don't know how to deal with emotional pain—so their primary response to pain is to anesthetize it. If men don't feel *anything*, then they won't feel pain, or fear, or grief, or loss.

The numbing effect of these myths works for a while, but over time men need more and more anesthesia—a need that leads to all kinds of destructive habits. Take alcohol, for example—men tend to drink to excess more than women by a ratio of about four to one. Men die at a greater rate than women from causes of death associated with excessive drinking. The most devastating loss men have suffered by accepting these distortions, however, is the loss of heart—the loss of their ability to feel, of their ability to be tender as well as tough, of their ability to be whole-orbed people, and of their ability to model what this looks like for their sons.

THERE IS HOPE!

Someone once observed that the paradox of this time in history is that we have taller buildings, but shorter tempers; wider freeways, but narrower viewpoints; we spend more, but have less; we buy more, but enjoy it less; we have multiplied our possessions, but reduced our values; we've learned how to make a living, but not a life. Problems and issues this deep can appear overwhelming. Yet we agree with futurist and author Alvin Toffler that "we must continue to search out solutions that offer hope rather than lament the thorny, knotted problems we face.... One of the most important things we can give to our kids is the sense that they live in a world being born, not a world dying."[13]

With God still on the throne, with the strong promises of God's Word, with the indwelling power of the Holy Spirit, and with moms and dads who are committed to gaining a greater understanding of the world in which they live, there is no reason to give in to despair. Author, educator, and psychologist Steve Lee reminds us of a wonderful truth:

> There is hope. For every disturbed adolescent killer, there are scores of teens who are serving people in community projects. For every teen who is playing violent video games or immersing himself in Internet pornography, there are hundreds of others who are involved in extracurricular activities. For every rebellious teen whose anger finds an outlet in crime, there are thousands of teens quietly going about the business of achieving in school and preparing for their future. And for every parent who neglects their child, oblivious to the hurts they feel and problem behaviors they perform, there are caring parents doing the best they can to give their teens what they need to be mature, godly, emotionally healthy adults. The perils of contemporary culture are powerful, but they are not inescapable.[14]

Christians put their hope in a Savior who brings healing to a lost and broken world. We can learn from Nehemiah, a leader whose vision was not clouded by the pain of adversity. As Nehemiah set out to rebuild the walls of Jerusalem, obstacles came from within and without. In the midst of that situation the people expressed their deep anxiety: "The strength of the laborers is giving out, and there is so much rubble that we cannot rebuild the wall" (Nehemiah 4:10). And the Jews' enemies were saying, "Before they know it or see us, we will be right there among them and will kill them and put an end to the work"(Nehemiah 4:11).

In spite of these obstacles, Nehemiah persevered through the hard times to accomplish the goal God had laid on his heart. "Therefore I stationed," wrote Nehemiah, "some of the people.... When our enemies heard that we were aware of their plot and that God had frustrated it, we all returned to the wall, each to his own work" (Nehemiah 4:13a, 15). God has given us the privilege and responsibility of helping our teenage sons reach godly adulthood. Let's not lose sight of the goal, even when our strength feels like it's giving out and cultural corruption and decay threaten to put an end to our work. Our God is able, for he *is* in control, and he *will* "meet all [our] needs according to his glorious riches in Christ Jesus" (Philippians 4:19).

SMALL BEGINNINGS

1. Think about your role as a parent. What morals and values are you now modeling for your son, based on what you say, what you watch, what you listen to, and what you do?
2. What are your son's three favorite music groups? What is his favorite radio station? What kind of movies does he go to? What's been his favorite movie in the past six months?
3. What proportion of freedom and responsibility do you give your son? Are the two balanced?
4. For the next thirty days, listen to your son's favorite radio station for at least ten minutes a day. If you don't like the music (or don't understand it), refrain from criticizing or dismissing it, but listen to it and ask God to help you understand the culture and values that are influencing your son. Use what you learn to help you pray with greater insight and wisdom for him and for his generation.

Chapter Three

ARE BOYS REALLY THAT DIFFERENT?

What are little girls made of?
Sugar and spice, and everything nice,
That's what little girls are made of.

What are little boys made of?
Snips and snails, and puppy dog tails,
That's what little boys are made of.

— OLD NURSERY RHYME

UP FRONT *In this chapter ...*

+ Understanding developmental and biochemical gender differences between boys and girls can help parents acknowledge the unique ways their sons relate to the world.

+ When comparing male and female brain structure, girls have a larger connection between the right and left sides of the brain and are better able to access both sides at the same time—a fact that explains why boys have more difficulty learning to read written material and to read emotions on other people's faces.

+ Boys have a lower level of serotonin (a neurotransmitter that decreases aggressive behavior) and a higher level of testosterone (a hormone associated with aggressive behavior). Parents and teachers can cope with this biological tendency toward rowdiness by providing creative activities that release excess energy.

◆ The right hemisphere of a boy's brain is better developed than the left hemisphere, enabling him to have more success in performing spatial tasks and in focusing intently on one task at a time.

◆ Boys take in less sensory data, have a shorter attention span, and use more space than girls do when playing. Action themes for home and school activities are helpful to use with boys.

◆ Because males prefer to view objects that move quickly in space, they are at risk to become addicted to television, video games, and the Internet. Rapid imagery overstimulates one side of the brain and can limit the development and growth of a boy's skills and intelligence.

◆ When an embryonic male is six weeks old, a surge of testosterone occurs that produces the male sex organs and influences the brain to develop differently from a female brain. Testosterone continues to have a powerful effect on boys as they grow and separate from their parents. Mood swings, temper flare-ups, bad attitudes, desire for instant gratification, and fascination with sex are common.

◆ Research has not supported the theory that increased levels of testosterone alone lead to increased incidences of violence. Parenting styles and societal pressures play an equally important role in the development of a boy.

I AWOKE TO A morning unlike any I'd yet experienced. "It's today!"

Carrie was wide-awake (not unusual, since she's a morning person), shaking my shoulder.

I must not have responded immediately, because she said, more loudly this time and with unmistakable enthusiasm, "Gary, it's today!"

I emerged just far enough into semiconsciousness to mumble, "I know it's today. . . . What day did you think it was?"

"No, Gary—my water broke!" Now I *was* fully awake, and it wasn't long before we were on our way to the hospital.

As it turned out, we needn't have hurried. Nathan was doing just fine *in utero* and in no particular hurry to come out. But when he did, our lives changed forever. Despite the graduate courses in parenting, despite the dozens of books on parenting, we still didn't understand that parenting boys and parenting girls are two distinctly different propositions. Besides, in 1982 there were very few books on raising boys.

Nineteen months later our son Matt made his appearance. By this time we had begun to notice that our friends with young girls were having significantly different child-rearing experiences than our friends with young boys. And as these children matured, it became resplendently clear that boys are different from girls. We began asking questions: *What are little boys made of, anyway? Why do they act the way they do? Did God deliberately make boys different from girls? And if so, what are some of those differences, and what are the implications for parenting?*

Gaining an understanding of gender differences is critical in order to successfully raise boys. The good news is that a variety of research is opening up a treasure: We now know more about how and why young boys act differently than young girls do. As we spent time at the playground with close friends and their first two girls, it didn't take a graduate degree in child development to notice some significant differences between their pair of girls and our pair of boys. Our boys seemed consistently more physical in their play—they climbed everything in sight (or tried to); they swung on the jungle gym rings from arm to arm to get to their next physical conquest. In contrast, our friends' girls were noticeably less aggressive, seeking corporate play as deliberately as our boys sought objects on which to climb. If the girls were going to swing, it would be next to each other. If they were going to climb the jungle gym, it would be for the purpose of huddling together at the top, talking and giggling. Relationship, not conquest, was their goal.

"One of my earliest memories is of playing with my little brother at a park near our house," an eighteen-year-old girl recalled in a recent conversation with me. "Even though he was a year and a half younger than me—and that's a *big* difference when you're so young—he climbed and played *so high* on the jungle gym, and I remember thinking that I couldn't let a *little brother* outdo me. So I'd end up climbing up to where he was—though with a lot of nervous caution, and never as quickly and fearlessly as he would."

Girls Are More Better Than Boys[1]

1. Girls chew with their mouths closed.
2. Girls have better handwriting.
3. Girls sing better.
4. Girls are more talented.
5. Girls can do their hair better.
6. Girls cover their mouths when they sneeze.
7. Girls don't pick their nose.
8. Girls go to the bathroom politely.
9. Girls learn faster.
10. Girls are more kinder to animals.
11. Girls don't smell as bad.
12. Girls are more smarter.
13. Girls get more things what they want.
14. Girls don't let stinkers as much.
15. Girls are more quieter.
16. Girls don't get as dirty.
17. Girls are cleaner.
18. Girls are more attractive.
19. Girls don't eat as much.

20. Girls walk more politely.
21. Girls aren't as strict.
22. Girls sit more politely.
23. Girls are more creative.
24. Girls look better than boys.
25. Girls comb their hair better.
26. Girls shave more.
27. Girls put deodorant on more often.
28. Girls don't have as much body odor.
29. Girls don't want their hair messed up.
30. Girls like to get more tan.
31. Girls have more manners.

HARDWIRED FOR MALENESS

It would be one thing if the differences between boys and girls were acknowledged, understood, and accepted without any value judgments. Unfortunately, many of the innate differences between boys and girls that lead to observable behaviors are viewed by some in our culture as bad or wrong.

Researchers have recently determined that in its physiological structure the male brain exhibits marked and measurable differences from the female brain. In the mid-1990s numerous researchers have used CAT (Computerized Axial Tomography), MRI (Magnetic Resonance Imaging), and other brain-scan equipment to measure the parts of the male and female brain that respond to various kinds of stimulation.

A boy's brain, for example, has been found to be at least ten percent larger than a girl's brain. On the other hand, a girl's corpus callosum—the bundle of nerves that connects the left and right hemispheres of the brain—is larger than a boy's corpus callosum. The female cortex, or brain, develops earlier in the embryonic stage than the male brain, which allows the female corpus callosum to become larger—which in turn means that the functioning female brain uses more of *each* hemisphere of the brain. In short, there is more cross-talk between the two sides of a female brain than in the average male brain. Meanwhile, the male brain uses primarily one hemisphere.

This developmental difference explains why girls tend to be better readers than boys, because reading requires using both hemispheres at the same time. So the male brain is at a disadvantage from the get-go—a disadvantage accentuated in traditional classrooms where reading is typically considered a predictive tool for how well a child will do in school.

A male's inability to draw from both sides of the brain at the same time also explains why boys commonly have a harder time identifying an emotion they see on someone else's face—an ability requiring a large corpus callosum to facilitate the travel of ample amounts of communication between both hemispheres of the brain. This physiological reality may help explain why many women feel that the men in their lives don't read their emotions well. Although many men could undoubtedly do far better at this, the truth is they just aren't hardwired for it. It doesn't come as naturally for a man as it does for a woman.

Males may also be hardwired for greater aggressiveness. The human brain uses neurotransmitters, which function as messengers communicating with the left and right hemispheres. When one such neurotransmitter called *serotonin* is low, a person may show symptoms of depression and respond sluggishly to various stimuli. Higher levels of serotonin, on the other hand, are known to inhibit aggressive behavior—and scientists have discovered that serotonin is measurably higher in girls than in boys. Furthermore, serotonin works together with hormones secreted from the hypothalamus—hormones such as testosterone. Males secrete higher levels of testosterone than females. Increased testosterone is associated with aggressive behaviors— all of which points to this conclusion: The lower level of serotonin combined with the higher level of testosterone in the male's brain gives a biological explanation to the observation that aggressive types of behavior are much more characteristic of males than of females.

Clinically and casually, we have seen aggression to be more of a problem for boys than for girls. One child and adolescent therapist we'll call Sandy tells of a thirteen-year-old client whose father had brought him to therapy. Jeff's parents had recently divorced, and visitation had become a huge conflict between his parents—with the teenager caught in the middle. By the time Sandy saw him, Jeff had made three appearances at the juvenile courts for three different incidents involving aggressive behavior. Such behaviors were relatively benign at first but were becoming more harmful and violent as he grew into puberty. During one particular therapy session, Jeff feigned indifference, but his anger was evident.

"I'm doing fine," he said. "Nothing much is bothering me. School is okay, although I'm failing. Dad is okay."

"So school isn't going too well?" Sandy asked.

"Yeah—but I don't care." The therapist told us later she had decided to ignore this rabbit trail of Jeff's apparent apathy and instead search for the root of why Jeff wasn't doing well in school.

"So how is your mom?"

Jeff's face contorted. "Oh, she's still a drunk," he said coldly, "but I don't need her anymore."

Jeff was a pleasant boy, ordinarily very kind to the therapist and to others. Yet underneath his pleasant demeanor was a storm of anger stemming from his parents' recent divorce—a storm that, combined with the typical developmental and chemical changes of adolescence, was leading to the display of more and more dangerously aggressive behaviors.

It is important to note that Jeff's sister, who was also a client of Sandy's, reacted very differently to the divorce of her parents.

Her anger went inward and turned into depression. Without the surge of testosterone, it was more natural for Jeff's sister to withdraw instead of to act out in an aggressive way. The difference in the way they reacted is tied to many factors, but you'd miss the boat if you overlooked a boy's naturally aggressive tendencies. When seeking the best solutions for treatment, Jeff's therapist found that knowing the different ways boys naturally react, and then looking for creative ways to direct the energy of the anger and aggression, is the most supportive, nurturing way to help teenage boys handle their aggression.

New advances in brain research have not only pointed out developmental and biochemical differences between males and females, they have also been used to study structural differences. Using brain-scanning equipment, researcher Robin Gur at the University of Pennsylvania has studied how different parts of the brain are activated depending on the task the brain is engaged in. The subjects in this study were asked to do a spatial task—like figuring out how two pieces of a puzzle fit together. Most of the male's right hemisphere, Gur found, lit up intensely, while the left hemisphere lit up less brightly. In the female brain, *both* hemispheres lit up equally, but less intensely than the male's right hemisphere. So it was no surprise to Gur when she discovered that, on the average, males do better at spatial tasks than females—presumably because they can draw heavily on one hemisphere to figure the problem out.

Gur also discovered that the male brain is not wired to be as verbal as the female brain. As a male brain works on a verbal test, much less of it is used compared to how much of a *female* brain is activated during a verbal test. Brain research also indicates that the female brain is at work *all* the time. Gur observes that the female brain is constantly on, while the male brain toggles off and on. This difference helps explain why males are typically so task oriented. While females can do a number of different kinds of tasks at once, males generally focus on one task—and they react more intensely to interruptions to their thinking.[2]

What all this data points to, of course, is that a boy is fairly hardwired to be who he is. Parents cannot change his innate natural behavior. Yet if they understand how he differs from his sister, they can teach him how to cultivate who he is, to have the right blend of solid confidence and appropriate self-esteem, and to become the man God has designed him to be.

Why Boys Are More Better Than Girls[3]

1. Boys can sit in front of a scary movie and not close their eyes once.
2. Boys don't have to sit down every time they go.
3. Boys don't get embarrassed easily.
4. Boys can go to the bathroom in the woods.
5. Boys can climb trees better.
6. Boys can hang on to their stomachs on fast rides.
7. Boys don't worry about "diet-this" and "diet-that."
8. Boys are better tractor drivers than girls.
9. Boys rite better than girls.
10. Boys can build better forts than girls.
11. Boys can take pain better than girls.
12. Boys are way more cooler.
13. Boys have less fits.
14. Boys don't waste their life at the mall.
15. Boys aren't afraid of reptiels.
16. Boys shave more than girls.
17. Boys don't do all those wiggaly movmets when they walk.
18. Boys don't scratch.
19. Boys don't brade another's hair.

20. Boys aren't smart alickes.
21. Boys don't cry and feel sorry when they kill a fly.
22. Boys don't use as mutch deoderent.
23. Boys were created first.
24. Boys learn to make funny noises with their armpits faster.
25. Boys can tie better knots—specially girls pony tails.
26. Boys get to blow up more stuff.
27. Without boys there would be no babies. [Now there's a new thought!]
28. Boys eat with a lot of heart.
29. Boys don't WINE.
30. Boys hum best.
31. Boys are proud of their odor.
32. Boys don't cry over a broken nail.
33. Boys don't need to ask for directions.
34. Boys can spell Dr. Dobson's name correctly.
35. Boys aren't clichish.
36. Boys don't hog the phone.
37. Boys aren't shopaholics.
38. Boys bait their own hook when they fish.
39. Boys don't hang panty hose all over the bathroom.
40. Boys don't wake up with bad hair.
41. Boys aren't stinker. [what?]
42. Boys don't take two million years to get ready.
43. Boys couldn't care less about Barby.
44. Boys don't have to have 21 pairs of shoes (three for every day of the week!!)
45. Boys don't put a tub of makeup on all the time.
46. Boys don't care if their noses aren't perfect.
47. Boys respect everything and everyone including GIRLS!

SHORTER ATTENTION SPAN AND A NEED FOR MORE SPACE

Jeanette Schmer was a preschool teacher. She genuinely cared for her students, with a natural and gifted way of cultivating each child's unique personality. She found that each of them behaved in their own special way and communicated in ways beyond words that demonstrated their unique characteristics. On top of all the individual differences, however, Jeanette constantly noticed how her boys in general needed creative ways to help them sit still. They loved stories about things that moved; they loved active games—basically, they loved everything that allowed them to expend energy in directed and constructive ways. Most of the girls, on the other hand, seemed to be able to sit still longer while listening to *all* types of stories, and they would enjoy activities whether or not the activities demanded physical movement.

Jeanette noticed other male-female differences evident even in infancy:

- While infant girls have longer attention spans, boys look at objects for shorter periods than girls—but the boys are more active in their looking. Getting boys to pay attention is simply harder than for girls.
- Boys tend to use more space than little girls, who are usually content to sit and play in one small area of the room. A boy, on the other hand, wants to use the whole room for his play. Boys don't enjoy prolonged touch as much as girls. The male brain can be overstimulated to the point of annoyance if he is given prolonged touch. A boy needs to run and explore his environment. *Prolonged* touch can actually become painful, because his brain is designed to take in quick bursts of information from *all* senses.
- Boys take in less sensory data than girls. They smell, taste, hear, and see less—which helps explain why many parents

can become frustrated when they think their son is not hearing them. Furthermore, males generally hear out of one ear better than the other, while females are better at hearing voices and noises out of both ears. From a very early age, males are reported to ignore voices and are less skilled at picking out background noises than girls. Boys generally don't differentiate sounds as well as girls, and at times they need to be spoken to louder than to girls.[4]

So if your son doesn't respond to you when you speak to him, he may not necessarily be ignoring you. Try replacing your frustration with an understanding that it may not be a bad attitude or intentional disregard. Learn which ear he hears best with, and then try to get the message to him through another sense—through the visual sense, say, or by wrapping the message in a story or a game.

Boys interpret visual information best if they see it with their left eye, which communicates to the brain's right hemisphere— the male's strongest and most developed side.

Boys' eyes generally need to keep moving, too. When Nancy Schmer Hoffmann worked as a pediatric nurse with infants at the children's hospital, she would often notice how boys seemed to gaze at any object that was moving in the room. Many times the child's gaze would move from Nancy's mouth to her eyes, to her earrings, and then back to her eyes—and then repeat the sequence. If the television was on, its bright and rapid images would attract their constant attention. The little girls, on the other hand, would stare more intensely into Nancy's eyes—and become upset if she would glance away.

MALES' NEED FOR RAPID SPATIAL MOVEMENT—AND TELEVISION

This need of the male brain for objects to move quickly through space is satisfied by television, video games, and the Internet—media that provide information through rapidly moving images. It's easy to see how an activity like a video game can become addictive for boys; add testosterone to the mix, and a quick-action video game with the almost obligatory violence can become downright destructive.

In his books *A Fine Young Man* and *The Wonder of Boys*, therapist and educator Michael Gurian expresses alarm about the effect of the content of television and video games on our boys, as well as how the media's use of rapid imagery influences the development of our boys' brains. Given these statistics, his alarm is well-founded:

- Average number of hours per day an American household has its television on: 6 hours and 40 minutes
- Average number of minutes per week that parents spend in meaningful conversation with their children: 3.5
- Number of hours the average American kid has watched TV by the time he reaches age eighteen: 22,000 (double the time he will have spent in classroom instruction—and more than any activity except sleeping)
- Percentage of American households that have a TV on while they are eating dinner: 66
- Number of hours per week of TV commercials an average kid in America watches: more than 5
- Number of TV commercials any given American will have seen by the time he is twenty-one: one million
- Number of violent acts on TV the average American kid will have seen by the age of sixteen: 200,000 (33,000 of which will have been acts of murder)
- Percentage of an average night's TV news about crime, disaster, or war: 54
- Percentage of airtime given to public service announcements: 0.7 percent
- Number of hours Americans watch TV each year: 250 billion

- Number of videos rented daily: 6 million
- Number of public library items checked out daily: 3 million[5]

It's not just the *quantity* of television watched. To researcher Gurian, the effects of rapid video imagery on boys' intellectual development is an equally great, if not greater, concern. Nor is it only a problem for boys. We live in a culture of stimulation that moves faster than our brains are capable of handling. In fact, today's hyperstimulating media/technology environment is judged by some researchers to contribute significantly to high rates of depression, thought disorders, and brain disorders. Furthermore, when we are bombarded constantly by rapid imagery, we may form an addiction. "The TV set ... using constantly changing short sequences, holds our attention by a constant sensory bombardment that maximizes orienting responses," Michael Gurian writes. "We are constantly drawn back to the set and to processing each new sequence of information as it is presented.... The set trains us to watch it."[6] This is especially true for boys.

For the sake of the development of boys in particular, we need to pay close attention to video games and advertisements. As we've seen, boys' brains start out emotionally disadvantaged because they use primarily one hemisphere. The stimulation by and addiction to visual media like TV and video games serve only to aggravate this disadvantage rather than to lessen it; in fact, researchers have seen that video games use primarily the one side of the brain and discourage the use of the other. Consequently, for the many boys who become addicted to visual stimulants in the media, the result can be a hindering of their limbic and neocortical development and a potential decrease in the growth of intelligence in general. "Overstimulating sensory functions of the brain with fast-moving images means less ability for other functions to develop," Gurian states. "Addicting oneself to the fast images means constantly returning to a well that provides only a very limited quality of drink."[7]

A UCLA psychiatrist agrees. "When the person is exposed to these violent media stimuli and it excites the psychoneurological receptors," writes Carol Lieberman, "it causes the person to feel this excitement, to feel a kind of high—and then to become addicted to whatever was giving him the high."[8]

The conclusion seems at least somewhat obvious: We need to limit the amount and kind of television programs children watch as well as the kinds of games they play.

TESTOSTERONE 101

After all the talk about fundamental neurological differences between males and females, you may be asking, "Where does testosterone fit it?" It fits in—well, early. And here's how:

Who we are as individuals comes from forty-six chromosomes—twenty-three from the mother and twenty-three from the father. Females carry only what are called X chromosomes; males carry both X and Y chromosomes. If a father contributes an X chromosome (via sperm) to the mother's X chromosome (in her ovum), the baby will be female. But if a father contributes a Y chromosome to the mother's X chromosome, the baby will be male.

Around the sixth week of embryonic development, sexual identity is determined. If the baby is to be genetically a girl, the hormones instruct the body to allow the development of the female reproductive system at this time. The six-week-old male embryo develops special cells that produce the male hormones and androgens, the main one being testosterone. These hormones steer the body away from developing female sexual organs and toward the formation of male genitalia. If the genetic pattern is female, nothing drastic happens at this time and the development of the female brain continues naturally along female lines.

Just as male hormones are required in order to change the reproductive system from female to male, the male brain also requires a radical intervention to change the naturally female brain structure to the male brain structure. In *Brain Sex* authors Anne Moir and David Jessel further explain:

> Embryonic boy babies are exposed to a colossal dose of male hormones at the critical time when their brains are beginning to take shape. The male hormone levels then are four times the level experienced throughout infancy and boyhood. A vast surge of male hormones occurs at each end of male development: at adolescence, when his sexuality comes on stream, and six weeks after conception, at the moment his brain is beginning to take shape.[9]

This dramatic sixth-week event is known as the *testosterone wash*—a very powerful moment in the development of an infant boy. It is this testosterone wash that is responsible for many of the structural differences in the male brain compared to the female brain. (Interestingly, the area of the brain called the hypothalamus—the part that secretes testosterone—is distinctly different in cell patterns and structure in the male and female rat.) Male hormones also alter the way the brain is structured and how it communicates between the two hemispheres. "A connection," writes Moir and Jessel, "—or at least a relationship—had been discovered, and experimentally demonstrated, between behavior, hormones and brain structure."[10]

Testosterone is one of the major factors as a boy navigates the rapids through adolescence and into adulthood. Boys high in testosterone will pursue their independence from parents earlier than girls as long as they feel safe and secure in the love of parents. If a parent doesn't grasp the developmental differences between boys and girls in this critical separation process— if Mom and Dad hold on to their boy longer than he wants to be emotionally controlled—or if his sense of safety and stability is disrupted through a circumstance such as divorce—then his natural, God-given, and very testosterone-driven urge to separate and launch himself out into the world will be disrupted.[11]

Divorce, of course, disrupts this adolescent male urge to individuate, and the natural process of separating from parents can become interrupted. Our therapist friend Sandy worked with Brian for nearly a year in therapy after his parents divorced. Before the divorce, Brian was active socially and athletically. He was well liked, and others sensed a healthy self-esteem that drew them to him. Brian admitted to Sandy that after the divorce, his perception of a safe family was destroyed. He continued to withdraw from reality into escapism—watching videos, browsing on the Internet for hours, reading comics, watching more videos—all the while retreating more and more from friends.

He was too insecure to leave home, and yet he didn't feel safe at home either. The crucial launching pad into independence—a safe family—had been broken; the natural development process of separation from his parents had been interrupted. "I'm afraid to be with friends and I don't want to be at home," Brian told his therapist.

Brian's emotional dilemma didn't leave much room for normal adolescent exploration. The safest place for him was simply to stay put developmentally, entertaining himself with television and the Internet.

It took time for Brian to come to terms with his parents' divorce, but he finally stopped blaming himself for their problems and gradually regained confidence. The trauma of the divorce, and the relational redefinition that divorce always necessitates, arrested Brian's natural inclination to go and "conquer the world." He needed to redefine his relationship with his mom and dad and regain his confidence in who he was before he could continue the process of healthy independence.

This natural desire for independence is only one effect of testosterone. Boys' rough-and-tumble playing style, the greater physical risks they take, and their generally more aggressive way of relating all reflect the significant influence of testosterone. If parents can acknowledge these unique physiological aspects of their boys, it allows them to work naturally with who boys are.

At no other time in their development (other than in the sixth week of embryonic development) does testosterone play such a vast role as when little boys enter into puberty, which for most boys begins around the sixth grade. Testosterone floods the boy's body, causing his genitals to increase eight times in size. During this *testosterone wash* the level of testosterone is ten to twenty times stronger in boys than in girls. The prepubertal and adolescent boy will have between five to seven surges of testosterone per day—an increase marked by a tendency to masturbate frequently, be moody and aggressive, want more sleep, lose his temper more often, be more negative and critical, act like his head is in the clouds, and have a significantly greater interest in sex. And this is just during his teenage years!

Some imagine a link between the increased testosterone and increased violence—a myth that comes out of the belief that testosterone is the *only* force that influences boys toward more violent behavior than what girls typically demonstrate. There are in reality *many* causes of adolescent violence—not just testosterone, but also cultural expectations and poor role modeling—that encourage a boy to be more rough-and-tumble in his play. Boys simply have a propensity to play more competitively and forcefully. They like games that involve large groups and occur in large places—while girls tend to engage in play that is more relational and less aggressive.

Testosterone in high levels can energize one male to play chess like he's never before played chess ... in another, to debate his opinion in front of a crowd with clear and concise thinking ... in still another, to play soccer to his greatest ability ... and in still another, to become passionately involved in a violent fight. "While testosterone does, in fact, contribute to boys' proclivity for action, scientists over the years have tried without success to establish an unequivocal link between testosterone and violent behavior," writes William Pollack in *Real Boys*. "The fact is that testosterone is just one of many biological factors (including serotonin) that have influenced aggression."[12]

Even beyond the age of adolescence, the young adult male continues to be more aggressive and competitive than the average woman. They tend to be more determined in the workplace, more inclined to compete for a superior position, more apt to try to one-up someone in conversation, more inclined to be competitive in sports. Behind all this is the male focus of *releasing tension*. He may be unconscious of it, but much of his behavior is aimed at decreasing the tension he feels. Michael Gurian in *The Wonder of Boys* states that the male's energy, "propelled by testosterone and guided by the specific structure and workings of male brain structure," leads to three behavior patterns most of us have noticed in our boys:

- The search for instant or quick gratification, whether in eating quickly, jumping from activity to activity, or seeking quick sexual conquest
- The tendency to move quickly to problem solving, even in emotionally complex experiences
- The tendency to find activities through which his body will build physical tension—like sports or other concentrated, single-task experiences—then release the tension with an "Ahh . . . "[13]

Boys need a parent's help to rise above the need for instant gratification. The first step for parents is to understand the natural way boys' unique chemistry inclines them to react and behave. It is futile, and even destructive, to try to make our boys respond and behave more like girls—that is, to have them be more "socially acceptable"—without understanding who they really are.

The truth about testosterone is that, though it does heavily influence how a male looks and behaves, testosterone is by no means the *primary* influence on the behavior of boys. How a boy is loved, nurtured, and shaped by his parents and by society constitutes the greatest influence on the growing boy. The way to help a boy develop favorably begins by knowing who and what he is, then helping him to direct his energy in ways that are most productive for him.

SMALL BEGINNINGS

1. What are your son's three favorite activities? What part do video games play in his life? What are some of his favorite video games?
2. What differences have you noticed between your son and girls of the same age? If you also have a daughter, what role does gender play in the different ways you parent them?
3. Name one insight from this chapter you can apply this week to help you be a more effective parent.

Chapter Four

MADE IN GOD'S IMAGE

Balancing Mind, Will, and Emotions

UP FRONT *In this chapter ...*

- ◆ If you teach sons that their worth is based on their likeness to Jesus Christ, they will be less likely to seek their identity and security in their own performance.
- ◆ Boys need to understand that they first must have a growing love relationship with Jesus—and that his power to transform their lives will free them from the world's expectations of what it means to be a man.
- ◆ God made humans with a three-dimensional soul—mind, will, and emotions—which he designed to work together in balance, but sin has distorted these roles.
- ◆ Boys are much more likely than girls to distrust their emotions (putting head over heart), and so must be shown that God intends for them to be whole persons, capable of feeling as well as thinking.
- ◆ The other extreme occurs when we so emphasize the emotional aspect of our humanity that we lose our ability to think things through logically (putting heart over head). Feelings are important, but our sons need to know that letting their feelings control them will only result in misery.

> ✦ *Head and heart in balance*—a better option. We do well to give equal play to both emotions and intellect—which for boys especially means understanding how their thoughts influence their feelings. Parents can teach sons to evaluate their thinking in the light of God's Word, prayer, the prompting of the Holy Spirit, wise counsel, time, friends, and experience. The result? They will be able to make wiser decisions.

You MAY REMEMBER THE scene in *Rebel Without a Cause* where the James Dean character and another man play chicken by agreeing to drive their cars off a cliff—and the first one to bail out of the car before it speeds off the cliff is chicken. When boys become adolescents and the testosterone kicks in, their need to prove themselves can lead to feats of bravery, daring, and strength that can put them in life-threatening situations. As our boys get older, the attempts might become a bit more sophisticated—and maybe even more ridiculous.

One guy took ridiculousness to new heights—literally. In 1982 a thirty-three-year-old North Hollywood truck driver, with no prior aviation experience, floated three miles above the southern California landscape in a lawn chair rigged with forty-two helium weather balloons. Armed with a two-way radio, a parachute, a pellet gun, and jugs of water for ballast, he expected to rise gracefully into the sky from his girlfriend's backyard, then shoot the balloons down to land gently on the ground.

When the mooring was cut, however, he unexpectedly rose into the sky like a cannon shot, and soon reached 16,000 feet. He passed a few private planes on the way up and was spotted by baffled jetliner pilots. The dizzy balloonist managed to shoot out about ten of the weather balloons before his gun fell overboard ninety minutes into the flight. His craft then drifted back toward earth. The balloons eventually became entangled in power lines near the Long Beach airport, and he was able to hop down from the lawn chair into the waiting arms of the law. He was informed that he now owed $1,500 to the Federal Aviation Administration, which accused him of flying in a reckless manner, operating too close to the airport, and failing to maintain contact with the control tower!

Now our three sons haven't done anything *quite* that crazy, for which we are very grateful. But when boys don't understand the basis for their significance, by nature they seek any number of ways to help them feel significant and secure—and not all of them are healthy. Boys will go to all sorts of lengths to prove themselves in order to shore up sagging self-worth and to demonstrate and validate their masculinity. Some tie helium balloons to lawn chairs, some bungee-jump off bridges, others parachute from skyscrapers. Some grow up to become workaholics who measure their success by the number of business calls they receive on their cell phones—including evenings, weekends, and vacations—or the number of overtime hours they put in, or how quickly they get pay raises or promotions.

The stunning truth that your son has been made in the image of God may be the most important thing to teach him at an early age—for at least two reasons.

MY SON, THE REDEEMED IMAGE BEARER

Why teach your son that he is made in the image of God? The first reason is this: This knowledge can be a sturdy source of strength and encouragement, for it is a powerful thing indeed to realize that one is a redeemed image bearer.

The foundation of self-identity is the realization that we are created by God in his image. When Adam and Eve sinned, it may have damaged and distorted the image of God in humans, but it didn't *destroy* it. Nor did the story end at the Fall, for afterwards came the cross and the empty tomb. Not only are we made in God's image, but our salvation was purchased with the blood of God the Son. Out of all the breadth and depth of God's creation, only human beings were made in his image—and redeemed by his blood for the purpose of becoming like him.

And here's what this theology means to our boys: Unless we help them understand what it means to be *in Christ*—what it means to be made in the image of God, to be redeemed by the Son of God—unless our boys understand this, their identity will be merely performance-based (that is, what they *do* on their own) rather than person-based (who they *are* in Christ).

Performance-based identity is such an easy trap to fall into, especially for males. Males typically look to some kind of ethical or social standard—family standards, youth group standards, school standards, peer standards, and the like—to steer them through what to embrace and what to avoid, instead of letting the clear teaching of Scripture do the steering. As boys move into adolescence, for example, the peer group often becomes a particularly potent influence. Yet Scripture will show them what they should and shouldn't *be*—more than what they should or shouldn't *do*—as they model their lives after Jesus, the ideal man.

The Pharisees (at least during Jesus' time) were infamous examples of performance-based identity. They followed the letter of all the biblical laws and even added some of their own commandments and regulations, which they followed to a T as well. Yet the obedience was all in their heads, not their hearts. It was little wonder they couldn't recognize the Messiah when he came. He simply didn't fit their mold of *doing* everything exactly as the law required.

True maturity, on the other hand, is measured by the degree to which our boys are becoming "conformed to the likeness of [God's] Son" (Romans 8:29), a maturity that is measured by their "love, joy, peace, patience, kindness, goodness, faithfulness, gentleness and self-control" (Galatians 5:22–23). This is a maturity demonstrated by a love that "never gives up, never loses faith, is always hopeful, and endures through every circumstance" (1 Corinthians 13:7, NEW LIVING TRANSLATION).

This is much more, and much more difficult, than just *doing* the right things at the right time.

The problem of most men today, including Christian men, is not about *doing* enough—most of them are doing plenty, and then some. Their problem is that they're not *being* enough, and not being *where* they should be. Their problem is that they're not *who* and *what* they should be. And these weaknesses, of course, rub off on our boys.

If you're a male or have lived with males for a while, you understand how head knowledge is always easier than heart knowledge for males. Men generally find it easier to discuss, debate, and dissect truth than to let the Holy Spirit use their life circumstances to help them become conformed to the image of Jesus Christ. It's one thing (and it is surely a *good* thing) to send our boys off to church school or to Bible clubs to hear Bible stories and memorize verses, and yet it's quite another to consistently cultivate Christlike character in them and in others around them.

Is head knowledge and good information important? Do our boys need to understand sound doctrine? Is it valuable for them to know *why* they believe *what* they believe? Yes, yes, and an emphatic yes! We want to be very careful not to give the impression that head knowledge is not important. It is important and can be valuable.

However what is *most* important, what is foundational to the Christian life, what must come *first* is for our boys to have an intimate, growing love relationship with their Lord Jesus Christ. Head knowledge *about* the truth is not an end in itself. The purpose of the truth is always transformation. When our sons are being transformed, they will be brave enough and secure enough to be themselves, to be real men.

A second reason we should teach our sons early that they've been made in the image of God is because this realization lets them escape the cultural myths of masculinity and sets them free from the unrealistic expectations that have bound so many men. Knowing he's made in God's image builds a boy's foundation for his growing understanding of what being a man really means.

MIND, WILL, AND EMOTIONS

In the Bible we are told that God loves us so much that he wants to help us become "conformed to the likeness of his Son" (Romans 8:29). The apostle Paul notes that we are "being transformed into his likeness with ever-increasing glory" (2 Corinthians 3:18). The apostle Peter writes that through God's wonderful promises we may "participate in the divine nature" (2 Peter 1:4).

What does this all mean—being conformed and transformed, being participants? Does it have something to do with being a whole person?

"May your whole spirit, soul and body," wrote Paul to the Thessalonians, "be kept blameless at the coming of our Lord Jesus Christ" (1 Thessalonians 5:23). A part of what it means to be made in God's image is that we have a *soul*—a personality, like God's, with three dimensions: mind, will, and emotions.

God gave us a *mind* for reasoning and for processing information, a *will* for making choices, and *emotions* for expressing our feelings. All three are God-given—a natural and healthy expression of our being made in his image. He designed these three parts to work together in balance and harmony. Like a tripod, each of these dimensions—mind, will, and emotions—is vital and necessary. If even one leg buckles, the tripod topples. If any aspect of our personality doesn't function the way God designed it to, we are not becoming all that God wants us to be.

Although it's natural to think of mind, will, and emotions as separate entities, they are intricately connected. Our choices and their consequences, for example, influence what we think and how we feel; our emotions influence what our mind takes in and what decisions we make; and our minds interpret our experiences and influence our feelings and the choices we make.

One night Gary came home after a particularly long, hard day at the office. There had been several crises, with tough decisions to be made (including the confronting of an employee about an ethical issue)—and when he walked in the door, Carrie greeted him pleasantly and said sympathetically, "Boy, do you look tired."

Gary's response was sharp and sarcastic. "Thanks, honey. I really appreciate your encouragement." He saw from her face that his shot had hit the target, then turned and went upstairs.

He knew as he unpacked his briefcase that he needed to apologize to Carrie. Apologizing is agonizingly difficult for him; yet, after doing his best to rationalize his unkindness, he finally gave in, went downstairs, and asked Carrie to forgive him. As usual, she graciously accepted his apology. As they talked it became clear that Gary was just plain physically tired and emotionally drained—just the kind of time when it becomes easy for him to be negative, defensive, to interpret comments in the worst way, and to jump to negative conclusions. Carrie had merely made an objective observation, but Gary's mind interpreted it negatively, his emotions were bruised, and his will opted to respond unkindly—all this without taking the time to process Carrie's comment with the same objectivity with which she said it.

Our emotions and our mind are two different yet equally valuable ways of experiencing, understanding, and interpreting the world around us. They provide two different kinds of information about ourselves and our world, and in so doing they can balance each other out. When our mind and emotions work together in harmony, our choices are more likely to be wise and responsible ones.

Yet the reality of sin gravely complicates the picture. Sin did not separate just God from humans and males from females; it also separated the three parts of our personality from each other—producing severely divided, damaged, and distorted humans. The division is especially obvious in the relationship between our minds and emotions; now what God designed to work together, in a complementary way, in reality often opposes each other.

Think of concrete, which requires a combination of proper amounts of cement, sand, and water. Too much or too little of one ingredient, and the concrete will be crumbly, weak, and short-lived. If you omit one ingredient altogether, the mix just won't set.

So it is with our personality. Healthy persons have learned to balance their mind, will, and emotions. The influence of sin, of course, makes the task immensely difficult and tends to make us vulnerable to one error or the other: either to deny, repress, suppress, and ignore emotions—to not trust our hearts and trust only in our minds—or to let emotions control us, never trusting our heads, but just going with our gut.

One of the goals for an adolescent's home and family is to be a place where, through trial and error, teaching and obser-vation, he can learn how his mind, will, and emotions work together. But what happens when a boy is raised in a home where this balance isn't modeled? And what happens when such a boy meets a girl whose home life wasn't ideal either?

BOB AND RITA

Bob grew up in a home where the male was the most impor-tant person in the house. His father had all the power—he was always right and his needs always came first. The function of Mom and the kids was to compliment, honor, and obey Dad. The reason Dad gave for this rigid domestic hierarchy was always the same: "It's the biblical model." The *functional* reason, however, was so that he could feel good about himself. He squelched independence, discouraged questions, forbade disagreements, and never openly displayed affection.

Bob's dad was the kind of father who needed his kids—especially his sons—to succeed in order for him to feel good about himself. He approved when they expressed socially acceptable emotions—that is, emotions that made *him* feel good and look good. But he discouraged them from expressing any emotions that communicated weakness or pain—and in fact he usually punished them when they did so. It made the family look bad—or so he believed.

The fact was that Dad simply didn't know how to deal with painful emotions.

His children learned their lessons well—especially his boys. They grew up believing that they should not experience certain emotions, and that if they did it would only show they were weak and inferior misfits—miserable failures. They believed if they were ever discovered to have these emotions, they would be criticized and rejected, and thereby suffer humiliation. And above all, they were constantly on their guard—especially against girls finding out about the real them.

Bob graduated from high school, went to college, and then—having been well trained to stuff his fears, hide his worries, and deny his doubts—met and married Rita. He was *the man* in the marriage—the authoritative one, the head, the one in charge—so he always knew what to do. At least he felt he *ought* to always know what to do. If at any time he was confused or discouraged, he hid it. He pretended everything was fine. Otherwise, he was sure that if Rita found out what an insecure weakling he really was, if she was aware of his deep pockets of insecurity, she would undoubtedly lose all respect for him—in fact, maybe even leave him.

Now Rita had grown up with an alcoholic father. When he was sober, he was a sensitive and wonderful father. When he was drunk, he was painfully unpredictable. As a child she listened for him to come home from work—and if the car tires screeched as he came up the driveway, she knew she needed to stay out of the way. If Bob grew up in an *emotionless* home, Rita grew up in a home where the expressions of raging emotions were always inconsistent and sometimes out of control. She learned early on that emotions couldn't be trusted, just as Bob had—but for different reasons.

After twenty-one years of marriage, Bob and Rita came to the point where they sought counseling. Bob was burned out from his job and on the verge of a nervous breakdown. His way of dealing with the fear of going under was to work longer and harder and to medicate himself with alcohol. The amount he drank gradually increased as his pain increased, until he was drinking regularly just to deal with daily struggles and complexities. He never got drunk—he just had "a couple drinks" every day.

Rita was burned out from twenty-one years of trying to create a relationship with someone who, in her words, had had "relational bypass surgery." She loved Bob, but from the early days of the marriage she realized Bob was capable of only so much intimacy. The warmth and emotional intensity he had expressed during their engagement period had seemed to vanish all too quickly.

When children came along, Rita's need for intimacy was met through them. She kept hoping and praying that Bob would change, but as the years rolled by Bob didn't change. Slowly they became "married singles"—they lived together, slept together, and shared the same home, family, and friends, but they were strangers. And now that the kids were growing up and leaving the nest, the stark reality of their relational bankruptcy hit her hard.

Bob and Rita's story has played out in different ways and to different degrees with millions of couples. Your own mom and dad might look a lot like them. And it's not just couples whose marriages have hit the rocks and end up in divorce court. We've seen lots of couples who stay in—who grit their teeth and endure—mediocre relationships.

Why does this happen? How can relationships that start out so good end up so bad?

There is no single answer to these tough questions. But part of the answer is rooted in the homes where children grew up, trained by their parents to become husbands and wives themselves someday. Both Bob and Rita grew up in homes with poor emotional modeling. As children, neither had seen a balance between mind, emotions, and will. Consequently they grew up with undernourished souls; they were victims of emotional malnutrition. And the cost was woefully high—isolation, frustration, pain, relational mediocrity—despite the fact that Rita and Bob's parents never intended to pass on to their children their own unhealthy legacy. Yet there is hope for parents who experienced a painful childhood at the hands of their own inept parents.

As Bob and Rita began to understand their emotions and the importance of balancing them with the mind and the will, things started falling into place for them. Many of their problems were stemming from opposite yet equally dysfunctional ways of dealing with their emotions. The lack of a healthy emotional education and the inability to balance all three dimensions of personality had caused them enormous heartache, robbed their children of a healthy model, and in the end almost cost them their marriage.

MIND OVER EMOTIONS

Here's how your three-part personality is designed by God to work optimally: Your will makes choices based on the information given by your mind and your emotions—and the best decisions are made when your mind and emotions work together.

But when one's personality becomes unbalanced, it tends to operate primarily in two ways: by relying overwhelmingly on the mind to make decisions (and thereby shortchanging the valuable influence of the emotions), or by relying overwhelmingly on the emotions to make decisions (and thereby shortchanging the equally valuable influence of the mind).

What do these two unbalanced states look like?

First, those who elevate their mind over their emotions, who magnify the head and minimize the heart, see the intellectual as more important than the emotional, even though they may no longer be able to hear God's voice through their emotions. Shutting down one's emotions long enough can numb them to their very ability to feel. Whenever people's feelings become frozen, their emotional life is in as much danger as their body would be if an arm or leg were frozen.

These people have concluded that emotions are untrustworthy and unreliable. "You can't base your decisions on your emotions," some preachers have been fond of stating. "Emotions change, but God's Word never changes. There is no room for emotionalism in the mature Christian life." Now these preachers undoubtedly had good intentions in reminding people not to be swayed by every emotional wind that blows, but they build an artificial and unbiblical dichotomy between the mind and emotions. Their interpretation is simple and clear: Emotions are a necessary evil. Listening to this kind of emotions-bashing, male listeners tend to tell themselves, "It's probably good to be aware of my emotions, but I can't take them too seriously. They may be helpful for getting along with women— but when it comes to making decisions, I'm better off if I ignore my feelings. Gotta go for the bottom line."

Indeed, many men have bought into this faulty line of thinking. As a result they conclude that their minds are trustworthy and their emotions are untrustworthy. Emotions become the black sheep of our personalities; they are written off as that part of us that comes as the result of the Fall, and a cause of the downfall of many.

Parents of boys must be especially aware of this unbalanced perspective, because in our experience boys are much more likely than girls to fall into the error of *dismissing* emotions. Males tend to favor their minds over their hearts anyway; add to this tendency the effects of sin and socialization, and many men become emotional cripples. If boys grow up believing that masculinity and emotionality are incompatible, they will invariably lose touch with a key component of what it means to be a whole person. When we teach our sons to elevate the mind to a position of superiority and relegate the emotions to the servants' quarters, we are splitting their personality in ways God never intended. We are teaching them to exchange their emotional birthright for an intellectual batch of pottage. This is a trade God never asked us to make.

EMOTIONS OVER MIND

Just as unhealthy as ignoring your emotions is letting your emotions control you at the expense of your mind. Some children grow up in homes where they're taught that if you don't feel it, you can't trust it. If it's rational, it can't be relational. In any case, they have learned to distrust the intellect.

Persons who *stuff* their emotions can suffer from frozen feelings; those who let their emotions *rule* their wills can suffer from flooded feelings. If the first kind of imbalance deifies facts, then this imbalance deifies feelings. For persons whose decisions are governed by emotions, it doesn't take long before their feelings *become* facts. "If I feel it, it must be true," they believe. No need to ask any questions. No need to check it out. No possibility that they might have misinterpreted what they heard: "It doesn't matter what you say, because I know what you're really thinking."

You undoubtedly know people like this—emotional jellyfish who float in and out with the tide, at the mercy of the winds and waves of their emotions. And the truth is, you feel drained after you've been around them for a while. When they say they've made up their mind, what they really mean is that they've made up their emotions. If you catch them when they're up, it's great; if you catch them when they're down, you could be in serious trouble. If you try to reason with them, your attempts are only proof that you don't really understand—and that you very likely aren't even capable of understanding them.

What they don't understand is that emotions need the mind as much as the mind needs emotions. If we teach our sons to ignore their minds and give the reins of their wills to their emotions, the results are often disastrous. The Bible tells of lots of people who ignored their mind and let their emotions determine their will:

- Saul was a mighty warrior and the first king of Israel. Then the young David killed Goliath and became more popular than Saul, and soon the city was singing, "Saul has slain his thousands, and David his tens of thousands" (1 Samuel 18:7). When Saul heard this, he allowed his emotions of anger and jealousy to control him. His out-of-control emotions distorted his perspective and interfered with his ability to learn from his mistakes and adjust his attitudes and behavior.

- When the ten Israelite spies returned from the Promised Land and could report only despairing news of giants and walled cities, the people of Israel allowed fear and depression to control them. These emotions so consumed them that they were unable to remember what God had done for them (see Numbers 14:1–4).

- Following a miraculous victory, Elijah succumbed to his fear of Jezebel and her threats to take his life. He fled the city and his problems (or so he hoped), found a broom tree in the desert, sat down under it, and waited morosely for death. His out-of-control fear led to a depression that caused him to lose not only his perspective, but also his desire to live (see 1 Kings 19:4).

Ignoring the emotions, as we've seen, tends to make one hard, cold, insensitive, unkind, and uncaring. Ignoring the mind, on the other hand, and letting emotions direct one's life, leads to an emotional roller-coaster ride. These riders are sensitive folks, to be sure, but they can become oversensitive to the point that their entire life is thrown off-kilter by the slightest twist or turn.

Now which of these imbalances are you most inclined to exhibit? Where did you learn your preferred way of making choices? Your patterns—the ways in which you function—are what your son will consider correct and normal. Which imbalance most characterizes your son right now?

Feelings are undeniably a necessary, positive, and valuable part of our personality—but feelings were never meant to be the *absolute* standard of truth, the infallible guide to what is right, the source to which we go for all decisions and actions.

Both imbalances reveal a significant misunderstanding of the biblical teaching on how God designed us to function. God designed our emotions to enrich our lives. But the effects of sin have damaged and distorted our emotions—and our minds and our wills as well.

HEAD AND HEART IN BALANCE

There is yet a third option: We can teach our sons to view their emotions from God's perspective and bring them into harmony with their mind. Maturity, after all, involves the whole person. It is impossible to be spiritually mature and emotionally immature. Maturity involves a balance between our heart and our head, between our feeling and our thinking. Both are important, both are designed by God for our good, and both demonstrate that we were created in his image. When they are in harmony, the third dimension of our personality—the will—can make wiser and stronger decisions.

Despite how highly the Bible regards our emotions, relatively few of the dads we have worked with understand or appreciate the importance of emotions in the process of becoming a real man. Furthermore, in several sets of systematic theologies in our library, we were amazed to find that the word *emotions* didn't warrant a notation in most of the indexes. A notable exception to the lack of teaching about the relationship between facts and feelings is found in psychologist William Kirwan's book titled *Biblical Concepts for Christian Counseling:*

> "Facts" and "feelings" are part of the same process. The brain does not separate feelings from facts or facts from feelings. There is little distinction between the two: All feelings are psychological and neurological arousal attached to facts. . . . Nor does the Bible make a distinction between facts and feelings. . . . We deal not with facts or feelings, but with facts and feelings. . . . By seeing emotions or feelings as a key aspect of the heart we see that they are also a key part of one's being. As a key to being, they are of vital importance in the life of the Christian.[1]

From our years of clinical counseling with men, we have become convinced that the majority of their dilemmas and difficulties come as a result of their lack of understanding their emotions. Too many men find it awkward or embarrassing to talk about their emotions—in fact, for some the very word *emotional* is a dirty word.

A prime duty of parents—and a difficult one, to be sure—is helping sons learn how to balance their head and heart, their thinking and feeling, their mind and emotions. As our boys grow in understanding what it means to have a functioning mind, emotions, and will, they are building a strong foundation for a healthy masculinity. There is no need to adhere again to the aggressive, domineering, and emotionally disconnected male role models that, unfortunately, are still *negatively* defined: Men don't cry. Men aren't weak. Men don't need affection, gentleness, or warmth. Men don't rely on others. Men don't need comforting. Men don't admit mistakes. Men don't need to be needed.

We must help our sons become proactive—to define themselves by who they are and who God has created them to become, by their person instead of by their performance or their production.

You can help your sons understand and deal with their emotions by giving them opportunities to test the accuracy of their private notions of themselves and of their world. We've worked hard to make our own home a safe place for our boys to express a wide range of emotions in healthy ways. When we as parents have fallen short and expressed emotions in unhealthy ways, we've tried to let them know, offered apologies, and asked for forgiveness.

No matter whether we ultimately fail or succeed as models for our boys, we want with all our hearts to convey to them that the essence of true manhood is not found merely in what a man does, in how big or strong he is, in how much money he has made or will make—but in who he is and in what he is becoming. The core of what it means to be a man is found within his heart, his moral character, his values and integrity. It is found in personal characteristics such as courage, steadfastness, responsibility, duty, fortitude, patience, and generosity, and in the demonstration of the fruit of the Spirit in his life.

Sons can be taught to value and listen to their minds as well as to their emotions. For example, boys need to know that their *minds* often cause them to *feel* a certain way—and that by changing their thoughts, they can change how they feel. During his elementary school years, our son Nathan went through a difficult stage. He behaved as though anyone who disagreed with him didn't like him. We couldn't figure out where he had gotten that idea—but once we became aware, we were able to help him understand that if he thought that everyone who disagreed with him actually didn't like him, then he'd be a very lonely little boy in a very short time. It was an instructive time for the whole family, as we explored the difference between constructive criticism, appropriate discipline, and deliberate hurt.

With your help, kids can be taught to give up irrational demands, to avoid tyrannical *shoulds* and *musts* and *oughts,* and to accept themselves as imperfect human beings who sometimes succeed, sometimes fail, and sometimes do stupid things. And they can learn that God can help them through *all* of these outcomes.

In the same way that Nathan interpreted other people's behavior, so our interpretations are lenses through which we see the world around us—lenses that are not necessarily accurate. They can color our world, or they can clarify reality. If we interpret events in a positive way, we have pleasant feelings. If we interpret them in a negative way, we have painful feelings. Unfortunately, many of us have inaccurate and irrational beliefs or assumptions about life that cause us to interpret events negatively—that is, to *misinterpret* the events. These irrational beliefs produce a distorted perception of reality in us—and we in turn pass them on to our sons. Common irrational beliefs of children include:

- It's awful if others don't like me.
- I'm bad if I make a mistake.
- Everything should go my way; I should always get what I want.
- Things should come easy to me.
- The world should be fair, and bad people must be punished.
- I shouldn't show my feelings.
- Adults should be perfect.
- There's only one right answer.

- I must win.
- I shouldn't have to wait for anything.[2]

Now it would not be fair to conclude that those boys who accept these beliefs will necessarily go bad. The degree to which irrational beliefs like these lead to emotional or behavioral problems in boys depends in part on the following:

- The number of irrational beliefs he holds
- The range of situations in which he applies his ideas (for example, school, home, peers, adults, work, play)
- The strength of his belief
- The extent to which he tends to distort reality as observed in errors of inference about what has happened or what will happen[3]

Our family has always liked to play games—board games, card games, games of all kinds. When Andrew was young, he went through a phase of dissolving into tears and stomping off if he lost. Somewhere he had picked up the belief, irrational though it may have been, that "if I don't win, then I can't have fun" (a belief not limited to children either). It took a couple of months, but we were able to help Andrew examine his misbelief by observing that, while it is always fun to win, when *we* lost we still had fun and enjoyed the game. This also gave us an opportunity to show how much fun we could have simply by being together—win, lose, or draw.

Many people function as though events *cause* their emotions, that if they could just change their circumstances they would feel better. These folks tend to be reactive—to go through life letting incidents determine not merely their feelings but also the very quality of their existence. The way they perceive it, they're victims—unlucky victims at that. *If only this deal had worked out, I could have paid my bills . . . if only I had met someone different, my life would have been different . . . if only I had gotten that promotion, I'd be happy now.*

No one denies that circumstances strongly influence how we feel, but even in the case of "victims" who have experienced awful things our circumstances are rarely the sole cause of our emotions. *The primary cause of our emotions is not what happens to us, but how we choose to interpret what happens to us.* "Feelings are often the end product of a series of irrational self-statements," explains Archibald Hart, professor of psychology at Fuller Theological Seminary, "and we can avoid prolonging the feeling or even triggering it in the first place by carefully examining the content of our thoughts, challenging their validity, and changing their content."[4] We may not be able to change what happens to us, but we can change how we choose to interpret those events and how we respond to them.

What our sons think about, then, holds the secrets to their feelings. Their misbeliefs, misperceptions, misinterpretations, and irrational thoughts contribute to the emotional problems they may be experiencing. Boys who look at reality through a distorted lens of irrational beliefs are at higher risk of a variety of emotional problems. And the sad fact is that most children are not taught how to identify, confirm, or disprove their assumptions and interpretations about events and interactions—so they enter adulthood with a limited understanding of their emotions and with a set of irrational beliefs that can cripple their ability to form intimate and healthy relationships.

Even to boys as young as six and seven years of age, we can begin to give a language that helps them identify and express their emotions. They can begin to learn to substitute healthy and positive self-statements for the negative and self-defeating talk that characterizes many sons. From the time our boys were young, we've both tried to label our emotions as we talk about them around the house. When Gary struggles with depression, he *talks* about being depressed. When Carrie feels a sense of anxiety creep up on her, she *talks* about being worried or anxious. When as a little boy our son Nathan ran into the house because "some big boys are out front," we listened and attached the word *fear* to his emotion, so he could identify what he was feeling.

As boys get older, they can be taught to evaluate their own thinking according to objective and rational criteria. They can learn to evaluate their self-talk in the light of what they have learned from the Bible, from their parents, and from their past experience. They can be taught to recognize their own irrational thoughts and beliefs as difficulties arise in the future. They can learn there can be more interpretations of a situation than the way they first *feel* about it.

When we say we can use our minds to help identify what we are actually feeling, we don't mean using a merely linear, left-brain evaluation, but rather the ability to stand back and put our emotions into perspective—to look at what we are feeling in light of the clear teaching of God's Word, prayer, the Holy Spirit, wise counsel, time, friends, and past experience. With this kind of help in examining their emotions, boys can learn that they can arrive at a much better place to make informed decisions about what they want to do. As they learn how to evaluate, retain, or reject the information they get from their mind and their emotions, they learn to make wiser decisions.

Helping our sons on the path to true manhood isn't giving them a destination as much as it is pointing them in the right direction. Real men haven't arrived; real men are *becoming.* They are open to change and growth.

We've come to realize there is a realistic way to look at "biblical masculinity." Biblical masculinity is *not* about perfection and possessing all the answers, but about having a purpose and opening oneself up to the process. Biblical masculinity is not about domination—about being the boss and having all the power—but about *demonstration:* being an example, practicing what we preach, and walking the talk.

SMALL BEGINNINGS

1. Explore with your son what the Bible has to say about who Jesus is. List some of his personal characteristics. Which of these characteristics would be reasonable for us to model?
2. For the next three days carefully observe your son and note the emotions he experiences and expresses most frequently, as well as the emotions he has difficulty expressing.
3. Look for opportunities to discuss specific emotions with your son—anger, fear, worry, depression, and the like.
4. For more information on males and their emotions, see *Real Men Have Feelings Too,* by Gary Oliver (Chicago: Moody Press, 1993).

Chapter Five

CULTIVATING THE EMOTIONS OF YOUR SON

UP FRONT *In this chapter ...*

+ Emotional intelligence involves self-motivation, persistence, delay of impulses and gratification, mood regulation, empathy, hope, and the ability to separate feelings from thoughts.

+ Researchers have found that emotional intelligence is more predictive of life success than raw intellectual ability (a person's IQ).

+ Satan has deceived many into believing that emotions indicate weakness.

+ Biological differences in boys have contributed to the underdevelopment of their emotional side. Their brains react to emotional objects tensely and tend to avoid processing emotional topics in-depth.

+ The presence of testosterone contributes to independent and physically aggressive behavior in boys. The male inclination toward dominance affects the way he reacts in social exchanges, often putting him at a disadvantage.

+ Parents need to teach their sons several things about emotions: what they are, where they come from, and why they're important.

WILLIAM POLLACK, AUTHOR OF the book *Real Boys* and director of the Center for Men at McLean Hospital in Belmont, Massachusetts, wants to help us rescue our sons from the myths of boyhood. One such myth says that the expression of emotions is incompatible with masculinity. In his book Pollack asks, "Have you ever noticed the way that boys begin shutting down their feelings once they reach school age?" He goes on to write:

> Little boys are full of feelings and energies. But in the jungle of the schoolyard they soon grow ashamed of useful and healthy emotions like sadness, fear, and tenderness. To help himself cope, a boy hardens his feelings and tenses his body.
>
> Then, one day, puberty strikes. In a shut-down body, one part suddenly springs to life like a crocus through the frozen soil! The boy is suddenly aware of a wonderful feeling of aliveness, of quickening, all located in one place! It's no wonder that a boy soon attaches all his feelings of closeness (and all his sense of aliveness and well-being) to the activities of his penis.[1]

Between experiencing the effects of sin and socialization, as we've seen, boys generally enter adolescence with their feelings numbed, believing the myth that emotions and masculinity are incompatible. What makes their condition particularly distressing is that research tells us that IQ, or intelligence quotient—a measure of raw intellectual ability—constitutes only about twenty percent of the factors that determine a person's potential life success. This leaves eighty percent to other forces.[2] Additional research clearly indicates the essential role mature emotional development plays in every aspect of our lives. In fact, many educators are saying that EQ, a kind of "emotional intelligence," is more predictive of success than IQ; in other words, people who are emotionally intelligent tend to have more success in their lives.

What is emotional intelligence? It includes the ability to motivate oneself, to persist in the face of frustrations, to control impulses, to delay gratification, to regulate one's moods, to empathize, to hope, to keep depression and distress from swamping one's ability to think.

Early in one of our parenting workshops we often lead participants (both men and women) in a word-association activity. "We'll read a list of words to you," we say. "When you hear each word, decide which gender—male or female—you would immediately associate with that word."

Try it yourself:

- love
- kindness
- gentleness
- patience
- thoughtfulness
- compassion
- tenderness
- meekness
- sensitivity

With few exceptions, all the men and women who responded (thousands to date) associate those words with a female—despite the fact that each of these words are used in the four Gospels to describe Jesus Christ! These words are obviously not feminine, but human. They describe emotions, attitudes, and actions of healthy females *and males* made in the image of God. Now, however, it seems that human characteristics designed by God for *all* healthy people characterize only women.

In light of this, we must underline the importance of raising sons with healthy emotional development, especially when we consider the many biological, cultural, and social hurdles that sons have to jump (which daughters generally don't). One such hurdle is the emphasis on mind and de-emphasis on emotions that most American men grow up with—their relative comfort with facts rather than with feelings. "If I can only think right thoughts and make right choices," many men try to convince themselves, "I won't have to deal with my emotions, and somehow those pesky emotions will take care of themselves."

We've met more than our share of Christians, especially males, who seem to be prejudiced against feelings. They have been deceived into believing that emotions aren't important, that emotions are somehow "feminine," that emotions signify vulnerability and weakness, that emotions aren't worth respecting or heeding.

So how did emotions become the "prodigal son" of our personality, especially given the fact that there are numerous biblical examples of emotional men—Moses, David, Peter, even Jesus? Perhaps some of these reasons help to explain:

- Many have seen and read about the outrageous, horrible things people do when their emotions are out of control. Acts done in the heat of anger, in the throes of deep depression, when consumed by grief, or when someone got "carried away"—such reports have led many to conclude that it's not safe to feel.
- Emotions have received a bad reputation because they can be unreliable, inconsistent, and difficult to understand. Emotions don't always make sense. We *want* to feel one way, but end up feeling another.
- Most men we've worked with have experienced poor modeling, or none at all, and have received frightfully little biblical teaching about the place of emotions in the Christian life.
- Many men become emotional invalids because their emotions force them to look at their real selves—to see their humanity, their weakness, their vulnerability, their "dark" side. God speaks to us through our emotions, and we don't always like the message.

ACKNOWLEDGING YOUR SON'S BIOLOGICAL WILD CARD

Why is it that more males than females enter adulthood with an undeveloped emotional side of themselves? It seems, for starters, to be because of striking biological and physiological differences between boys and girls.

For years we assumed that this peculiarly male difficulty was due to sin, socialization, and a stubborn unwillingness to grow. To be sure, these can be, and often are, part of the problem— but only a part and not the whole. Decades of personal and clinical experience, as well as the results of recent research, have convinced us that physiology also plays a significant role in the male struggle with emotions. In fact, replicated medical research suggests that boys bring what some call a *biologically hardwired emotional disadvantage* to emotional and relational development.

Thanks to increasingly sophisticated neural imaging scans, we now know more about the differences between the male and the female brain. Consider these male distinctives as they relate to emotional and relational development:

- The male brain is hardwired to be better at spatial relationships than emotional ones.
- The frontal lobes of the brain, which handle many of the social and cognitive functions related to emotional relationships, develop more slowly in the male brain than in the female brain.
- The female brain has more gray matter (the active brain cells that carry out thinking) than does the male brain; the female brain activates both sides of the brain more often, while the male brain "lateralizes" more often—that is, activity is restricted to one side of the brain (thus, males may focus on computer or television screens and not hear what spouses or parents are saying).

- With the increased blood flow, higher gray matter content, increased electrical activity, and greater ability to use both sides of the brain, adolescent and adult females on average score higher on communication and social-skills tests than males, and higher on emotional-recognition tests as well.
- The male brain is tuned to relate with less tension to non-emotional objects than to emotional objects.
- The male brain system is actually emotionally fragile and often chooses to avoid emotional stimulation; meanwhile, the effects of testosterone compel males to take huge physical risks. Many males experience a deep conflict between the awareness of their internal fragility and their need to express external aggression. When a boy becomes an adolescent, this conflict increases.
- The male brain tends to avoid processing emotive data intensely. The way men tend to use the television remote control illustrates their brain formation. Males do not spend as much time as females focused on one topic of emotional or relational depth. If they do linger, they are more likely than their female counterparts to seek a quick solution.[3]

Testosterone appears to be a major contributor to this *biologically hardwired emotional disadvantage* in boys. This male hormone stimulates independence and physical aggression, propelling the male toward dominance patterns—all of which puts him at a disadvantage when it comes to forging emotional connections. In *You Just Don't Understand,* sociologist and author Deborah Tannen clearly demonstrates that male conversation, even when it's engaged in with women, relies on one-upping and dominance patterns. Testosterone also affects how males react to the emotional content of a situation: Females tend to process the emotional content of a situation—an argument, a moving film, a social interchange—long before the male does.[4] When it comes to using words that reflect emotional content, males are at a profound disadvantage. Studies demonstrate that, compared to men, women use on average five times the number of words in a week with a significantly higher amount of emotional content.

If your boy is an adolescent, consider this additional factor: The wash of testosterone through his body and brain during adolescence causes adaptations in his emotional system that *minimize* the emphasis on feelings and *enhance* emphasis on projects and activities.

Other research has revealed that when males experience emotions, there's not as much activity inside the male brain as inside the female brain—the brain is less active in fewer brain centers; there is less cross-talk between hemispheres, creating less verbal expression. In other words, a male's emotional experience is much more limited and localized due to the structure of the male brain in comparison to similar emotions experienced by women.

As you begin to understand these physiological differences, you will be better equipped to discern where your boys are coming from and to parent them in ways that will stimulate their emotional growth.

WHAT DO WE NEED TO TEACH OUR SONS ABOUT THEIR EMOTIONS?

As a result of our years of clinical work with men and women, we've identified seven specific principles we must pass on to our sons:

1. God Gives Us Our Emotions—and They Are Magnificent

Like the magnificent fall colors in our own Ozark Mountains, emotions add zest and beauty to life. Emotional insensitivity, though, is like experiencing life in black and white. Unless we teach our sons about the passion and intensity that emotions were designed to add to their lives, they may become paralyzed by the very emotions they ignore and disown.

Emotion is derived from the Latin word *emovaré*, which means "to move," and deals with motion, movement, and energy. It's been said that emotion could be spelled *E-motion,* since emotions are energy in motion.

Author Dorothy Finkelhor defines emotions this way:

> Emotions are the motivating forces of our lives, driving us to go ahead, pushing us backward, stopping us completely, determining what we do, how we feel, what we want, and whether we get what we want. Our hates, loves, fears, and what to do about them are determined by our emotional structure. There is nothing in our lives that does not have the emotional factor as its mainspring. It gives us power, or makes us weak, operates for our benefit or to our detriment, for our happiness or confusion.[5]

"I am fearfully and wonderfully made," declares the psalmist (Psalm 139:14). Nowhere is the delicate complexity of God's creation more evident than in our emotional makeup. Our emotions are complex, involving sensory, skeletal, motor, autonomic, and cognitive aspects, and they influence the spiritual, social, intellectual, and physical aspects of our lives.

2. Far from Being Negligible or Inherently Untrustworthy, Emotions Are Critically Important

Our generation has paid a high price for persuading men to ignore their emotions—and individuals and families will continue to pay unless and until we parent our sons differently. Denying our emotions—as it is when we deny any reality—distorts our perspective, limits our perception, and trains us to distrust our experience. What's worse, in denying our emotions we deny the very things God wants us to face in order to grow. Denying our emotions only increases the pain and alienation from a fundamental part of our personality, putting us out of touch with a significant part of who God made us to be. A body and mind are incomplete, even paralyzed, without emotions to empower them. God speaks to us through our emotions, as through a sixth sense. Emotions are to our personality what gasoline is to a car—the source of our passion and intensity. Emotions help us to monitor our needs, alert us to good and evil, and provide motivation and energy.

If boys don't learn how to understand and deal with their emotions, as adults they will likely lack the ability to understand and deal with emotional pain when it strikes. Emotional ignorance or insensitivity accompanies many men through life and either weighs them down or overcomes them with feelings of hopelessness and helplessness. The inner pain they experience can be just as draining as a headache or a wrenched back. When the pain becomes too much, the only option for many is to anesthetize it, which increases the risk of becoming addicted—often to more subtle things than just alcohol or drugs.

Unfortunately, some groups within evangelical Christianity have only encouraged the male discomfort with emotions, at least in part because of perceived *excesses* of emotion-driven religion. Yet the Bible makes it clear that maturity involves more than acquiring facts and possessing head knowledge—it's the transformation of the total person, including mind, emotions, and will.

The Bible is by no means silent about emotions. We have emotions, the Bible suggests, because God has emotions. From Genesis to Revelation we read about God's emotions—he is jealous, angry, loving, kind, sorrowful, and the like—and humans have been created in his image, which means males as well as females have the capacity to feel and to care.

When God told King Saul of Israel that his dynasty would end, he put it this way: "Your kingdom will not endure," he said through the prophet Samuel, for "the LORD has sought out a man after his own heart" (1 Samuel 13:14). Notice that God didn't want someone "after his own head." God was not particularly interested in a king with a rational mind, a monarch who could quickly calculate the bottom line and make objective decisions unfettered by emotions. No, God was looking for someone after his own *heart*. And David was that man—the same David who made many mistakes, who was flawed and fallible. But David was a passionate man who had a *heart* for God.

In the four Gospels we read that Jesus experienced and expressed anger, distress, sorrow, disappointment, frustration, fear, amazement, love, compassion, joy, and delight. Even in the Upper Room the night before Jesus died, he left his disciples a mandate by which, he said, all people would know they were his disciples. That identifier was an emotion: By their *love* for each other, Jesus said, all would recognize them as Christ-followers. Jesus said, "A new command I give you: Love one another. As I have loved you, so you must love one another. By this all men will know that you are my disciples, if you love one another" (John 13:34–35).

3. The Same Emotions Can Be Healthy or Unhealthy

In our seminars we ask participants to make a list of frequently experienced emotions. Of the hundreds of lists we've compiled, the shortest list included eleven emotions (this was from an all-male group), the longest included eighty-two emotions (need we say this was from an all-female group?). Here are the emotions listed as most frequently experienced.

loved	happy	pleased	surprised
confused	confident	anxious	concerned
indifferent	fearful	hurt	frustrated
embarrassed	frightened	humiliated	angry
appreciated	accepted	excited	grieving
confused	scared	lonely	proud
bored	glad	elated	worried
delighted	uncomfortable	shame	generous
depressed	unsure	sad	terrified

These emotions—*any* emotions—are not inherently good or bad. There are no good emotions and no bad emotions—just healthy and unhealthy expressions of those emotions. Not even love is an inherently good emotion; it's *what* we love and *how* we love that determines how healthy or unhealthy it is for us. We've counseled many men who appeared to love their job—or their car or their golf clubs—more than they loved their families. Yet if we love *things* rather than people, or even if our appreciation for who we are in Jesus Christ turns into a narcissistic preoccupation with *our* uniqueness and giftedness—even that can be unhealthy.

Or take the emotion of anger. Even this emotion is not fundamentally wrong, bad, or negative. Like all emotions, anger is something that is God-given and, when understood and used as God intended, is something that has tremendous potential for good. The fact is, when we don't understand our emotions we are more likely to express them in destructive and unhealthy ways.

4. Emotions Have a Physical Effect

We've lost count of the number of times we've heard a husband minimize or negate his wife's emotions by telling her sincerely, "Honey, it's all in your head!" To the contrary, emotions are not only in our head, but throughout our entire body.

Emotions trigger changes in our central and peripheral nervous systems by means of a variety of chemicals and neurotransmitters. Emotions can make your heart beat faster and your pupils dilate; perspiration increases, you may tremble, tears may come to your eyes, you may get goose bumps, and you may experience a tremendous surge of energy or a depleting drain of energy. While it's been established for many years that unhealthy responses to emotion can cause or complicate disease, more recently researchers have been studying the role emotions can play in healing.

Health writer Henry Dreher, author of *Your Defense Against Cancer,* has reviewed research suggesting that the inability to express emotions may play a role in weakening the body's defenses, and that people prone to this problem tend to be self-deprecating, nice to a fault, and unable to express their frustration and anger. "Many people who contract cancer," he writes, "seem to be out of touch with their emotions and their own needs and desires as individuals."[6]

5. Males Don't Naturally "Do" Emotions

Despite the critical need for males to value, understand, and respond in a healthy manner to their emotions, for the most part it's just plain difficult for them to do. Look at what men typically call out when we ask them at men's conferences for one-word descriptions of where men are today:

afraid	discourage	inadequate
angry	isolated	stuck
misunderstood	trapped	dependent
confused	numb	apathetic
running scared	guilty	lonely
ashamed	sad	wounded

Even the word *emotions* still seems to catch men by surprise. Listen to their responses: "Emotions are like a foreign language to me" ... "Emotions are what women have" ... "I rarely feel any emotions." One man admitted that "I'm not even conscious of my emotions during the day. I don't even think about my emotions at work, only about my actions. If I have a bad day at work, I remind myself why I'm here. I'm trying to make a living. I'm trying to finish a task. I'm paid to move on to the next task, not to focus on how others respond to me or how I feel."

At best, many men associate emotions only with times of crisis or excitement—during sporting events, for example, when they are most likely to show joy and excitement.

While there aren't distinctively male and female emotions, most women are nonetheless more aware and more expressive of their emotions. This difference becomes obvious in childhood, and the effects of our childhood training persist into adulthood. A comprehensive review of research related to emotional differences between men and women revealed that men tend to be both less able to identify with and feel the pain of others—that is, less *empathetic*—and less emotionally *expressive* than women. Several studies also reveal, however, that men can learn these important skills as adults.

One of the most devastating consequences of male role socialization is the high incidence of at least a mild form of *alexithymia*—the inability to identify and describe one's feelings and fantasies in words.[7] Family therapy expert Ronald Levant from the Center for Psychological Studies says that this common male problem is a result of being socialized to be emotionally stoic. Not only were boys not encouraged to learn to identify and express their emotions, but, more pointedly, they were told not to. They might have been told that "big boys don't cry." In sports they were taught "no pain, no gain" and admonished to learn to "play with pain." These exhortations trained them to be out of touch with their feelings, particularly those feelings on the vulnerable end of the spectrum. As a result of such socialization experiences, men are often genuinely unaware of their emotions. Lacking this emotional awareness, they tend to rely on their cognitive powers and try to logically deduce how they should feel. They cannot do what is so automatic for most women—simply direct the senses inward, feel the feeling, and let the verbal description come to mind.[8]

Males, then, can learn to express their feelings, yet their early training still makes them play catch-up to women. We must teach our sons how to demonstrate and verbalize their feelings—which they may very well be repressing or ignoring as a result of years of habit.

6. *If We Don't Understand and Control Our Emotions, They Will Control Us*

Our eleven-year-old stormed into the house after soccer practice, slammed the door, and headed out the back door to his backyard fort. Nathan is something of an introvert, so I gave him time by himself before going out to talk with him. We chitchatted about his fort, then I asked him what he was feeling. My question seemed to catch him off guard.

"I wish," he said after a pause, "that Coach would find a new job."

More chitchat, then I repeated my question. I guessed he was so focused on the flood of emotions that he couldn't nail down exactly *what* he was feeling. "I'm not sure, Dad," he said. "But I know I'd like to embarrass *him* the same way he embarrassed me."

"If you feel like telling me, I'd sure like to hear about it," I said. And Nathan continued to open up. As we talked about how hard he tried at practice, how he was really trying to follow the coach's instructions when the coach embarrassed him and (from Nathan's perspective) ridiculed him in front of the other guys—when these details came out, it became easier to make sense of his feelings. He was able to identify several emotions—fear, hurt, humiliation, frustration, and disappointment. And before his attention span expired, Nathan ended up expressing more than a little bit about what he was feeling.

Many males (and some females) suffer from the disease of *overcontrolled emotions*. Like Nathan, they come home from a draining or frustrating or humiliating day and retreat to their "fort," where they deny, repress, suppress, or ignore their emotions—in a word, they *overcontrol* their emotions. Now observe the cause-and-effect sequence: When they are out of touch with their emotions, they are out of touch with their true needs. (Such people often find other people and *their* feelings easier to deal with than their own; consequently they can become very selfless and service-oriented—but very unhealthy.) Gradually they can become either emotionally numb or dependent on and addicted to others who supply the significance and security for the "selfless" ones. Such "other-focused" people don't really have a life of their own, but depend on others and vicariously live their life through them.

Though they may possess the best of intentions, these individuals become sensitive to everyone's feelings but their own. When they think of being aware and sensitive, it's awareness and sensitivity to the emotions and reactions of *others*, not to themselves.

Overcontrolling their emotions is one of the quiet ways in which men can avoid dealing with them. Another way to avoid constructively dealing with emotions is to let them explode all over the place. It's ironic that an emotionally overcontrolled male often turns into an emotionally out-of-control male who eventually (or regularly) blows up verbally and physically. Like the two killers at Columbine High School, these are the ones we hear about in the media. When we let the river of emotion get out of control, its floodwaters can wreak havoc.

Both overcontrolled and undercontrolled emotions are signs of emotional immaturity. The price tag for such immaturity is high—we can pay now or pay later, but we will surely pay. Whether we are overcontrolled or out of control, we will typically have less energy and be less creative, our decision making will be impaired, and we will become more negative, critical, and preoccupied.

In a similar way, emotional maturity—typically expressed by a resolve not to bottle up emotions or let them explode—is a strong influencer of thinking patterns. Psychologist Alice Isen of the University of Maryland spent seventeen years studying the ways in which positive emotions affect the way people think, concluding (at the annual meeting of the American Association for the Advancement of Science) that positive emotions not only tend to make people more helpful and generous toward others, but appear to improve thinking processes such as judgment, problem solving, decision making, and creativity.

"Good feelings seem capable of bringing out our better nature socially and our creativity in thinking and problem solving," Isen said—which means that good feelings such as joy, appreciation, and gratitude can be a source of interpersonal cooperativeness and personal health and growth. Her research has implications for any situation where you want to bring out the best in someone. "Positive emotions," Isen says, "encourage people to look beyond the normal problem-solving method to try different options."[9]

7. *An Emotionally Healthy Boy Is More Likely to Become an Emotionally Mature Man*

We can look to the Bible for guidance on how God wants our sons to grow and become emotionally mature. From the teaching of the apostle Paul, we can glean the following insights:

God wants to renew our sons' minds. Our sons can be "transformed by the renewing of [their] mind," Paul writes in Romans 12:2. To the Philippians he writes, "Your attitude should be the same as that of Christ Jesus" (Philippians 2:5).

God wants to heal our sons' emotions. "Follow the way of love," Paul tells the Christians in Corinth (1 Corinthians 14:1). Elsewhere the apostle suggests that anger and sin are by no means synonymous—that we can be angry, and yet not sin (see Ephesians 4:26). In the same letter we read that we can be imitators of God as we "live a life of love, just as Christ loved us" (Ephesians 5:1–2).

God wants to direct our sons' choices. "Put aside the deeds of darkness and put on the armor of light," Paul urges the Roman Christians (Romans 13:12). To the Ephesian Christians he explains that we can choose to "put off [our] old self" and "put on the new self, created to be like God in true righteousness and holiness" (Ephesians 4:22, 24). Finally, Paul tells the Philippian Christians that it's pointless to dwell on past behavior, and instead we all should reach forward to what lies ahead (see Philippians 3:12–14)

CONCLUSION

Just because we are psychologists and counselors doesn't make it any easier to raise our boys according to biblical norms. Our boys have so much in common with your boys—a sin nature, a male brain, exposure to the same stereotypical myths and cultural misconceptions.

What *has* helped us, however, can help you, too. We've learned that a problem defined is a problem half-solved. We've learned to talk to other parents to find what's worked for them. And we've created opportunities for our boys to mingle with our adult male friends, who reinforce what we are trying to teach them.

SMALL BEGINNINGS

1. Recognize the importance of your own emotions. Develop a vocabulary for emotions—especially for the vulnerable ones like hurt, sadness, disappointment, fear, rejection, and abandonment, and also for the tender ones like sensitivity, warmth, appreciation, and affection. Take an emotional inventory of your boys. Which emotions are the easiest for them to experience or express? Which emotions are the hardest for them to experience or express? Which emotions seem to be causing them the most difficulty?

2. If you haven't started reading through the Bible with at least one child (if not with the entire family), start now— and pay particular attention to emotions in men like Abraham, Moses, David, Peter, and Jesus. What are some of

the emotions Jesus experienced? How did he choose to express them?

3. Play *Name That Feeling.* The game is easy—when you or one of your boys experiences a strong emotion, try to name it. Use as many names as possible for the emotion. Let the person who is experiencing the emotion talk about what it looks like from the inside out. Then others can share what they thought the emotion was, based on their interpretation of how the other person expressed it.

Chapter Six

WHAT TYPE OF SON DO YOU HAVE?

UP FRONT *In this chapter ...*

- ✦ Children from the same family have distinctly individual personalities. Parents need to adjust to their son's unique temperament and style of relating to the environment.
- ✦ Parents can appreciate and better understand the value of each child's differences by recognizing that God has given different spiritual gifts and types of service for the growth of the church. *Different* does not mean inferior or wrong.
- ✦ Boys are born with natural preferences and tendencies that have a strong influence on their personality type. Identifying a son's psychological type can help parents appreciate his differences and seek ways to promote the healthy use of his preferences.
- ✦ The Myers-Briggs Type Indicator (MBTI) identifies four sets of contrasting personality traits that people typically exhibit when facing the world: Extrovert/Introvert, Sensor/Intuitive, Thinker/Feeler, and Judger/Perceiver. Individuals manifest all eight traits, but tend to prefer one in each pair.
- ✦ When a boy is forced to use a less-developed trait to handle a situation, the results are often inferior. Parents need to be

> sure to send the message to their son that God made him in his image and made no mistakes in placing him in his particular family with his particular personality.

In HIS CLASSIC 1978 study of temperament styles titled *Please Understand Me*, David Keirsey writes the following:

If I do not want what you want, please try not to tell me that my want is wrong.

Or if I believe other than you, at least pause before you correct my view.

Or if my emotion is less than yours, or more, given the same circumstances, try not to ask me to feel more strongly or weakly.

Or yet if I act, or fail to act, in the manner of your design for action, let me be.

I do not, for the moment at least, ask you to understand me. That will come only when you are willing to give up changing me into a copy of you.

I may be your spouse, your parent, your offspring, your friend, or your colleague. If you will allow me any of my own wants, or emotions, or beliefs, or actions, then you open yourself, so that someday these ways of mine might not seem so wrong, and might finally appear to you as right—for me. To put up with me is the first step to understanding me. Not that you embrace my ways as right for you, but that you are no longer irritated or disappointed with me for my seeming waywardness. And in understanding me you might come to prize my differences from you, and, far from seeking to change me, preserve and even nurture those differences.[1]

If you came from a family where you were not an only child, if *you* have more than one child, if you know of a family with more than one child, you have undoubtedly noticed that children from the same gene pool, raised by the same parents, living in the same neighborhood, eating the same foods, drinking the same water, going to the same school, and attending the same church—children who apparently have very, very similar heredity and nurture can nonetheless be totally different. They may be the same gender; they may even be identical twins—yet each is unique in his or her own way.

And it doesn't take long for very clear distinctions to emerge in their little personalities. Infants show significant individual differences essentially from the time of birth. Each child is born with unique temperamental characteristics and behavioral traits. Psychologists have described several dimensions of such differences, including activity level, sensory threshold, responsiveness, curiosity, irritability, soothability, and the capacity to signal needs and inner states. Because each infant has a distinctive way of interacting with the environment, parents must seek to understand and adjust to their infant's particular makeup.

Even more fascinating than examining psychological studies was watching our own kids develop. Why did Matt love to be cuddled and rocked and Andrew push us away after being held for a short time? Why is one of our sons more compliant and another more argumentative? Why as babies did Nathan like to stack blocks or lay them in a straight line and Matt like to rearrange whatever Nathan had organized? Where do those differences come from? How do we explain them?

With individual differences that run so deep, parents cannot depend on understanding and communicating with their sons without *learning* how to understand and communicate with them. And, if truth be told, it's a lot like learning a different language. It's almost impossible to get some boys to be quiet, and almost impossible to get others to talk. Some boys are like tightly wound machines, while others are calm and reflective. Some are aware of all the nuances of what's going on around them, and others are oblivious to anything but what they happen to be doing at the moment. If you let them, some boys would watch television or play video games from morning till night, while others couldn't care less about the television and would be happier reading a good book.

Each one of your children talks differently, listens differently, moves differently, feels differently, and sees the world differently. "Thank you for making me so wonderfully complex!" is in essence how the psalmist says it, with hearty gratitude to God: "Your workmanship is marvelous—and how well I know it" (Psalm 139:14, NEW LIVING TRANSLATION). Made in the image of God and endowed with infinite worth, every person is clearly, unmistakably, wonderfully unique.

DIFFERENT IS A GOOD THING

Different is a powerful word. When you were a child, did your mom or dad ever tell you that you were different? What did it feel like? What do you think of today when you hear the word *different?* Is *different* primarily a positive word for you, or a negative word? A compliment, or a criticism?

The word *different* suggests simply that the different thing— or person—is partly or totally unlike another. Something or someone *different* doesn't quite fit the mold, whatever "the mold" may be. *Different* implies a deviation or variation from the norm. Unfortunately, children in particular often take the word to mean *not the way something or someone should be*—unusual, inappropriate, inferior, deviant, wrong. And sadly, that's the message many of our boys get from society, especially from their predominantly female elementary school and church school teachers—and sometimes even from their parents. ("Tommy is just like me, but I'm not sure where David came from. He's so different from the rest of us.")

Not only do we live in a place and time that generally celebrates individuals and their distinctivenesses (rather than in a place and time that celebrates society and its community), but the Christian religion also celebrates differences, or diversity, as opposed to division. Paul wrote to the Corinthians that there were different spiritual gifts, different ways to serve the church, different ways in which God works in our lives—and that God is the author of those differences (see 1 Corinthians 12). Rather than shaving away our individual differences, we need to maximize their value. Indeed, this is a key to raising healthy sons who love Jesus and who can become good husbands and fathers: We must understand and appreciate their individual differences.

We've already commented on the implications of the significant gender differences between boys and girls. However, significant personality differences will also determine the degree to which we are able to understand and truly hear our sons, as well as the degree to which they will feel heard. It's impossible to overstate the enormous value in learning to appreciate differences.

TEMPERAMENTS AND TYPES

There are several routes to better understanding such differences. Cultures have been identifying different personality styles for thousands of years. Hippocrates identified four temperaments. Native Americans have the four points of the medicine wheel. In the 1930s Norwegian theologian Ole Hallesby proposed the idea of sanguine, choleric, phlegmatic, and melancholic temperaments, later adapted and popularized in the United States by Tim LaHaye and Florence Littauer.

Psychological type has been found to be another eminently helpful way to understand and appreciate innate personality differences. Psychological type provides something of a map to a person's personality. While this map, like any map, is short on details about terrain, climate, and the like, it *does* point us in the right direction. In fact, identifying personality type has been critically important to us, whether with respect to parenting our three sons or providing professional counseling.

Your son's personality type consists of several broad inborn preferences or tendencies that shape his personality. Everyone begins life with a small number of inherited personality traits—the fundamental building blocks of personality. These inborn traits determine the unique distinctives of personality.

While these core traits are present at birth, they are influenced and modified by the environment. Every child is an *initiator,* who in part makes his own environment. He is a *reinforcer,* who selectively rewards or punishes agents in his environment for the way they behave toward him. And he is a *responder,* who modifies the impact of the environment on his personality.[2]

Of the several tools used to measure psychological type, we have found the Myers-Briggs Type Indicator (MBTI) to be one of the most helpful. The MBTI identifies four pairs of contrasting personality traits: extrovert/introvert, sensor/intuitive, thinker/feeler, and judger/perceiver. Each pair represents opposite ways of perceiving, deciding, and so forth:

Extroversion (E)	*Focus Attitude*	(I) Introversion
Sensing (S)	*Perceiving Function*	(N) Intuition
Thinking (T)	*Deciding Function*	(F) Feeling
Judging (J)	*Lifestyle Attitude*	(P) Perception

According to type theory, every person uses all eight traits—but in each pair, one is preferred and better developed. It's something like playing the piano: You learn to play with both hands, but the fact of your right-handedness (that is, your preference for using your right hand over your left hand) determines the relative ease of playing scales with your right hand and the extra practice your left hand needs if you are to play the piano well with both hands.

Here's a simple demonstration of how preferences affect a task. Take a pen or pencil, hold it with your *less*-preferred hand, and write your name here as quickly as you do when you use your preferred hand:

_____

Do it again, now writing with your preferred hand:

_____

You get the point. Most people say that using their less-preferred hand is awkward and frustrating, takes more time and concentration, and yields an inferior result. When using your most-preferred hand, tasks are usually easier and less frustrating, take less time, and the end result is usually better.

That's the way it is with different personality types. When we or our children are forced to carry out certain relational tasks with one of our less-preferred, and thus less-developed, traits, the activity is usually more awkward, threatening, and frustrating—and it usually takes more time and concentration, and it often produces an inferior result. Working with less-preferred traits usually leads to results we're not proud of—so we try to avoid such situations in the future.

The four pairs of traits in the MBTI make sixteen possible personality types. In each four-letter combination the first letter is always either an E or I (extroversion or introversion), the second letter an S or N (sensing or intuition), the third letter a T or F (thinking or feeling), and the fourth letter a J or P (judging or perception):

ISTJ	ISFJ	INFJ	INTJ
ISTP	ISFP	INFP	INTP
ESTP	ESFP	ENFP	ENTP
ESTJ	ESFJ	ENFJ	ENTJ

That's an overview of the personality types represented in the Myers-Briggs Type Indicator. Let's now look at the pairs in more detail.

Extroversion/Introversion

Extroversion and *introversion* describe two basic ways of relating to the outer world. They identify where we are most comfortable focusing our attention and where we are energized. Again, every person uses both extroversion and introversion in relating to the outer world, but each prefers, or is more comfortable with, one of them over the other.

Extroverts get their stimulation primarily from the environment around them, from the outer world of people and things. They are generally more comfortable when they focus on people and activities outside of them and around them. Extroverts do not necessarily talk more, nor are they necessarily "party animals." They simply draw energy from the outer world of people and things.

Our middle son, Matt, leans toward extroversion. He has a bubbly personality, enjoys lots of friends at school, and would much prefer playing with several friends than being alone. He's the sort of boy who readily talks with strangers, tells them his name and the names of his brothers, and then asks a personal question about the stranger. He is comfortable in the outer world. He processes information by talking about it, not thinking about it. When Matt comes home from school, he immediately wants friends over or wants to call a friend on the phone.

Introverts, on the other hand, get their stimulation primarily from within themselves, from their inner world of thoughts and reflections. They are energized by being alone. They aren't necessarily quiet and unsociable, but simply more comfortable when they focus their energy *inside* themselves rather than *outside*.

Our introverted son is Nathan, who loves spending time by himself reading, thinking, or working on a project. Nathan is friendly and likes people, but he doesn't seek out large groups—he simply likes being alone. He has only a couple of close friends, and that's enough for him. When Nathan comes home from school, he usually heads to his room. Unlike Matt's easy self-revelation to strangers, Nathan tends not to reveal much about himself to someone until he has known that person for a while. When you ask Matt a question, he may start to answer it before you're finished *asking* it. Ask Nathan a question, and he'll want to take time to think about it.

Here's an extroversion/introversion summary.[3] Which trait generally describes your son?

Extroversion (E)	Introversion (I)
Can feel drained if he spends too much time alone.	Can feel drained if he spends too much time with people.
Feels drawn outward by external requests and opportunities.	Feels pushed inward by external requests and intrusions.
Energized by other people and external experiences.	Energized by inner resources and internal experiences.
An interruption is an opportunity.	An interruption is an intrusion.
Enjoys people.	Enjoys pondering.
The unlived life is not worth examining.	The unexamined life is not worth living.

May be unaware of what is going on inside of him.	May be unaware of what is going on around him.
Acts and then (maybe) reflects.	Reflects and then (maybe) acts.
Seeks activity.	Seeks solitude.
Is often friendly, talkative, easy to know.	Is often reserved, quiet, hard to know.
The whole world knows what he is feeling.	Only a few people know what he is feeling.
Solves problems externally.	Solves problems internally.
Thinks while speaking.	Thinks before speaking.
Values relationships.	Values privacy.
Gives breadth to life.	Gives depth to life.
To *introverts*, he may seem shallow.	To *extroverts*, he may seem withdrawn.

Sensing/Intuition

At any given time we are either taking in information or making decisions that are based on information we have received. To use the MBTI terms, *sensing* and *intuition* are two different ways of perceiving or gathering information.

While our son Matt can and does use his intuitive side, he prefers the sensing function. Consequently, he's influenced more by what he sees, hears, touches, tastes, and smells—that is, by what he learns with his senses—than by the possibilities of what might be. He is *not* necessarily more sensible or sensitive; he simply tends to be very observant and attentive to details. He has a here-and-now orientation that keeps him focused on the task at hand. He prefers to deal with practical things.

The intuiting function processes information not so much by one's five senses as by "hunch," or a kind of sixth sense. Our youngest son, Andrew, prefers intuition. Because he has more of a future orientation, it can be difficult for him to concentrate on what his schoolteacher is saying—he's constantly thinking about the possibilities inherent within a previous statement. He can get bored with details or mundane tasks. He loves to create. When he colors, he isn't much concerned about staying within the lines. He is not limited by *what is*, but imagines what *might be*. When Andrew is asked a question, he usually gives a more general answer and tends to answer several other questions at the same time—in contrast to Matt, who tends to answer a question with a specific answer.

Here's a sensing/intuition summary. Which trait generally describes your son?

Sensing (S)	Intuition (N)
Looks at specific parts and pieces.	Looks at broad, overall patterns and all possible and probable relationships between specific parts and pieces.
Focuses on the immediate, enjoying what's there.	Focuses on the future, enjoying the anticipation of all the exciting, important things that might be.
Likes things that are definite and measurable.	Likes opportunities for being inventive, and if not given the opportunity will go ahead and be inventive anyway.
Prefers handling practical matters.	Prefers imagining all potential possibilities for himself, family, friends, his world, and even other worlds.

Asks "Will it work?"	Asks "Is it possible? If so, what do we need to do? If not, why not? And who says why not?"
Can't see the forest for the trees.	Can't see the trees for the forest; in fact, he may not even be looking at the forest in front of him because no matter where his body is, his mind is probably somewhere else, especially if he is an adolescent.
Starts at the beginning and takes one step at a time.	Isn't sure where the beginning is, doesn't think it's important, jumps in anywhere, leaps over steps, and doesn't usually know that he's skipped anything.
Enjoys reading instructions and notices details.	Skips instructions and follows hunches, until he's tried two or three times and can't figure it out; then he either calls an "S" friend for help or, as a last-gasp effort, looks at the instructions, if he can find them.
Likes set procedures, established routines.	Likes frequent change and variety. May have found three or four different ways to come home from work because it's too boring to come home the same way every day.

Looks for the evidence.	Looks for the potential, the possibilities, the options, the way to take what isn't and bring it to pass, the way to find new solutions to old problems.
To *intuitive* types, he may seem practical to a fault, boring, and literal-minded.	To *sensing* types, he may seem fickle and impractical.

By the way, be sure to note the difference between the writing styles of these two lists. Someone who prefers sensing (like Matt) would love the list on the left—it's precise, concise, and specific; there's no rambling, no nonsense, no wasted words. Someone who prefers intuition (like Andrew) would appreciate the list on the right, which is much more creative and expansive, wandering a bit here and there—which makes it all the better to an intuitive type.

Thinking/Feeling

According to the MBTI, *thinking* and *feeling* are the two ways of making decisions. Of course, most people use both functions when making a decision, but they prefer or are better at one than the other. Those who prefer the thinking function tend to decide on the basis of logic and of objective considerations. The feeling function, on the other hand, decides more on the basis of personal subjective values.

Our seventeen-year-old Nathan prefers the thinking function when making decisions. When he's asked to do something, he is likely to ask why—not necessarily in a rebellious manner but simply because he prefers to make decisions based on reasons. "Just because" is not an acceptable answer for him. You don't disagree with Nathan without being prepared to explain your reasons. Nathan's matter-of-fact style of making decisions can come across as cold, uncaring, and impassive. To the contrary, Nathan is a very tender and sensitive young man—yet honesty and fairness are very important to him. He tends to see things as black or white, right or wrong. There just aren't a lot of gray areas.

Andrew's preferred decision-making function is feeling. (In fact, Nathan can get irked that his little brother "gets so emotional.") In the MBTI lexicon, *feeling* doesn't mean that a person is overly emotional or illogical, but simply that the person makes decisions based on people or values rather than on black-and-white principles. While his older brother approaches problems objectively, Andrew prefers a subjective approach. If you disagree with Andrew, he will often let it go because of his desire to maintain harmony and not make waves. When it comes to making a decision, Andrew will weigh heavily the feelings of others. Empathy comes easily for him. He makes decisions primarily on the basis of how they will affect others—so much so, in fact, that he sometimes forgets to pay attention to his own needs.

When Andrew is asked to obey in a situation he doesn't understand, he doesn't ask why (as Nathan usually does)—he'll simply do what he's asked because he wants to please. Children who prefer feeling can be especially sensitive to the emotional climate in their homes. Constant conflict at home can lead to emotional or even physical problems.

Here's a thinking/feeling summary. Which trait generally describes your son?

Thinking (T)	Feeling (F)
Decides with the head.	Decides with the heart.
Decides by linear logic.	Decides by relational logic.

Needs to understand emotions before he experiences them.	Needs to experience emotions before he understands them.
Concerned for truth and justice.	Concerned for relationships and harmony.
More firm-minded.	More gentle-hearted.
Experiences life as an onlooker, from outside a situation.	Experiences life as a participant, from inside a situation.
Takes a long and detached view.	Takes an immediate and personal view.
Spontaneously finds flaws and criticizes.	Spontaneously appreciates, encourages, and praises.
Has a hard time keeping criticism under control.	Has a hard time making a critical observation.
Can speak the truth, but not always in love.	Can have difficulty speaking the truth if it might hurt someone's feelings.
Analyzing plans comes naturally.	Understanding people comes naturally.
May have the gift of justice.	May have the gift of mercy.
Sees things in black and white.	Sees a lot of gray areas.
To *feeling* types, he may seem cold and condescending.	To *thinking* types, he may seem fuzzy-minded and emotional.

Judging/Perception

Judging and *perception* are what the MBTI calls the "lifestyle attitudes," reflecting two different lifestyle orientations—two different ways people relate to the world around them.

A judging lifestyle is decisive, planned, and orderly. Nathan prefers a judging lifestyle, but that doesn't mean he is judgmental.

He relates to the external world in a structured and organized way. Even as a baby Nathan lined up his toys in a straight line. He had a certain place for everything, and he got upset if things weren't where they should have been. He can be spontaneous, but he prefers order and structure. He enjoys knowing what the schedule is and keeping to it. Too much change can throw him off.

Those who prefer a perceiving lifestyle, on the other hand, tend to be more flexible, adaptable, and spontaneous. Perception types aren't necessarily more perceptive than judging types, but simply more curious and flexible—able to handle change well. Matt, for example, relates to the outer world in a laid-back, casual manner. He doesn't care if his clothes and homework and other stuff are lined up in a straight line or scattered across the floor. He enjoys surprises and responds well to the unexpected. Consistency and follow-through aren't Matt's strong suits, because he can be easily distracted. He starts a lot of projects and completes few of them, usually because something new catches his attention. He is fun-loving by nature, and he brings a lot of laughter to our family.

Judging (J)	Perception (P)
Prefers an organized lifestyle.	Prefers a flexible lifestyle.
Enjoys definite order and structure.	Enjoys going with (or against) the flow.
His motto is "Work now, play later."	His motto is "Play now, work later"—or, even better, "Play while you work."
Likes to have life under control.	Prefers to experience life as it happens.
Enjoys making decisions, but may make them too quickly.	Enjoys getting more information, but can become so fascinated with the information that he forgets to make a decision.

The product is more important than the process.	The process is more important than the product.
The most important part of a trip is arriving at the destination.	The most important part of a trip is the traveling.
Likes clear limits and categories.	Likes freedom to explore without limits.
Feels comfortable establishing closure.	Feels comfortable maintaining openness.
Finds it hard to relax until the task is completed.	Can easily interrupt a task if something more fun or interesting comes along.
Enjoys deadlines and likes to plan in advance.	Thinks there is plenty of time, so tends to meet deadlines with a last-minute rush.
To *perceiving* types, he may seem demanding, rigid, and uptight.	To *judging* types, he may seem disorganized, messy, and irresponsible.

Go back and skim all four descriptive lists. Now imagine what it would be like to have a preference *opposite* that which you were expected to have—for instance, to be by personality a *perceiving* boy who was talked to and expected to act like a *judging* boy— who constantly was told (or otherwise picked up the message) that "good" boys were organized and structured? What kind of miscommunication and conflict might there be in such a household? Chances are, you'd feel out of place . . . you'd think something was wrong with you . . . you'd worry that God had made a mistake in placing you in your particular family.

DISCOVERING YOUR SON'S TYPE

Now it's time to take a closer look at your own son's preferences in particular. (Remember that the younger he is, the less fixed his personality is—so while some of his preferences might be perfectly clear on some scales, on others there may still be a lot of ambiguity.) Choose your responses in light of how your son *usually* behaves.[4]

1. Does your son . . .

_____ act quickly, sometimes without thinking?

_____ get tired of long, slow jobs or games?

_____ enjoy learning by doing?

_____ chatter?

_____ enjoy new activities?

_____ want to do things with others?

_____ care what other children think?

_____ unload emotions as they occur?

These are all characteristics of *extroverts*. When your son does these things, he is extroverting.

2. Does your son . . .

_____ think before acting?

_____ work or play patiently for long periods of time?

_____ enjoy learning by reading?

_____ keep things to himself?

_____ hesitate to try something new?

_____ have a few close friends?

_____ want a quiet space to work or play in?

_____ set his own standards despite others' opinions?

_____ bottle up emotions?

These are all characteristics of *introverts*. When your son does these things, he is introverting.

3. Does your son . . .

_____ enjoy familiar activities and routines?

_____ want to know the right way to do things?

_____ observe carefully and remember lots of details?

_____ memorize easily?

_____ ask, "Did it really happen?"

_____ like coloring books?

_____ enjoy collecting things?

_____ enjoy working with his hands?

_____ seem steady and patient?

These are all characteristics of *sensing* types. When your son does these things, he is perceiving through the senses.

4. Does your son . . .

_____ enjoy learning new things?

_____ enjoy being different?

_____ learn quickly but forget details?

_____ have a vivid imagination?

_____ enjoy imaginative stories?

_____ use toys in new and original ways?

_____ often lose things?

_____ quickly go from one new interest to another?

_____ work and play in fits and starts?

These are all characteristics of *intuitive* types. When your son does these things, he is perceiving through the intuition.

5. Does your son . . .

_____ ask "why?" a lot?

_____ insist on logical explanations?

_____ get alarmed if someone is treated unfairly?

_____ like to arrange things in orderly patterns?

_____ show more interest in ideas than in people?

_____ hold firmly to his beliefs?

_____ seem uncomfortable with affection?

_____ want rules in games established and kept?

_____ like to be praised for doing something competently?

These are all characteristics of *thinking* types. When your son does these things, he is making thinking judgments.

6. Does your son . . .

_____ like to talk or read about people?

_____ want to be praised for caring for others?

_____ get alarmed if someone is unhappy?

_____ tell stories expressively, in great detail?

_____ try to be tactful, even if that means lying?

_____ show more interest in people than in ideas?

_____ generally agree with his friends' opinions?

_____ want to be told you love him?

_____ relate well to other children, teachers, relatives?

These are all characteristics of *feeling* types. When your son does these things, he is making feeling judgments.

7. Does your son . . .

_____ like to know what is going to happen?

_____ know how things "ought to be"?

_____ enjoy making choices?

_____ usually work before playing?

_____ discipline himself?

_____ have definite goals?

_____ have strong opinions?

_____ keep a well-ordered room?

_____ want to be in charge?

These are all characteristics of *judging* types. When your son does these things, he is relating to the world through his judging function.

8. Does your son . . .

_____ enjoy spontaneity?

_____ show a lot of curiosity?

_____ enjoy sampling new experiences and ideas?

_____ turn work into play?

_____ overextend himself?

_____ adapt well to changing circumstances?

_____ keep an open mind?

_____ not object to having things out of place?

_____ want to understand whatever's happening?

These are all characteristics of *perceiving* types. When your son does these things, he is relating to the world through his perceiving function.

LEARNING AND SPEAKING YOUR SON'S "PERSONALITY LANGUAGE"

A normal part of life within a family unit is learning to deal with each other's differences. Family members are hardly immune to frustration and conflict due to personality differences. But when parents understand personality type—the different relational languages God has given each of us—they can significantly decrease the unnecessary conflicts and misunderstandings that plague many families. If you understand personality type, you are less likely to try to squeeze your son into your own mold and instead you can focus your energy on raising him to become the unique person that God designed him to be.

Understanding your son's personality type will contribute to responsible and more effective rearing, teaching, counseling, and overall understanding of him. It can help him to better understand himself and to improve his relationships with parents, teachers, and friends. By identifying individual strengths, you can help him strengthen self-esteem, enhance achievement, and build social interaction.[5]

Parents wield the most influence on how their boys learn, how they understand themselves and others, and how successfully they grow according to their individual, God-designed bents. You can begin to find out how your own personality preferences and expectations either blend or clash with those of your sons. You can learn how to speak your sons' language and thus increase the probability of clear communication. If you understand some of the most important personality differences between you and your boys, you are likely to be more successful in nurturing their growth.[6]

The most accurate way to identify your personality type is to take the Myers-Briggs Type Indicator (MBTI); have your children take the Murphy-Meisgeier Type Indicator for Children (MMTIC). To find those in your area who are qualified to give it, ask your pastor or a Christian counselor, or contact the Association for Psychological Type (APT), P.O. Box 5099, Gainesville, FL 32602, (904) 371-1853; they'll put you in touch with someone who can help you. Or go to their web site at www.personalitypage.com for an overview and a short form of the MBTI.

For more information about the MBTI, consult these books:

Keirsey, David, and Marilyn Bates. *Please Understand Me.* Del Mar, Calif.: Prometheus, 1978.

Kroeger, Otto, and Janet M. Thuesen. *Type Talk.* New York: Delacorte Press, 1988.

Mayhall, Jack, and Carole Mayhall. *Opposites Attack: Turning Your Differences into Opportunities.* Colorado Springs: NavPress, 1990.

Myers, Isabel Briggs, with Peter B. Myers. *Gifts Differing: Understanding Personality Type.* Palo Alto, Calif.: Consulting Psychologists Press, 1980, 1995.

Neff, LaVonne. *One of a Kind.* Portland, Ore.: Multnomah Press, 1988.

Wright, H. Norman. *The Power of a Parent's Words.* Ventura, Calif.: Regal Books, 1991 (especially chapters 12 and 13).

SMALL BEGINNINGS

1. What are the benefits of understanding your son's preference, whether it is: extroversion or introversion; sensing or intuition; thinking or feeling; judging or perceiving?

2. What are some consequences of *not* understanding your son's preferences?

3. As you begin to identify personality type in yourself and in your son, what are some ways you could relate to him that would be consistent with the unique person God has made him to be?

4. Think about your son's personality type. What does he like to do? What are his interests? His favorite activities? Where are his blind spots? How can you help him in these areas?

5. Most parents who read this chapter will realize that some of the disagreements you've had with your son have centered around personality differences rather than around things that are right and wrong. How are you and your son different? Share these observations with your son and talk about ways you can make your differences work *for* you rather than against you.

Chapter Seven

ANGER

Understanding the Fundamental Male Emotion

UP FRONT *In this chapter . . .*

+ Violent acts by boys have escalated in recent years. We must begin teaching boys to understand their emotions and control their anger.

+ As a necessary and natural protector from danger, anger can be used to work *for* us rather than against us.

+ Anger is a God-given emotion; in the Bible it is mentioned in frequency second only to *love*.

+ Anger is a secondary emotion, an automatic response to pain that often disguises the underlying emotions of fear, hurt, and frustration.

+ Anger can be a signal that something is wrong, a warning of a problem that needs attention.

+ Parents need to model constructive ways of coping with emotions. This can be accomplished by:

  • keeping an "anger log" identifying situations likely to trigger anger

  • being aware of the emotional climate at home before you return home from work in the evening

  • making sure the family doesn't bear the brunt of any displaced anger that really belongs to others

  • having developmentally realistic expectations of the children

VIOLENCE BY BOYS HAS dramatically escalated during the past few years, from schoolyards in Kentucky and Oregon to basketball courts throughout the country. In fact, the overwhelming majority of violent acts are committed by boys.

If our sons are to control their anger, they have to first understand the emotion. So just what is anger, anyway? At its core, it is a multidimensional emotion, which makes it difficult to define. Dictionaries render *anger* as "emotional excitement induced by intense displeasure." The word *anger* names the reaction but in itself conveys nothing about intensity or justification or manifestation of the emotional state. Anger is a "hot" feeling, and when allowed to burn out of control, leads to rage. In fact, the English word *anger* is derived from an old Norse word that means "affliction." The German *arg* means *wicked*— so the noun *arger* is the emotional response to "wicked" stimuli. The Spanish *enojar*, which means "to get angry," derives from *en* and *ojo*—something that offends the eye. In these languages *anger* connotes uneasiness, displeasure, and resentment.

Yet anger is not necessarily negative. We've considered the literal definitions of the word; now ponder these emotional and psychological insights about anger:

- Anger involves physiological arousal, a state of readiness. When you are angry, your body shows an increase in energy that can be directed in whatever way you choose.
- Anger is an intense emotional reaction that can remain at times largely unexpressed and bottled up inside; at other times it is directly expressed in outward behavior.
- Anger is one of the many God-given emotions that can be a potentially powerful and positive force for good in our lives.
- Anger is a secondary emotion that is usually experienced in response to a primary emotion, such as hurt, frustration, or fear.

- Anger is a natural and normal response to a variety of life's situations and stresses.
- Anger is a God-given emotion intended to protect us and to provide energy for developing solutions to life's inevitable problems.
- Anger—along with the ability to understand it and appropriately express it—is a sign of emotional and spiritual maturity.

To make our anger work *for* us rather than against us, we do well to recognize and discard three myths about it.

MYTHBUSTER: ANGER IS A GOD-GIVEN EMOTION

The Bible has a lot to say about anger. Clearly God acknowledges the significance of this powerful emotion. In fact, the only emotion the Bible mentions more than anger is love. Anger, or wrath, is first mentioned in Genesis 4:5 and last mentioned in Revelation 19:15. In the Old Testament alone, anger is mentioned 455 times, with 375 of those references dealing with *God's* anger.

The New Testament uses several different Greek words that are translated in English as simply *anger*. It is critical to understand the distinction between these words; otherwise Scripture appears to contradict itself (in English translations, at least) because the Bible says we should not be angry ("Get rid of all bitterness, rage and anger, brawling and slander, along with every form of malice"—Ephesians 4:31; see also Colossians 3:8 and James 1:19–20), and yet another verse admonishes us "in your anger do not sin" (Ephesians 4:26). So what does it all mean?

The most common New Testament Greek word for *anger* is *orge*. It appears thirty-six times and suggests a more settled and long-lived attitude of anger, slower in its onset but more enduring—like coals in a barbecue grill that slowly warm up through red to white-hot, then hold this temperature until the cooking is done. The enduring nature explains why *orge* often includes revenge—but *not always*. There are two significant occurrences of this word where revenge is *not* implied:

- In Ephesians 4:26 Paul writes to those Christians, "'In your anger do not sin': Do not let the sun go down while you are still angry." The word *anger* in the first part of this verse is the Greek word *orgizo*—an entirely different word than the one translated *angry* at the end of the verse *(parorgismos)*. Even the Bible illustrates the value of understanding our anger.
- In Mark 3:5 the writer records that Jesus looked at the Pharisees "in anger" *(orge)*—an implication that at least this kind of anger is justified.

In these two verses the word *orge* (or its derivative *orgizo*) means an abiding habit of the mind that is aroused under certain conditions against evil and injustice—the *healthy* type of anger Christians are encouraged to have, an anger that does not include revenge or rage.

Another New Testament Greek word used to describe the emotion of anger is *thumas*, which characterizes anger as a turbulent commotion or a boiling agitation of feelings. *Thumas* anger doesn't simmer reflectively like *orge*, but explodes—it bursts out from a spring of inner indignation, like a match that flares up in an instant and just as quickly burns out. This *thumas* anger is mentioned eighteen times (Ephesians 4:31 and Galatians 5:20, for example, where it is translated as "rage," or "fits of rage"). And it is *this* kind of anger we are told to control.

MYTHBUSTER: ANGER IS A SECONDARY EMOTION

Anger is an almost automatic response to any kind of pain, an emotion we feel almost immediately after we have been hurt. When you trip and fall or drop a hammer on your toe, it hurts, and you may experience mild anger. When your son talks back to you in public, it hurts, and you may respond to him (probably in the car on the way home) in anger.

When your teenage son stays out two hours past his 11:00 P.M. curfew and doesn't bother to call, you experience concern and fear. When he waltzes in the door and calmly announces, "Sorry I forgot to call, Dad," you probably experience anger—and he may experience your expression of that anger.

Anger is often the only emotion that a male is aware of, though they've surely experienced a myriad of other emotions as well. For just below the surface, a man has many other, deeper emotions that need to be identified and acknowledged. Hidden underneath (sometimes deep underneath) the surface emotion of anger is fear, hurt, frustration, disappointment, vulnerability, and a longing for connection. Boys learn early on that anger can help them deflect attention from these more painful emotions. Anger is safer, and it provides some protection for the frightened and vulnerable self. Anger helps him avoid, or at least minimize, his pain. Anger provides a surge of energy. It decreases his vulnerability and increases his sense of security. What's more, he tells himself, all real men get angry.

In short, boys learn quickly that it's easier to feel anger than it is to feel pain.

MYTHBUSTER: ANGER IS A SIGNAL

Through our expression of the emotion of anger, God gets our attention and makes us aware of opportunities to learn, to grow, to mature, and to make significant changes for the good. Like love, anger has tremendous potential for both good and evil.

Anger is like a smoke detector, like a car's dashboard warning light, like a flashing red traffic light on a dark road. Anger warns us to stop, look, and listen. Anger tells us to take caution, because something may very well be wrong. In *The Dance of Anger* clinical psychologist Harriet Lerner notes the following:

Anger is a signal and one worth listening to. Our anger may be a message that we are being hurt, that our rights are being violated, that our needs or wants are not being adequately met, or simply that something isn't right. Our anger may tell us that we are not addressing an important emotional issue in our lives, or that too much of our self—our beliefs, values, desires or ambitions—is being compromised in a relationship. Our anger may be a signal that we are doing more and giving more than we can comfortably do or give. Or our anger may warn us that others are doing too much for us, at the expense of our own competence and growth. Just as physical pain tells us to take our hand off the hot stove, the pain of our anger preserves the very integrity of our self. Our anger can motivate us to say "no" to the ways in which we are defined by others and "yes" to the dictates of our inner self.[1]

Boys who never learn how to listen to their anger miss out on benefiting from one of anger's greatest functions. If boys can learn to recognize anger's warning signs, they are more likely to be able to deal with the anger—and the issues behind the anger—while things are still manageable.

WHAT THEY SEE IS WHAT WE GET

We like to think that our home is generally stable, quiet, and peaceful—a refuge from a frantic world. The reality, however, is that our home can be a real battleground, complete with arguing, shouting, fighting, and power struggles. We sometimes surprise ourselves at how quickly we can go from a spirit of calmness to a spirit of frustration and exasperation. Despite great intentions and frequent morning times together in Bible reading and prayer—even on the days we're working hard at listening to each other and trying to maintain a healthy environment—car rides still deteriorate into stress-filled disagreements, meals end with one or more of the boys frustrated and angry, and bedtime turns into wartime. Our experience is similar to that of parenting expert and acclaimed speaker Nancy Samalin, who makes this observation:

> Whatever its source, we often experience parental anger as a horrifying encounter with our worst selves. I never even knew I had a temper until I had children. It was very frightening that these children I loved so much, for whom I had sacrificed so much, could arouse such intense feelings of rage in me, their mother, whose primary responsibility was to nurture and protect them.[2]

It seems that the greater your love for someone, the greater your capacity to experience a wide range of emotions toward them—*including* the harmful emotions of irritation, resentment, anger, and rage. It doesn't matter whether the target is a parent, a spouse, or a child. The people to whom you give the most time and energy and in whom you invest the most love are the ones of whom we have the highest expectations—and the ones with the greatest potential to trigger emotions such as fear, hurt, and frustration—and anger.

In unhealthy homes, this natural inclination to wound the people closest to us goes unchecked. The home environment becomes rigid, restrictive, and demanding. Love is expressed conditionally, and children learn to ignore who they are by nature and are forced to shape their behavior to meet the needs of their parents. Instead of developing their real selves—instead of discovering what it means to be made in God's image and to be who God designed them to be—they develop false selves that learn how to read the environment (including Mom's and Dad's moods) in order to get the love and approval these false selves desperately need.

When children grow up in unhealthy homes—when their basic needs are not met, when they are abused, neglected, exploited, or deceived—they become emotionally, psychologically, and spiritually damaged. Their normal development is at best hindered and at worst arrested. We've worked with hundreds of men and women over the years who were chronologically in their thirties and forties, yet who were emotional and psychological adolescents.

Yet, even granting the normal emotional commotion and inevitable conflicts of living together, a home can be a wonderfully nonthreatening environment that is supportive, nurturing, and flexible, a place where the uniqueness of each family member is encouraged. And it's through *watching* their parents—that is, through modeling—that children learn who they are, gauge their value and worth, and discover how to love, how to communicate, how to deal with conflict, and how to understand and express emotions; it's the way they find out what it means to be a boy or a girl and the way they begin to grasp who God is and how relevant he is for them.

Remember this, though: You can't give your kids what you don't have yourself. If you want them to have healthy emotional development, they need to see you deal with your emotions in healthy ways. If you want them to learn constructive ways to deal with anger, they will learn it best from what they see you *do*—which simply means you need to grow in how you deal with your own anger toward them.

GREAT EXPECTATIONS—ACTUALLY, TOO GREAT

Few things trigger anger toward children like a parent's expectations. And Gary for one has surprised himself with how easily he holds our sons to adult standards and expectations—despite the fact that the very nature of living with children breeds frustration, disorder, contradictions, aggravation, and chaos—as well as surprise, delight, wonder, joy, humor, warmth, vulnerability, creativity, and energy.

So take some time to study your son. Learn his unique characteristics, his idiosyncrasies. Then set your expectations accordingly. If your son is young, what is he capable of learning at his age? What kinds of concepts are his young mind capable of grasping? What are age-appropriate expectations? What are age-appropriate behaviors? For example, your son the toddler will reach into every closet, every door, every cupboard in the house. He will indiscriminately taste, touch, smell, pull on, lick, jerk, bite, and swallow every particle he can reach (and he will reach them all). He will have no fear of deep water, no fear of fire, no fear of moving vehicles. And he will only resent, ignore, and crawl or toddle away from all your warnings. (Now look at these expectations again with your *teenage* son in mind . . . funny how similar toddler and teenager can be!) Whatever the age of your son—whether toddler or teenager—keeping in mind his developmental limitations gives you more realistic expectations of him. And appropriate expectations decrease your frustration and anger.

SIX O'CLOCK ANGER

Unrealistic expectations of your son aren't the only things that can trigger anger in you. *Displacement* is a fancy name for what happens when you're angry at some thing or person, then dump it on an innocent party—who in many cases happens to be your child.

Take Marilyn, for example. Her day had gone about as unpleasantly as possible. In the morning her car wouldn't start, so she had to ask a neighbor for a ride to work. She arrived late and didn't have time to put the finishing touches on a presentation she had to make that day. The computer was down for two hours, which put her even further behind. And then at 4:30 P.M. her husband called to tell her he'd be late for dinner.

On the way home, she fantasized about unwinding on the couch for a little while before making dinner; instead she walked into what looked like a nuclear test site. When she stormed into the backyard and yelled at her kids to "get into the house right now!" they knew what that tone of voice meant. She ranted and raved about how hard she worked, how no one appreciated her, how sick and tired she was of doing all the work, and how they thought of no one else but themselves. She ended her tirade by questioning whether they would spend their entire lives being selfish and irresponsible.

The kids disappeared into their rooms, tail between legs and feelings bruised. Marilyn felt better—for the moment—but the kids had barely left her sight before she came back to her senses and realized that not only had she *not* solved her problem, she had created other ones. Yes, the house was a mess; yes, the kids should have picked things up a bit; yes, there were times when her kids didn't appreciate her. But her anger wasn't really aimed at the messy home; it was the result of her frustration and disappointment at work. Her anger was about the selfishness, lack of appreciation, and unrealistic expectations of her boss, not the attitudes or behaviors of her children. This is *displacement* at its most ignominious.

Learn to ask yourself the question, "What is my anger about?" Is it about my children; is it about things in my past or in my present—or some combination of all three? Parents surely bring emotions from their own childhood into their parenting. They can introduce unresolved childhood anger into current relationships—especially at a point when a child reaches the age *you* were when a traumatic event or crisis happened in your life.

And sometimes, like Marilyn, it's not so much the remembrance of childhood traumas as it is simply the toll of a string of hectic or hurtful days. Coming home at the end of a day has always been a vulnerable time for Gary. When he identified this point of vulnerability—how anger lurked just beneath the surface when he walked in the door—he was able to make some changes in his preparation for coming home that virtually eliminated this as a problem. In fact, just being aware of the problem helped him develop a solution.

As we talked and prayed about his inclination to experience "six o'clock anger," the first solution we agreed on was for him to work harder at not being so frazzled while still at the office— which means becoming more aware of his schedule, saying no more often, and getting adequate aerobic exercise. Gary has also learned to call home for a "weather report" before leaving the office. If it was a particularly demanding day, either on the home front or at the office, he'll spend an extra ten minutes or so at the office praying and emotionally and spiritually prepping himself for the evening with the family. And he's found that prayer refreshes him, relaxes him, and renews his perspective. Gary can come home and "be there" in spirit as well as body.

KEEP AN ANGER LOG

Keeping an "anger log" is a simple way to help you clarify what is making you angry. Such a log helps you discover the frequency, intensity, and duration of the anger you express at your kids. When are you most likely to lose it? When are you most likely to respond in healthy ways? (You may want to photocopy the anger log form on page 148, or simply keep track of the information listed in *Small Beginnings* on page 147.)

One benefit of such a log is that it can help you identify situations where your anger is most likely to be triggered. Here, for example, are common triggers expressed by parents at parenting workshops. Check the ones that apply to you.

❏ When they defy me
❏ When they won't do what I say
❏ When they refuse to take no for an answer

❑ When they want to negotiate every issue
❑ When they "hang" their clothes on the floor
❑ When they won't clean up their room
❑ When I see them making the same mistakes I made
❑ When they stay on the phone for hours
❑ When they embarrass me or throw tantrums in public
❑ When they act like helpless babies
❑ When they don't do their homework
❑ When they whine or argue in "that voice"
❑ When they don't eat what I've prepared or complain about the meal
❑ When they tune me out or ignore me and become "parent deaf"
❑ When they won't take responsibility for their belongings
❑ When they won't go to or stay in bed
❑ When they won't share with their friends or siblings
❑ When they try to boss me around
❑ When they don't show appreciation for the things I do for them
❑ When they fight and argue with each other
❑ When they give me that "attitude"
❑ When they talk back and say things that hurt or insult me
❑ When they seem to go as slow as possible, knowing I'm in a hurry

HOW TO HANDLE YOUR ANGER TOWARD YOUR SON

When you get angry with your son, express it in ways that will heal rather than hurt, build up rather than tear down, encourage rather than discourage. Here are some tips that may help:

Remember that the best way to teach your son what it means to be "slow to become angry" (James 1:19) is *for him to see it in you*. Don't overreact. Don't minimize or maximize. Don't assume you know what the problem is. The most important issue isn't what *you* think of the problem, but how *your son* thinks and feels about the problem. Listen. Ask questions. If there is more than one person involved, hear all sides of the story. Give him time to explain his perspective.

Anger involves strong feelings that shouldn't be ignored or denied. An angry outburst or a temper tantrum is not necessarily the sign of a major problem. When parents overreact to their son's anger, a covert message is being communicated that "anger is bad; anger is wrong. When you get angry, you are bad and you are wrong."

Examine your motive. When anger comes, ask yourself what you hope to accomplish. Determine how you can use the situation to communicate your love and concern, to draw you closer to your son, to strengthen the bonds of trust, and to help your son learn. How can you communicate your anger in such a way that will let him know you value him? Parents who react emotionally to their boy's expression of anger, or whatever emotion or behavior he is expressing, are more likely to make negative and critical statements that communicate that their son is unworthy and unlovable. Before responding, ask yourself how you can acknowledge his rights, values, and concerns. How can you respond in a way that will encourage him? How can you help him become more responsible?

Be specific. Focus on the essential. Make the expression of your anger descriptive, accurate, and to the point—not a ten-minute tirade filled with as many details as you can cram in, but *one* point. What's the bottom line? What is negotiable, and what is nonnegotiable? Do you and your children even *know* what's negotiable? Are your rules, standards, and expectations consistent, or do they change regularly?

When you confront your son, use the first-person singular pronoun—say I, *not* you. Clearly own what you are saying by making *I* statements rather than *you* statements, which tend to come across as demeaning, demanding, and accusatory. *I* statements, on the other hand, make the point with greater clarity and with less damage to your son's sense of value and worth. Some examples of *I* statements include:

- I am very angry right now. I need to take a time-out to think and pray about what I'm feeling before I decide what I'm going to do.
- It's hard for me to concentrate on my driving when you're yelling and throwing things. I'd like you to be quiet.
- I'm disappointed and hurt that you lied to me.
- I'm exhausted and I need some peace and quiet right now. I'll be glad to help you after dinner.
- I don't like it when you talk to me like that.

Stay in the present. Don't dredge up all of the past failures. When Gary is expressing his anger with one of our boys, he still tends to list this son's entire list of recent transgressions. Of course, this doesn't do what Gary intends—which is to add more weight to his argument—but only overwhelms and discourages the boy, who gets more frustrated, or simply turns Gary off. You may very well know what it feels like to be on a ranting roll, all the while suspecting that your son has turned you off. Your own frustration only increases and leads to more anger. It's a lose-lose situation.

Keep it short and simple. Have you ever been in a situation where a parent, spouse, or boss was chiding you, and he or she seemed to go on and on, ad infinitum, ad nauseam? Do you remember what it felt like? Do you remember what you would have liked to say to the person? Did this approach motivate you to listen? If *you* as an adult can't stand someone's lengthy tirade, imagine how much more difficult it will be for your child. The shorter and simpler your message, the more of it your son will receive.

SMALL BEGINNINGS

Complete the following statements:

1. I am most likely to experience anger when . . .
2. When I get angry I . . .
3. If I could change any one thing about the way my son expresses his anger it would be . . .
4. If my son could change any one thing about the way I express my anger it would be . . .
5. One of the most important insights gleaned from this chapter to help me be a more effective parent is . . .
6. Learn to identify your anger pattern. Keep an "anger log" for thirty days.[3] You may want to photocopy the form on page 148, or simply keep track of the information below. Whenever you become aware of anger, grab your log and record these details:

   - What is the date and time of day?
   - Rate the intensity of your anger from 1–10 (1 = barely noticeable, 10 = a rage that is out of control).
   - Where possible, identify the primary emotion or emotions that led to the secondary emotion of anger.
   - What issue led to your anger? (Be aware that you won't always be able to identify the issue.)
   - What is your self-talk about this situation? Does your self-talk reflect passive or aggressive reactions, or an assertive response of some sort?

Date:_____ Time:_____

Intensity:
1   2   3   4   5   6   7   8   9   10

Primary emotion *(circle one):*
hurt   frustration   fear   other
_____

Issue:

Self-talk:

Stress or pressures in past seven days:

Date:_____ Time:_____

Intensity:
1   2   3   4   5   6   7   8   9   10

Primary emotion *(circle one):*
hurt   frustration   fear   other
_____

Issue:

Self-talk:

Stress or pressures in past seven days:

Chapter Eight

HELPING YOUR SON CULTIVATE HEALTHY ANGER

UP FRONT *In this chapter ...*

+ As early as possible, identify unhealthy patterns in your son's responses to anger so you can begin to teach him healthy coping skills and prevent poor anger habits from carrying on into adulthood.

+ Seven ways to help your son cultivate healthy anger.

+ Temper tantrums are typical of children ages two to four. Most are caused by a combination of high energy and low self-control. The cure: setting appropriate boundaries for the child.

+ Educate your sons to manage their own arguments. Sibling relationships provide an excellent venue in which to develop assertiveness, compromise, and problem-solving skills.

+ Boys often view criticism as an attack on their self-worth or masculinity. Parents must discern which reproofs are necessary and be sure to precede them with a compliment and deliver them in private and in a spirit of love.

IN THE PREVIOUS CHAPTER we explored how important it is for parents to understand and deal with their own
anger first. Now we need to look at how to help our sons deal
with *their* anger.

Child training takes time—one step at a time, one skill at a
time, one habit at a time, through lots of trial and error. "Teach
your children to choose the right path," the wisdom writer
observes, "and when they are older, they will remain upon it"
(Proverbs 22:6, NEW LIVING TRANSLATION). Teaching your son is
something like helping him put together a jigsaw puzzle—you
first point out how to build the border, then how to round up
pieces of the same color—all the while coaching with encouragement as you work together on the project. Often the "border" to your son's jigsaw personality consists of unhealthy ways
of responding to anger. The sooner you can help him clarify his
anger, the sooner you can coach him in developing healthy
anger skills. If his anger patterns are not identified and worked
on, however, they can become automatic, deeply entrenched,
and lifelong.

The first step is to ask yourself, "Is anger a problem for my
son?" Spend a few moments with this inventory that identifies
common signs of anger in children.[1] All children occasionally
manifest these signs—but if several of these signs are continually observed in your son, then anger may indeed be a problem
for him. Using the 0–1–2–3 rating system, assign a rating to
each of the fifteen items:

0 = My son never or rarely does this
1 = My son occasionally does this (no more than once a month)
2 = My son often does this (once a week or so)
3 = My son does this frequently (daily or several times a week)

____ 1. My son blames others for his troubles.

____ 2. My son throws or breaks things whenever he feels frustrated or irritated.

____ 3. Whenever my son gets angry, calming him down takes a lot of placating.

____ 4. My son does not like change of any sort and becomes angry when change is forced on him.

____ 5. My son changes the rules of games when playing with other children.

____ 6. My son says spiteful or hateful things whenever he is thwarted.

____ 7. My son is negative and deliberately slow, and he resists doing what he is told to do, to the point that discipline becomes a standoff.

____ 8. My son seeks out arguments or reasons to become upset, even when everything is at peace.

____ 9. My son ostracizes, scorns, and complains about others.

____ 10. My son loses control when he is angry and shows it with facial expressions or body language.

____ 11. My son uses foul language whenever he gets angry.

____ 12. When my son is learning something new, he easily becomes frustrated and wants to do something else.

____ 13. My son is stubborn and refuses to do what he is told to do unless you use the right tone of voice or approach.

____ 14. My son's friends don't like to play with him because he is such a bad sport.

____ 15. My son gets into fights with other children and has great difficulty controlling his temper when teased.

Total Score _____

0–5	Your son is remarkably free of anger and is not prone to frustration. If anything, he may be a little too passive—but don't try to change this!
6–10	Your son is showing a normal degree of anger and irritation. (Children under six years old can score 9 or 10 and still be near the norm. Scores on the low side, like 6 or 7, are typical for older children.)
11–15	Your son is beginning to show an above-normal degree of anger response. Some attention to your child's response may be needed. (Again, higher scores are more typical for younger children, and not as great a cause for concern.)
16–20	Your son clearly has a problem with anger and should receive your attention.
20+	Your son has a serious problem with anger, especially if he is already of school age. Take immediate steps to help your son cope with his anger, seeking professional help if necessary.

HOW TO HELP YOUR SON CULTIVATE HEALTHY ANGER

Help Your Son Identify His Anger Pattern

Begin by identifying your own anger pattern—you can either let your son watch you do so or you can tell him about it. One of the best gifts we can give our sons is to give them words formed out of our experience for what they are feeling, that is, put a name to what it is they are feeling.

When our boys were young we would use the word "angry" at those times we were experiencing and expressing it. By doing so we were helping them to know what anger looked like. We remember well the day Gary helped Andrew, who was five at the time, stack plastic blocks, only to see the tower tumble every time he got to the seventh or eighth block. Finally, in exasperation, our five-year-old announced, "Dad, I'm angry." Gary was able to say, "I'm glad you know what you're feeling. It's frustrating when you keep on trying to do something and it doesn't work. I get frustrated and angry when things like that happen to me too."

If your son isn't quite as forthright about what he's feeling, you start the conversation. First, calmly acknowledge his behavior: "Honey, I can see you are very upset. Do you know what's bothering you? Do you want to talk about it now, or later?" When possible, link their behavior with the secondary emotion of anger. Then gradually, over a period of time, start linking his anger to the primary emotion—fear, hurt, frustration, and the like.

Giving a boy words to describe his feelings is one way to help him identify his anger pattern. Keeping an "anger log" is another, whether you do this exercise yourself for a younger son, or give one to an older son to do himself. (You may want to photocopy the anger log form on page 148, or use the questions listed in *Small Beginnings* [under point #6 on page 147] as you do this exercise on behalf of a younger son.)

Help Your Son Own Up to His Anger and Accept Responsibility

What began with Adam and Eve is alive and well in us and in our children. Kids love to blame something or someone else— especially a brother or sister.

When your son blames someone else for "making" him respond in anger, acknowledge the reality of what the other person did—but then let your son know that he *could* have responded differently: "Yes, David took your toy and that wasn't very nice. But you didn't have to hit him. What other ways could you have expressed your anger?"

Don't dwell on what your son did wrong. Focus instead on what his choices were and what he can learn that could help him next time. Show him you accept his feelings, as you suggest other ways to express those feelings: "Let me share what some other boys might have done in this situation."

Help Your Son Decide Who or What Will Have Control

It may take some time and patience, but kids can learn to distinguish between the *emotion* of anger and their *expression* of anger. If a parent models it, boys can learn to take time to respond. Your son can understand that thinking, feeling, and doing aren't the same thing—that he has the freedom to choose his response.

Help Your Son Identify and Define the Source of His Anger

It may be difficult for children, but it's not impossible for them to identify and define the source of their anger. They obviously will not understand the difference between a primary and secondary emotion—all they know is that what they feel isn't good. So avoid the temptation to explain fine distinctions to them. Start simply by using questions to help them understand *what they are feeling*.

Boys feel anger for the same fundamental reasons adults do, but they don't have the abstract reasoning skills of adults—and no history of experiencing the consequences of unhealthy expressions of anger. They just cannot stand back and look at a situation from another perspective. Without consciously realizing it, children use anger to express *many* emotions—sadness, depression, hurt, fear, frustration, feelings of dependency, failure, anxiety, rejection, and the like. If you think *you* have a difficult time understanding your emotions, imagine what it must be like for a child.

So when *you* are angry, think aloud with your son about your anger. Identify the primary emotion that led to your anger. As you discuss your son's emotions with him, it will become fairly easy for him to identify the emotion of anger. In time he will be able to identify the emotion or emotions that led to the anger.

Help Your Son Choose His Response

Without a plan to deal with anger, we are more likely to say things that hurt rather than heal—more likely to do things we will regret. One way to help a boy choose healthy responses to his anger is to remind him of what has or hasn't worked in the past.

Take this common scenario, for instance. Timmy storms into the house, slams the front door, stomps up the stairs to his bedroom, and slams *that* door too. So far, fairly predictable eight-year-old angry male behavior. His mother goes to his room and asks what's wrong.

"Aaron said he's not going to invite me to his birthday party, and I invited him to mine. I hate him, and I never want to see him again."

Karen waits for a moment, just in case Timmy wants to add anything, before saying, "Sounds like you're really hurt by what Aaron said. I know four different ways you can handle this hurt, and some of them may work. If you want to hear them, let me know." She gives her fuming boy a hug, then leaves the room.

A few minutes later Timmy appears at the door to his mom's home office. "So what are they?" he asks.

"Do you really want to know?"

Timmy mumbles a "Yes."

"Well," she said, "here they are. Some of them might be better than others, but you can decide. One: I could set the timer for fifteen minutes and go into my room and kick and scream and pound on the floor until the timer goes off. Two: I could call three of my friends and tell them what a terrible, awful, horrible person Aaron is. Three: I could write a letter to God and tell him how sad and hurt I am, and then read the letter to a friend. Four: I could tell my mom how sad and hurt I am, and then maybe we could pray and talk about how I can choose to respond."

Timmy opts for number four, and he and his mom end up having a profitable discussion. Coached by a parent, Timmy chose a healthy response and felt good about his decision in the end.

Help Your Son Express His Anger in Healthy Ways

Don't even try to handle your son's anger for him. It's *his* anger, and he has to deal with it. But you *can* help him. After asking his older brother several times to stop teasing him, our seven-year-old took off his snow boot and threw it at his nemesis. The boot bounced off Nathan's head, prompting him to run down the stairs yelling, "Matt hit me with his boot!"

What was the best way to respond? We certainly could have been upset at both of them, or told them, "Now you really shouldn't get mad at each other," or "There's no excuse for that kind of behavior." Our dilemma was this: How do we honor the feelings and concerns of both boys and yet help them deal with the real issue? The situation had occurred before, and so we were a bit better prepared to help them take responsibility for their own problem and thereby learn something valuable from this incident.

"It's probably frustrating to be teased," said Carrie, "and I know it hurts to have a boot bounce off your head. But, Nathan, do you know what it feels like to be teased? You've been teased before—how did you like it? And, Matt, did Nathan's teasing make it right for you to throw your boot at him? What could you have done besides flinging your boot at him?

"So I'm giving you this opportunity to go to your room and discuss the choices you have. What do you need to say to each other? What can you learn from this situation? How can you respond differently if this happens again? When you've come up with a solution, let me know. I'm sure you guys can work this out!"

Sure enough, Nathan and Matt went off, talked together, and resolved the conflict: Nathan acknowledged that being teased was no fun, and Matt decided that, while it sure felt good to throw the boot, it would be better to just walk away or to come to one of us for help.

Of course similar incidents did happen again, but over time we've made progress in helping our sons develop the awareness that there are always options for expressing our frustration and anger. These were opportunities to help them validate the reality of their own emotions, while at the same time to recognize that other people had valid emotions too. Another seed planted, another truth reinforced, another healthy example modeled. And the next time this kind of conflict erupts, maybe, just maybe, it will be resolved a little more quickly and with a little less parental energy.

Help Your Son Review His Response

Learning to experience and express anger in a healthy way is a process that takes time and involves trial and error. But the product is worth the process. When your son takes even the slightest step in the right direction, congratulate and praise him for a job well done. Ask him to describe what he learned from this situation and how he can be more effective the next time such a situation arises.

TEMPER TANTRUMS—PROBABLY THEATRICS

In only a matter of minutes your son's irritation can roar like a runaway train through frustration and anger into full-blown rage—out of control and running full tilt into a temper tantrum—which, frankly, can be quite impressive. The cute little tyke shouts, screams, holds his breath, jumps up and down, kicks wildly, bangs his fist (or his head) on the nearest flat surface, throws himself on the floor (or throws the nearest objects he can reach), and rolls around. Tantrums leave everyone exhausted—participants, perplexed parents, and observers alike.

Social psychologist and researcher Carol Tavris has observed that temper tantrums first appear during a child's second year, peak between the ages of two and three, and decrease by the age of four—an age when the child is forming a sense of self, when the toddler is old enough to have a sense of "me" and "my wants" but is too young to get what he wants when he wants it. A temper tantrum is most likely to happen when your son is frustrated by a boundary you've set around his behavior. Children want to be grown-up, independent, in control, and able to do whatever Mom and Dad do—despite the fact that they are small, dependent, not in control, and limited in what they can do. In short, it's a perfect recipe for frustration. While some tantrums result from organic disturbances or allergies, most are caused by the combination of high energy and low self-control. Most children throw tantrums only in a particular place and with a particular person. Tantrums usually last as long as it takes to get what they want or until they realize that their outburst isn't going to work.[2]

Consider the mom who takes her three-year-old son to the grocery store. The cart rolls into the checkout line, and the child spots the strawberry-lemonade Nerds on the candy rack. He is a normal, healthy child, and so he wants what he sees—and he tells his mother as much. She refuses, and he increases the volume of his demands. His blocked desire leads to frustration, and frustration leads to temper-tantrum anger. If his mother gets sufficiently embarrassed by his dramatics, she may give in and buy him the candy—which teaches the boy that if he loses his temper and screams long and loud enough, he will get what he wants.

While there may be a physiological reason for your son's temper tantrum, in many cases the tantrum is evidence of a power struggle—maybe even the result of not setting appropriate boundaries. The tantrum is your clue that it's time for a lesson in impulse control that might go something like this: Your son wants the strawberry-lemonade Nerds, and you say no. He responds with the opening notes of a dramatic tantrum—but you interrupt him by picking him up, holding him firmly, and saying, "I love you, and you cannot have the candy."

Don't surrender to theatrics. Your response to your son is much more important than what anyone in the grocery store might think of you. "The child should gain no request by anger," an ancient philosopher is reputed to have said. "When he is quiet let him be offered what was refused when he wept." That's still good advice today.

THE JOYS OF SIBLING RIVALRY

"MOM!" Nathan screamed. "Matthew got to watch the Turtles, but he won't let me watch Inspector Gadget." Then a scream—so bloodcurdling you would have thought that a human limb had been cut off without anesthetic. Into the kitchen runs Matthew with a "Mom, Nathan hit me, and I didn't do *anything!*"

Sooner or later most parents confess to other parents that "my kids fight all the time." Sibling rivalry, parents say, is a significant source of anger for their children. When other children are competing for the same toys, parental attention, or space, it's normal for a child to experience frustration. As the children's frustration increases so does the parents'. Yet we parents need to understand that sibling rivalry is an excellent venue for teaching our sons the socializing skills of assertiveness and compromise.

First, try to ignore the minor everyday disagreements. If you try to solve every fight, or use the wisdom of Solomon and try to figure out who is right or wrong or who really started it, you will go crazy—and you will rob your kids of the opportunity to develop their own problem-solving skills.

When things start getting nasty and you *must* intervene, do so in such a way that the kids are responsible for solving the problem they have created. Listen to them. Clarify what they are saying. Let them know you understand—"I can see why both of you would be frustrated. It sounds like a tough problem, but I know you two can work it out." Teach them how to manage their own arguments. Provide ideas on how they might compromise. Help them generate and weigh various options, and then coach them to follow through on their conclusions.

One possible and insidious result of uncontrolled sibling rivalry can be a child's feeling that he is unprotected. Children need to know that they are safe. They need to know that it is never acceptable to hit a brother or sister. They need to understand that there are clear consequences for certain kinds of behavior. When these safety conditions are in place, kids are more likely to move into a problem-solving mode.

Surely in the course of dealing with sibling rivalry you'll make mistakes, you'll lose your temper, you'll get discouraged. But if you're candid with your kids about your own emotions, through much practice, a consistent approach, and a dependence on prayer you can gradually minimize unhealthy sibling rivalry in your home.

MALES AND CRITICISM—AN ATTACK OR A CRITIQUE?

Males tend to view criticism not as an opportunity to learn and grow, but as an attack on their adequacy or even their masculinity. Many men and boys are convinced that to be criticized implies an admission of failure, inadequacy, or incompetence. Psychiatrist Willard Gaylin makes this poignant and helpful observation:

> In modern life, no new element of danger need be introduced to make a man feel less secure, less manly, less worthy. Simply raise doubts about his strength, his ability, or stature, and you will diminish his self-respect or self-confidence. The same environment is then perceived as more hazardous.
>
> The extremely insecure man in today's society will receive any criticism as a threat. There need not be rejection, humiliation, abandonment; it is enough for someone to raise questions about his essential worth to produce a sense of stress, introducing either a frightened or an angry response. In the ghettos of our cities, "disrespect" is offered as an excuse for "wasting" an

opponent, and "turf" is a leading cause of gang wars. Any criticism can be interpreted by a man as questioning his power and his competence.[3]

This way of understanding criticism starts early in a male's life. One "masculinity myth" in particular has a powerful effect on our sons—the myth that says, *When a man's power and competence is questioned, his very value and worth are at stake.* One wife put it this way: "Because he's the man of the house, my husband acts like he always has to be right." Many of us grew up believing the myths that real men have all the answers; real men aren't weak; real men don't lose.

About halfway into his first counseling session, a respected Christian leader told Gary that for several years he knew he needed to get some help. "But coming to counseling seemed like an admission of failure," he confessed to Gary. "I've encouraged others to do it, but I told myself that I'm a leader, therefore I shouldn't need it.

"I'm not sure what I expected from counseling. Maybe to be criticized and condemned—or that you would immediately go for my emotional jugular vein."

Thankfully he discovered that the experience wasn't as bad as he thought it would be.

Here's a rule of thumb for beginning to train boys *out of* this fear of criticism: If you must be candid and criticize (in the neutral, healthy sense of that word), learn to distinguish between high-ticket and low-ticket concerns so you don't become like a dripping faucet. When it is necessary to speak a critical word to your son, never do it in public, but choose a time when he will really *hear* you. Start with a compliment, and let no hint of sarcasm infect your voice.

MY SON, MY ADVERSARY

It had started as a pleasant evening at home, David told us. He was downstairs working on the family finances, and his twelve-year-old son was upstairs practicing the piano.

"We've had our struggles with Ben's piano practicing," said David. "What he was playing sounded great, so I decided to take a break, go upstairs, and compliment him." David did just that, then asked how the rest of his lesson was going. "Want to play a couple other pieces for me?" he asked his son.

Things quickly went south. Ben immediately became frustrated with his dad, a frustration that quickly turned to anger. Ben then turned his anger into blame.

"Nothing I do is ever good enough. I don't know why I even try."

Then David did what every normal parent would do: He became frustrated as well. "Well, fine," he bristled. "And I really don't appreciate your attitude, Ben." He can't remember what else he said, but whatever it was caused Ben to become even *more* defensive. "What I had imagined would be a positive moment," David said, "suddenly turned into emotional combat." Ben went to his room and slammed the door.

David returned to his desk and just sat there thinking, trying to figure out what had happened. He had discussed situations like this with Gary in therapy, so some key things were still fairly fresh in his mind—specifically, a set of questions he knew he needed to ask himself:

- What did I do in this situation that was healthy?
- What did I do in this situation that was unhealthy?
- Did I speak respectfully to him—or did I raise my voice or threaten him in any way?
- What could I have done differently?
- What do I do now? How do I handle this?
- In similar situations, what has been helpful?
- What do I need to take responsibility for?
- What can I learn from this interaction?

He answered these questions to his own satisfaction, decided on a course of action, and headed upstairs to talk with his son. He knocked on Ben's closed door (instead of just opening it and walking in uninvited) and asked if he could come in. Ben gave a halfhearted "Yeah," which David interpreted to mean yes.

"Ben, I'd like to talk with you for a few minutes," his dad said. "Would you be willing to talk to me?" Almost before David got the words out of his mouth, Ben answered, "Sure, Dad." David sat on the edge of his son's bed, and they began to chat.

"After some banter about the magazine he was looking at, I moved into my agenda," remembered David. "I apologized for my own actions and acknowledged my anger, and then I asked Ben for forgiveness. As we talked, the primary issue began to emerge: He wanted to rush through his lesson so he could catch *Babylon 5* on TV. My wonderfully affirming moment got in the way of his finishing his piano practicing in time to watch his show. He was very frustrated, but he couldn't tell me."

David learned that even before he had knocked on his son's door, Ben had been lying in bed thinking about coming down to talk to *him*. "We talked through what happened and came up with different ways he could have responded. During our conversation, we both got a little irritated with each other, and we both got a little weepy too. We prayed before I left as well."

This dad did several things right: He took responsibility for his own actions, he knocked instead of barging into Ben's room, he acknowledged his anger, he apologized for his unhealthy expression of frustration, he asked for Ben's forgiveness, he invited Ben to give his own perspective, and he prayed with Ben.

We happen to know that David doesn't succeed as splendidly in all of his challenging child-rearing circumstances. Yet by coaching your son to clarify his anger, by listening and seeking to understand, by candidly sharing your own struggles to make anger a healthy emotion for you rather than an unhealthy and destructive emotion—these principles will gradually help your son respond to his own anger in a creative and healthy way.

SMALL BEGINNINGS

1. It's been said that "*crazy* is to find out what doesn't work, and then keep on doing it." Name some of the unhelpful ways you've tried to deal with your son's anger.

2. One of the best ways to teach your son healthy anger management is to model it for him. Name at least one thing you've learned in this chapter that you can model for your son in the next twenty-four hours.

3. Criticism can be devastating to anyone, and boys are especially sensitive to any message that suggests they've fallen short. If you precede a criticism with one or two sincere compliments, it is much more likely that he will hear and accept your criticism. List at least three strengths or positive attributes of your son that you could compliment him on. (Hey, get crazy on this one—and list seven or eight strengths!)

Chapter Nine

RESPONDING TO THE EMOTIONS YOUR SON EVOKES FROM YOU

UP FRONT *In this chapter...*

- ✦ A crucial task of effective parenting is learning to control your emotional reaction to your son's emotions. Otherwise, you will likely be a poor example of maturity for your son, and you may end up feeling guilty and ineffective.
- ✦ Your unhealthy response to your boy's emotion is not his problem—it's *your* problem.
- ✦ Parents must recognize what triggers their emotional reactions—that is, what in your relationship to your son sets off your unhealthy responses to his actions.
- ✦ Know when you tend to be particularly vulnerable to losing control of your emotions. Fatigue, hunger, frustration, stress, and discouragement can all contribute to weakened defenses.
- ✦ Identify what works and what doesn't work when you find yourself in stressful situations—then make a realistic plan (with as many alternative responses you can think of) for dealing with future problems.
- ✦ Genuine and lasting change takes time, so look for small signs of growth in the decreasing intensity and frequency of your unhealthy responses.

Y OU IDIOT! YOU ARE absolutely worthless! Can't you do anything right?" the father yelled at his child in as sarcastic a voice as Gary had ever heard. The large man, well over six feet tall, towered over his son, who was all of seven or eight years old. As Gary pedaled his bike past the pair, he caught the painful look on the boy's face—a mixture of sadness, shame, and devastation.

Although Gary was soon far away from them, the rush of emotions continued within him. Tears came to his eyes. In his chest he felt the fear, the hurt, the pain, the rejection, the sense of failure and worthlessness that he had seen on the child's face. The little guy had tried to hold back the tears, but he couldn't. And Gary couldn't either.

He felt anger as well. He wanted to grab that father, shake him, and ask him if he had even the slightest clue what he was doing to his boy. Okay, so the man's son had made a mistake. Maybe the boy hadn't listened to his dad. Maybe he had gotten into something he had been consistently warned about. And maybe he had made this very same mistake several times before. But whatever his misdeed, the child did *not* deserve this kind of treatment.

A SHORT PARENTAL FUSE

It's one thing to help your sons understand and deal with *their* emotions. But it's another thing—and a necessary thing if you want to fill your parenting role well—to deal with your own emotional responses to your sons.

In short, this chapter is not about your boys; *it's about you.*

Look at what happens when you don't deal well with your emotional responses to your boy's emotions:

- Reacting inappropriately to your boy's emotions undermines the very principles you're trying to teach him. A parent then becomes a poor role model, not to mention feeling guilty, discouraged, and defeated.

- Reacting inappropriately to your boy's emotions gives him power over you. At a very early age kids learn the principle of cause and effect. They learn that doing this or not doing that will almost always evoke a certain response from one of their parents. I've known of children who would behave in a way they knew would get them in trouble just for the "kick" of seeing Mom or Dad spinning out of control.

- Reacting inappropriately to your boy's emotions clouds your perspective, causing you to disregard the actual issue. You are more likely to react to surface issues than to address root causes. It's easy to become so focused on the intensity of your own issues that you become blind to the needs of your children.

- Reacting inappropriately to a boy's emotions may put a parent at risk of becoming an abusive parent. Very few parents wake up one morning and say, "I think I'll be an abusive parent today." In fact, most have no idea when their inability to deal with their own emotional responses became a problem. I've worked with many parents who were appalled by their abusiveness, shocked by the fact that they had hit one of their children. They never dreamed they were capable of this kind of behavior. But over a period of several years they had gradually let their emotions control them more and more, until they became numb to the inner voice of warning. Later they woke up to the reality of having become an abusive parent who had spun out of control.

Dan knew only too well this scenario of letting an unhealthy emotional reaction rage out of control.

"I can't believe I blew it again," this father said despairingly. "I feel like a total failure. I have these good intentions and these great expectations of myself, and then, once again, some little thing happens and I lose it."

Dan was a committed Christian man who loved his wife and their two boys. He really wanted to be a great dad and help his kids experience a better childhood than he had had. But Dan had a low tolerance for frustration and a short fuse with his sons. "I've gone to seminars, listened to tapes, and read books on how to be an effective parent. Most of the time I think I do a great job. But when I lose it and start dumping on the kids, I feel like all of the good I've accomplished has been undone. It's so discouraging."

When Dan became frustrated with his children, he made threats. But because he seldom followed through on his threats, the kids soon learned they didn't have to worry about what Dad said—all the smoke would blow over in a couple hours. Once he had announced that the kids were grounded for the evening, then walked out of the room—but not before he overheard his youngest son say to his older brother, "Don't worry—Dad will chill out before nine."

So to get even short-term responses from his sons, Dan found himself increasing the volume of his voice and increasing the seriousness of the consequences. Fortunately for Dan and his boys, he admitted the problem and got counseling before it got completely out of hand.

HOW TO RESPOND TO YOUR SON'S EMOTIONS

Dan asked us the same questions we've heard so many times: "Is there any hope? Can I really change how I respond to my sons' emotions?"

The answer is yes—and here's how.

Acknowledge, Own, and Define the Problem

A problem defined is a problem half-solved. The first and most important step in the change process is to acknowledge to ourselves, to God, and then to one or two others that there is a problem.

First, acknowledging the problem to oneself brings those problems out of the shadows and into the light. It brings clarity to the problem and makes it easier to deal with. As parents acknowledge the problem before God, they can admit this is something they can't handle on their own. They can claim promises such as Romans 8:28, Philippians 4:13, and Philippians 4:19. It is wonderfully encouraging and energizing to look at a problem in light of who God is and what he has promised to his children.

Second, when parents acknowledge the problem to a couple of trusted friends, they add a much-needed degree of accountability. It's one thing to admit a problem and ask God for help in dealing with it, but it's another thing to share the problem with friends and ask them not only to pray for you but also to periodically check up on you.

Third, go on to accept responsibility for the problem. Own it. Dan had been defining one of the problems with his son this way: "If he would just pick up after himself, I wouldn't get so angry." While in some ways this statement reflected genuine truth, Dan would come to see that he was placing the responsibility for *his* emotions on his seven-year-old son, and that while there surely *were* situations that increased the probability he would feel angry, he was nevertheless free to choose how he would express that anger.

Dan finally came to the point of owning another problem he had with this same son: "I don't like the way I respond to his complaining. When he whines and complains, it's easy for me to get frustrated, and then when he doesn't stop, I get angry. All too often I allow my anger to control me—and yet it doesn't feel good to me and I know it's not helpful for him. With God's help I want to change this response pattern. I want to learn how to communicate my anger in ways that heal rather than hurt."

In this simple admission Dan acknowledged that there was a problem, that he accepted it as *his* problem, and that it revealed an unhealthy expression of anger toward his son. He didn't condemn himself or beat himself up emotionally. He simply told himself the truth and decided to learn, to change, and to grow.

Dan also started with just a couple of parenting problems, not *all* his parenting problems. He chose to start there, because these two problems were particularly frustrating and discouraging. His goal was practical, realistic, limited, and achievable.

Identify the Triggers

Children can trigger a negative emotional response in their parents by specific words, behaviors, or perceived attitudes. So what are the triggers for you? List your son's behaviors that tend to spark an unhealthy emotional response from you. To do so is a simple step in the direction of resolving the problem, yet most parents never actually sit down, focus on this part of the problem, and write what their kids do or say that makes them vulnerable to an unhealthy expression of their emotions.

Different situations trigger different responses in different parents. We've found that the following tend to be some of the most common triggers:

- Fighting and name-calling
- Talking back, showing disrespect
- Whining, complaining
- Talking, yelling, interrupting when on the phone
- Not doing something he said he'd do
- Being late
- Borrowing things without asking
- Not putting things away after he's borrowed them

Dan took the time to compile his own list, and soon he saw that he was allowing his son's whining, complaining, and back talk to trigger his own unhealthy responses.

Determine What Increases Your Vulnerability

Furthermore, Dan observed that sometimes his son's behaviors didn't bother him, while at other times it only took about five minutes and he was "ready to ship him off to a boarding school." So it wasn't *just* his son's behaviors that triggered Dan's unhealthy responses—there were other factors that made Dan more vulnerable to unhealthy responses.

So you'd do well to take some time to explore what it is *in you* that makes you more likely to respond negatively. Recall three or four recent episodes in which you've responded negatively, and ask yourself these questions:

1. In the last twenty-four to forty-eight hours, what's been going on in my life? Was I busier than usual? Were there any crises that took place? Were there any great successes or failures? Did I get less sleep or exercise than usual?
2. Do these episodes seem to occur at about the same point in the week? (Some people we work with say they're much more vulnerable to "losing it" in the middle of the week when they feel overwhelmed, while others say the weekend is their most vulnerable time.)
3. Am I more vulnerable at a certain time of the day? When is my "danger zone"? (Many parents find they are at greatest risk during the times preceding the evening meal or right before bedtime.)
4. Was I preoccupied with other problems? The anxiety and stress that come from dealing with problems in other areas of our lives can spill over into our relationships with our children. We have less energy and thus a lower tolerance for frustrating situations.

The vast majority of people we counsel do identify patterns to their unhealthy responses. When Dan thought back to his most recent blowups, he discovered he was much more vulnerable in the evenings during the middle of the week. "By the middle of the week I'm more likely to be exhausted by what I've already done, frustrated by what I haven't gotten done, and discouraged by what I think I need to get done before the weekend," he said. "On the weekends it's easier for me to kick back and relax, but for some reason during the week I seem to get much more intense. It's like I'm on a treadmill."

By identifying times of increased vulnerability Dan was able to ask his wife and his friends to pray more specifically for him. His increased awareness also made it easier for him to catch his anger at an earlier stage and replace unhealthy responses with healthy ones.

Recall How You Responded in the Past, and Note What Hasn't Worked

"*Crazy* is to find out what doesn't work, and then keep on doing it," someone has said. Many parents suffer from this kind of craziness, responding for years to parenting challenges in ways that simply don't work. They didn't work five years ago, and they're not working today. But there's a positive side to all this: A great resource for parents is the opportunity to learn from *what hasn't worked for them.* Your own mistakes and failures are a gold mine of information for becoming more effective parents.

We say gold *mine* deliberately—for there can be some difficult digging to do as we examine old ways of dealing with problems and look for new ways. Yes, sometimes the gold is the invaluable insight, as Dan discovered, that the emotional responses of yelling, threatening, overgeneralizing, labeling, and sarcasm didn't work—none of those responses had produced any positive change. Yet those behaviors had comprised ninety percent of Dan's responses to his son. As Dan began to recognize what hadn't worked, he could begin to look for more effective approaches.

Identify More Effective Ways to Respond

What responses haven't you tried yet? What haven't you tried with consistency? What have other parents done in this situation? What kinds of responses are most consistent with what you *want* to model for your children?

Dan read several parenting books and talked with friends as well as his children's teachers. We worked with him to develop a two-page list of suggestions, which included:

- Study his son's personality type and discover the unique ways he perceives his world.
- Study the differences between his and his son's personality types, and how Dan could make those differences work *for* their relationship rather than against it.
- Work hard to identify, understand, and deal with his own emotions first.
- Articulate to himself and to others his frustrations and the problems he faces as he parents his son.
- When tempted to raise his voice, determine instead that he will speak more softly; when tempted to speak more quickly, determine to slow down and be more deliberate.
- Cultivate a prepared heart for those vulnerable times when he knows he's more stressed than usual and therefore more susceptible to being negative, critical, and on the verge of losing it.
- Look for ways to be a Barnabas to his son and give him at least one encouraging compliment every day.[1]
- Determine to pray with his son before confronting him about a problem.
- Embrace his son and play with him when he complains and is whiny.

Develop a Realistic Plan

Dan began to see some change as he worked through several steps. He had acknowledged, owned, and defined the problem. He had identified his son's triggers and the factors in himself that made him more vulnerable. He had recalled what *hadn't* worked in the past, as well as ascertaining what might work in the future. His friends regularly asked about his progress—how he was doing, what he was learning, and what specific things they could continue praying about.

Now to make a plan—a *realistic* plan with realistic expectations. He had lived for too many years trying to be the perfect father, which only meant he crashed that much harder when he blew it. He had what some call the *overcompensation syndrome.* Failing to live up to his expectations of perfection only led to guilt and shame, which led to the "I'll do better next time" response, which of course never works. In fact, trying to be *perfect* (instead of simply trying to be *better*) usually guarantees failure on the next go-around.

So Dan traded his pursuit of perfection for a pursuit of *growth.* He also scaled back his expectations for his kids. He began to take into account age-related developmental differences as well as differences in personality type. He began to feel he was understanding his children better, and soon he found himself responding in ways that cleared up problems rather than increased frustration.

A big goal in his realistic plan was to retrain himself to pause before dumping on his son. The Bible was a key source of insight and help for Dan. There he discovered the truth that "a patient man has great understanding, but a quick-tempered man displays folly" (Proverbs 14:29). He learned that "better a patient man than a warrior, a man who controls his temper than one who takes a city" (Proverbs 16:32), that "a man's wisdom gives him patience" (Proverbs 19:11). And *wisdom* was what Dan knew he needed a lot of—a wisdom that would give him a cautious spirit and a gentle tongue, a wisdom that would help him make responsible decisions about his kids. We encouraged him to take a brief time-out before reacting to an explosive situation, to give himself the time and space to ponder and pray about his response.

Finally, Dan's realistic plan included using a new set of responses available to him. Through prayer, conversations, and reading, he realized there were a variety of positive ways to respond to his son that he hadn't tried—though in the heat of battle he knew how difficult it would be to respond in a new and different way, even if that way was a lot healthier. So Dan addressed the problem before he met it in battle: He wrote down just three new responses and put each one on a three-by-five card. Every morning he asked God for strength to help him get out of his behavioral rut. His wife helped him role-play problem situations so he could hear himself respond in new ways.

Dan's plan was simple, specific, practical, achievable, and measurable; it went beyond good intentions to specific strategies. And within six months, Dan's plan was working pretty well.

Assess Your Results, Then Set New Goals

Many people wish they could be different, but few relish the process of change. Change takes time; it can be frustrating and discouraging; it inevitably involves failure. Yet unless we allow God to help us change, we aren't likely to become the man or woman, the spouse, or the parent we want to be.

So be content to let change trudge along slowly, knowing that it won't occur overnight. When you assess your results, look for *small* signs of growth. You can measure growth by three relatively simple yardsticks: a decrease in the *frequency*, a decrease in the *intensity*, and a decrease in the *duration* of the unhealthy response. By the way, realize that you don't stand much chance seeing decreases in all three of these at the same time! Be encouraged by improvement in just one area at a time. Dan first noticed a decrease in the intensity of his negative responses. Later he noticed that when he did lapse into a negative response, it was of shorter duration. Finally he noticed a clear decrease in the frequency of his unhealthy responses.

A few months down the road, Dan's realistic plan was working—and it was time to set a new goal, and a realistic plan to meet *that* goal. It was still hard work, but he found that his small initial victories produced a new sense of confidence and hope.

SMALL BEGINNINGS

1. What are some of the uncomfortable or unpleasant emotions you are most likely to experience with your son? How long have they been a problem for you?
2. Has your spouse or friends ever expressed concern at how you handle your emotions around your kids? How have you responded to their concerns? Is it possible that at least some of their concerns are valid?
3. What pattern (or patterns) have you fallen into that has been shown not to work for you or your son?
4. If you were to pick one emotion to which you could begin to apply the seven steps to responding in a healthy way to your son's emotions, which one would you pick? When can you begin working on it? How about today? Whom can you share your "project" with and seek prayer support from?
5. When working through these steps make sure you spend adequate time with steps two and three. Remember that a problem defined is a problem half-solved. If you can identify the triggers and the factors that increase your vulnerability, you will have solved half of the problem.

Chapter Ten

WHAT BOYS NEED FROM THEIR DAD

UP FRONT *In this chapter...*

- ✦ Despite its lifelong consequences, no training is required to be a parent. On the other hand, all the training in the world cannot prepare you for parenting. Yet child-rearing help from extended family and community, two groups that have traditionally supported parents, is dwindling these days.
- ✦ The physical absence of the father from the home is a critical social problem in America. To have a father in the home is as critical as having a mother there in order for boys in particular to be raised with a sense of wholeness.
- ✦ Effective fathering includes nurturing your sons; being a man of prayer; sharing your heart with your sons; loving them unconditionally; being mentally and emotionally present to your family; playing with your sons; keeping your promises; and encouraging your sons to dream dreams and imagine possibilities.
- ✦ Boys notice what their fathers measure themselves by—and those standards influence how boys gauge themselves and others. Building a strong relationship with your son doesn't require perfection—just time, commitment, courage, and faith.

Dad. FATHER. POPS. ALLOW yourself a moment to think of the man you called Father. Capture an image of him from your childhood—in his favorite chair, the way he dressed, his characteristic look or mood. Do you recall the power he had to delight you with his approval, to create dread in you with his displeasure, or to wound you with his indifference? Did you ever stay awake just to hear his voice when he came home? Did you long for his attention or praise? Can you imagine that even at a young age your children will already have longings, images, and apprehensions regarding you? One day these will become old memories of delightful things *you* said and did, *your* characteristic moods, perhaps even the hurtful things you did or didn't do. *Father* will become a powerful, evocative word for your children, just as it is for you.[1]

Despite the developmental theories I had digested in my graduate studies in psychology, despite my biblical and theological training, despite my training as a marriage and family therapist, despite my years as a clinical psychologist, despite all the patients I had counseled over the years—despite all this, I was unprepared for what fatherhood really meant until I had my own children:

- I was unprepared for the overwhelming feelings of love and protectiveness I would feel toward my sons.
- I was unprepared for the energy my boys would require of me.
- I was unprepared for the ambivalence I would feel about their presence.
- I was unprepared for the ongoing demands they would make on me.
- I was unprepared for the ensuing, continuous struggle to find a balance in my own life.
- I was unprepared for how the importance of my family would change my life perspective forever.

- I was unprepared for how much pleasure my sons would give me.
- I was unprepared for how anxious and frightened I would feel about my sons.
- I was unprepared for the profound changes that would take place in my marriage after my sons were born.
- I was unprepared for the awesome God-given opportunity and responsibility to shape confident, happy little guys.[2]

I just thought I'd be better prepared for fatherhood than I was. And I discovered that most men are like me—no matter how little or how much training they've had, they just aren't prepared to parent. It is one of the greatest opportunities, one of the most challenging roles, one of the most significant tasks, and one of the highest honors that God can give to any man—and we're pretty much left to figure it out on our own!

WHY ARE FATHERS IMPORTANT?

When you hear the word *father*, what do you think of? Your own father? Someone who was a father figure to you? God? What images come to mind? What pleasant, or painful, memories does that word evoke?

Most men would agree that being a father to children in the home is one of the most significant and sacred times in a man's life. Yet fatherhood is the role that men are least prepared to fill. Where did you learn about what it means to be a father? Who taught you? What preparation did you have? When your first child was born, did other fathers visit you and give you tips on how to be a new dad?

We live in a generation that places a high value on education and training for almost everything we do—*except* fathering. There is more preparation for driving a car than for being a dad. Let us say it again: Most men enter fatherhood massively unprepared for one of the most important and challenging roles they will ever fill.

"Becoming a father is a precious and sacred time in a man's life but, unfortunately, it is rarely acknowledged as such," writes parenting expert Will Glennon. "We arrive at this moment almost completely unprepared—no wise, elderly male relative takes us aside and impresses upon us the importance of seizing the chance for deep bonding. Too often, the moment passes without our even understanding the opportunity that is already slipping away."[3]

Is this lack of preparation because we believe fathering skills are instinctive or innate and will somehow magically appear when the first child is born? We don't think so. In previous generations, men learned how to be fathers through their relationships with significant males—their fathers, uncles, grandfathers, teachers, coaches, or friends of the family. Today most boys grow up isolated from extended family systems. To complicate the picture, most dads spend most of their time away from home and family to support home and family.

Many voices in our society attest to how important fathers are to their families—and why this is so.

In his book *The Wonder of Boys,* Michael Gurian cites the following observation from former Delaware governor Peter du Pont, now policy chairman of the National Center for Policy Analysis: "Four out of every ten children in America will go to bed tonight in a home where their father doesn't live. By the end of the decade, it may be six out of ten. . . . Sixty percent of rapists, seventy-two percent of adolescent murderers, and seventy percent of all long-term prison inmates are boys who grew up without their fathers in the home."[4]

The latest survey by the National Center for Fathering revealed that nearly three-fourths (seventy-two percent) of Americans agreed with this statement: "The most significant family or social problem facing America is the physical absence of the father from the home." Yet, even when the father *is* present at home, there can be problems. Fifty-six percent of Americans believe that "most people have unresolved problems with their fathers." Young adults in particular (sixty-seven percent of eighteen- to twenty-four-year-olds) felt strongly that unresolved problems with fathers are a significant issue; seventy percent of nonwhite respondents expressed agreement with the statement that most people have unresolved problems with their fathers.[5]

Men are starting to wake up to the fact that few honors are greater, few responsibilities more significant, and few privileges more meaningful than to be a father to a son or a daughter— or to be like a father to those boys or girls who are without fathers.

The way we fill and fulfill our fathering role is important to God, and it's important to us too. We've never met a man who didn't want to be successful at the role he plays in the workplace—men worry about it, work hard to achieve it, plan for it, prepare for it. And when things aren't going well in their work, they just might even pray they would achieve greater levels of success at it. Yet we've met thousands of fathers who say they never *imagined* all that it took—or that they didn't have what it takes—to be a dad.

Moms and dads fulfill different needs in their same-sex and other-sex children. Contrary to the claims of some radical feminists that fathers are unnecessary, research is validating what the Bible has told us for thousands of years: Fathers are as important as mothers—not more important, but *as* important. Studies tell us that children with effective fathers:

- Get along better with their peers
- Display more social confidence
- Are more comfortable in new situations
- Adapt to change more easily
- Score higher on intelligence tests

- Demonstrate better thinking ability
- Have increased empathy for others
- Have a greater ability to rely on their own judgment[6]

When it comes to raising boys, a father's role is especially significant. From Gary's experience as a dad and as a marriage and family specialist, from our own research, conversations, and interviews with thousands of dads, as well as from reviewing the results of many surveys, we have identified several key tips to becoming an effective father.

BE A PASSIONATE MAN

Why is it that a relatively recent study revealed that only twenty percent of the fathers surveyed felt they had a close emotional relationship with *either* their own fathers or their sons?[7] It could be, at least in part, because most men are very good at controlling their feelings. They are especially skilled at gutting it out and getting on with things in the face of hardship, danger, pain, and turmoil. "When the going gets tough, the tough get going"; "no pain, no gain"—it's our masculine legacy and part of our cultural mythology.

Men generally have a limited emotional vocabulary and little experience in emotional dialogue; what experience they do acquire is usually negative. Men are all too capable of numbing their emotions or becoming stoic problem solvers and unemotional security providers. Because they were trained to stuff, repress, deny, and ignore their emotions, they find themselves untrained, unsupported, unsure, and uneasy in the crucial task of emotionally nurturing their children. Consequently, they don't know how to share their emotions—and if *they* don't know how to model healthy masculine emotionality, how will their sons learn this essential dimension of what it means to be made in the image of God?

Most women will tell you that reintroducing a man to his emotional side is a very tall order—at least in part because men have grown up in a culture that encourages males to avoid anything that looks like weakness or sentimentality. Fathers, how recently did *you* feel something so deeply you were moved to tears? Where were you? What did it feel like? Were you uncomfortable? Embarrassed? Surprised? Relieved? What did you do with those feelings? Did you express them to someone, or keep them to yourself?

The deeper the emotion, the more difficult it is for most men to share it with someone else. Have you ever felt like you cry—or laugh or get angry—at the wrong time? Men think nothing of investing in years of training for communicating their *ideas* with clarity, yet receive precious little training in clearly communicating their *feelings*. When they do try to express their emotions, they often come on either too strong or not strong enough. They get embarrassed. People misunderstand them. They get criticized and corrected—and, not surprisingly, they learn to avoid the risk of humiliation, of being laughed at or rejected.

A common male device (though by no means exclusively male) is to hide inside his intellect in order to avoid the pain of feeling what he never did understand. With unusual candor, former pastor and radio host David Mains, now director of Chapel Ministries, writes about the big padlock he had slapped on his emotions:

> For a large part of my life I was tuned out emotionally. I wasn't aware of where others were coming from, and I didn't even understand my own feelings.
>
> I was probably extreme in that regard. I didn't know when I was tired. I seldom paid attention to whether I was hot or cold. I wasn't in touch with what I liked or didn't like. If someone would ask me what was wrong, instead of saying, "I feel trapped with no way out of this situation," I'd reply, "I'm OK, why do you ask?"

Most of the time if someone accused me of expressing a negative emotion like anger or pride or frustration, I denied it. Was I stomping mad? No. Did I swear? Had my words stopped making sense because of my intense emotion? Never. What do you mean I was angry? You're accusing me of not acting the way a Christian should!

"You were emoting," my wife would tell me the next day. "It was as if you were sending out waves and waves of high voltage electricity. I don't understand how everybody can sense that except you."

Well, I wasn't in tune with my anger, my pain, my loneliness, my defensiveness, my fears, delights, moods, embarrassment, jealousies, whatever. I functioned relatively well in the objective world of ideas and facts and words. But the more subjective realm of feeling was atrophying, shriveling up within me.

Thank God that in recent years the Lord has been doing a major healing in me for which I'm extremely grateful. One of the signs of health is that my feelings are coming back into play.[8]

When David Mains reads the Bible now, he says he sees how much it has to say about emotions. When he goes to church, he often finds himself filled with inexplicable joy. He is able to shed tears when he is hurt or when he discovers he has hurt someone else. He is better able to discern when he has let himself become too busy and requires a time of rest.

Only if fathers allow God to cultivate their hearts, to allow his love to pour through them, will they begin touching what their sons need to see in their fathers, what their sons need to hear and feel from them—so that their boys can someday become whole men.

Although being a dad is often about *doing*—something for which most fathers prepared their sons quite well—being a Christlike father is primarily about *feeling*, about sharing your heart with your son. The first challenge for fathers, then, is to heed the divine call to become emotional warriors, and in doing so to return to the heart of fathering.

Be Passionate in Your Love for Jesus

Being an effective father starts with a Person, not a performance. The starting place of wise fatherhood is our relationship with God the Father. Even Jesus said as much: "The Son . . . can do only what he sees his Father doing, because whatever the Father does the Son also does" (John 5:19). At another time Jesus confessed that "I do nothing on my own but speak just what the Father has taught me" (John 8:28).

A passionate love for Jesus can be expressed, for example, through the practice of a spiritual discipline. In the weeks prior to one of the Promise Keepers conferences, Gary let our boys know that he was going to fast one day a week—and he asked if they wanted to pray for him during that time. Each one of the boys, entirely on his own, said he'd also like to join him in the fast. We talked about what fasting is and what it isn't, and about some of the reasons people fast. We looked at some of the writings of John Piper and Richard Foster and discussed various types of fasts. Gary and the boys decided to do a liquids-only fast. Even that seemed a bit much for then eight-year-old Andrew. After some creative thinking, he decided to abstain from sugar one day a week—a huge sacrifice for this boy!

If Gary has a passionate love relationship with God, our boys will notice it. They'll notice what he embraces and what he shuns, and they will be drawn to do the same. To use pastor and Bible expositor John Piper's analogy, the boys will note what Gary hungers for and what dulls his hunger. They will begin to realize it is not the banquet of the wicked that dulls our appetite for heaven, as Piper insightfully teaches, but our endless nibbling at the table of the world; they will begin to see that the most deadly appetites are not for the poison of evil, but for the simple pleasures of earth.[9]

Be Passionate in Your Love for Your Children

What children need most from parents is to be acknowledged and loved for who they are—which is why the most basic duty of parents is to discover who their children are, help *them* understand who they are, and then love them unconditionally for their uniqueness.

It's particularly important to let go of our sons' blunders, mistakes, and embarrassments—which, for some reason, dads seem to have a harder time doing than moms. Boys make mistakes and fall on their faces; so do we all. They will say and do things no one would ever want to be reminded of. Thus, one key to good fathering is a willingness to *remember to forget*. As Will Glennon observes, to be a good father is to cultivate empathy that reaches beyond performance:

> True empathy goes beyond simply understanding how our children feel. It is the emotional discipline of taking yourself outside of time, putting yourself in the position that they now occupy, and then actually experiencing their feelings. . . . The range of our children's emotions is quite broad, but the span of our own emotional experiences is considerably broader. We have been there and beyond. . . . When we experience their feelings, they cannot help but know it. And the better we get at sensing, decoding, and understanding the flow and texture of their emotions, the more they will feel known, loved, safe, and secure. . . . When we are able to put ourselves in their place and feel what they are feeling, the rest is easy. . . . Our willingness to feel—rather than just understand—their feelings is both a demonstration of their importance to us and the proof of our love for them. . . . The rewards of empathy are many.[10]

If a father's love for his son is conditional—if there are strings attached—then the son will most likely begin to doubt his significance and lose his security. Much of his energy will be invested in trying to solve the mystery of what he needs to do in order to receive his dad's approval, love, and blessing. Instead of focusing his energy on discovering the unique person God made him to be, a son whose father loves him *conditionally* will likely spend his adolescent years (and beyond) studying his dad's every move and mood shift in order to successfully anticipate what he must do to please Dad.

A man once told of a weeklong visit he had made to his parents' home. As he stood in the kitchen talking to his mother, he watched his father and his own boy—grandfather and grandson—working in the vegetable garden. His father was showing the boy the "correct" technique for turning over the soil. It reminded the man of the endless corrections he had undergone while growing up in that house. "I'm sure he just felt like he was doing his duty, teaching me 'the right way,'" the man recalled later, "but I hated it. I felt stupid and grew up convinced I couldn't do anything right."[11] What our children need from us is care, concern, unconditional love, and access to our years of experience. What they do *not* need is a live-in know-it-all.

As fathers become fully engaged with their own emotions, they will learn to share deep feelings with their sons. In fact, a father's ability to share his heart with his son may be the most significant legacy he can leave. When fathers open up to sons, the boys will, in a sense, receive permission to share their hearts with their fathers. As they watch fathers who are comfortable with their own emotions, sons are more likely to hear God speak to their hearts and weave their minds, wills, and emotions together in a chord of strength that will sustain them throughout their lives.

BE PRESENT

For years Gary prided himself on how many evenings a week he was home with Carrie and the boys; he *was*, in fact, doing better than most men we knew. But God eventually convinced him that, while he was home physically, he might just as well have worn a sign around his neck that read: "I've got a lot of important things on my mind. Do not disturb."

Gary was at home, but he wasn't mentally and emotionally present with the family. It's not so hard for men to be present physically and to interact regularly with their sons—but to sense that the powerful flow of vital energy is missing. Men can easily create a zone, a safe place inside themselves to which they can retreat, an island unto themselves. You know what we're talking about—you may have already visited this island several times this week.

"Father absence" has become a critical problem. The emotional distance that has increasingly come to characterize men's lives has begun to reverberate out into the world. A United States Census Report (Princeton Survey Research) tells us the following:

- Nearly half our children live outside traditional two-parent homes.
- Fathers in the United States spend less time with their children than fathers in any other country.
- Among those fathers who *do* live with their children, the average amount of time spent with them is twelve minutes a day.[12]

Many dads have sentenced their sons to the bewildering experience of growing up with a desperate need to feel loved by a father who, all too often, is simply *not there*. And the effects are devastating:

- Nearly eighty percent of those who end up in our juvenile justice system lived in homes without a father.
- The overwhelming majority of our adult prison population grew up without fathers.
- The single strongest predictor of violent juvenile crime—specifically robbery and murder—is that the child grew up without a close relationship to his father.[13]

It doesn't matter if you are a Boomer, a Buster, or an X-er. Each generation has had its song that bemoans the effects of a distant, absent, or preoccupied dad: Harry Chapin's "Cat's in the Cradle"; Faster Pussycat's "In My House of Pain"; Shaquille O'Neal's "Biological Father Didn't Bother"; and Everclear's "Father of Mine."

When Gary helped his sister move from California to Colorado, he took our middle son Matt with him. Together they drove one of the cars to Denver. When they crossed the border into Nevada, the first thing they saw was a gigantic roller coaster on the grounds of a big casino. They had been sitting in the car for a few hours, so Gary let his son talk him into stopping for a couple of rides. Besides, they were hungry, and casino meals are cheap.

As they walked through the casino to get to the ride, Gary was amazed to discover an entire section of the casino dedicated to children—games, rides, shops, even a day care facility. He saw a brochure promoting family vacations to this casino. Casinos have traditionally been known for many things, he thought, but never for family services.

Matt immediately noticed the men and women standing in front of the slots and video poker machines, glassy-eyed, pouring coins in, one right after another.

"I thought people came to casinos to have fun," he said. "You know, I haven't seen one person here who looks like they're happy, like they're having fun."

What had started out merely as a quest for a great roller coaster ride and a cheap meal turned into a marvelous teaching opportunity.

It's easy to talk about the dangers of gambling and criticize the folks who allow their habit to preoccupy them and take them (and their money) away from those they love. But if Gary wants to become a better dad, he needs to stop and look at himself and ask what habits or hobbies or pastimes take *him* away from *our* kids. A hobby or interest or business venture doesn't have to be inherently wrong to keep him from being physically or emotionally present with his boys.

"No problem," some of you are saying. "At least I've got *this* one down. I'm home at least four nights a week." Don't gloat quite yet. It's easy for men to be present but preoccupied—and when you're preoccupied, you might as well not even be there physically. There are two kinds of absence: *not there,* and *there, but not really there.* Gary knows. It's still easy for him to slip into showing up, but not being present.

Don't worry about working late once in a while when you must. It's okay to stay in your bowling or racquetball league. But keep your eyes open for whatever it is—work commitments, recreational opportunities, even church activities—that consistently rates a higher priority than your family.

BE PLAYFUL

"If I could start my family again, one thing would be changed," writes family counselor J. Allan Petersen. "I would play more with my three boys and cultivate more family-sharing experiences. By sharing good times, a family builds cohesiveness and unity. They learn to enjoy each other and compensate for each other's weaknesses. The play of children is something of a rehearsal for life, and parents who share these times of play will have a great opportunity to teach their children how to live."[14]

Read what the Report to the President, White House Conference on Children, concludes:

A child learns, he becomes human, primarily through participation in a challenging activity with those he loves and admires. . . . It is in work and play with children, in games, in projects, in shared responsibilities with parents, adults, and other children that the child develops the skills, motives, and qualities of character that enable him to live a life that is gratifying both to himself and those around him.[15]

The report adds that the alarming decline in the amount of time adults are spending with children is causing a breakdown in the process of "making human beings human."

Who do you most enjoy being around? Who do you eagerly anticipate spending time with? Who leaves you feeling encouraged because you've been with them? Chances are they are the people you feel safe with—people you can laugh and play with.

Parenting expert Will Glennon comments on the joy of playing with our children:

> Truly, deeply, enthusiastically enjoying our children is one of the fundamental building blocks of an enriching lifelong connection. When we play with our children, we need to throw our expectations overboard and turn control over to the play experts—our kids. Playing need not be about teaching, about solving problems, or about building something. . . . Playing should be about enjoying ourselves, and it is an art form at which children are extraordinarily talented.[16]

When we as a family look at the times that have been the most meaningful and enjoyable, they have been without exception the times we played together. With Nathan, Matt, and Andrew, we have discovered that the spontaneous moment is often the most enjoyable. Yes, we have structured times where we go camping, biking, fishing, and hiking—but those times when Gary puts down his "important" projects (which five years from now he will have forgotten) and leaves the house with a boy or two in tow to explore a new part of northwest Arkansas or to get a strawberry milkshake at the Sonic drive-in or to catch a movie at a local theater—these are the times our family enjoys most.

What often says *love* to our sons the most is to simply *be with them* in the moment—to forget teaching and problem solving for that point in time and just enjoy their presence in our lives.

BE A PROMISE KEEPER

The story is told of a father whose game with his small son consisted of repeatedly throwing him in the air—and catching him just before he hit the ground. Relaxed and having a great time, the boy punctuated each toss in the air with "Do it again! Do it again!"

If I were that child, I'd be stiff as a board, thought a watching neighbor, as he sauntered over to the hedge and asked the father, "So the boy's not afraid of being tossed, huh?"

The father first caught his son, then looked at the neighbor. "It's simple," he said. "We have a history together. We've played this game before, and I've *never* dropped him."

Being a dad is, among other things, about keeping promises. If you promise something, deliver on it. If you break a promise, apologize and ask for forgiveness—and that includes truly recognizing when you've hurt someone. It sounds simple, but it's something a lot of fathers don't do easily.

Sometimes a dad's apology is a reflex, and he doesn't fully understand the pain he's inflicted. "Sorry," he mumbles, hoping that the hastily spoken apology will heal the rift in the family. Then there's the classic "Whatever I did to upset you, I'm sorry," which is even worse. Apparently a genuinely offered apology leaves some males too vulnerable to suit their fancy.

So keep it simple, and keep it heartfelt. When you realize you've bruised your son's feelings, apologize *and ask for forgiveness*—"Taylor, I was wrong for yelling at you. I'm sure that embarrassed you in front of your friends. I shouldn't have done it. Will you forgive me?"

BE POSSIBILITY FOCUSED

The movie *October Sky* tells the story of Homer Hickam, a teenage boy in Coalwood, West Virginia, who in 1957 dreams of leaving Coalwood to become a rocket scientist. One of several barriers Homer must overcome if he's to achieve his dream is, unfortunately, his father—a coal-mining boss—whose own dream is to see his son follow in his footsteps down into the mine to become the town's next mine boss.

October Sky is an inspirational movie for teens because it encourages them to buck the odds and never give up in the pursuit of their dreams. It's inspirational for dads, too, as they recognize the true love that Homer's dad has for him, but also the struggle that his dad has in expressing his love. This dad is exhausted and distracted by the pressures of the job. He perceives his mistakes, but finds it hard to admit when he's wrong. When Homer rejects Coalwood, his dad interprets it as a rejection of him as a father.

Good fathering is not simple. It is a father's job to encourage his children to take risks, to expand their world, to expose them to new experiences; at the same time, it's a father's sacred duty to support his children simply for who they are. There are few things an adolescent enjoys more than seeing a man he respects get excited about the teenager's vision.

Dads must encourage their sons to reach for the stars, but dads also need to be ready to hit the brakes when the drive for their sons to succeed becomes more important than nurturing their own relationship with them.

DADS MAKE A DIFFERENCE

You can be a dad who makes a difference. While dads in television programs like *The Simpsons, Home Improvement, Everybody Loves Raymond,* and *The Nanny* often depict mindless, incompetent, bumbling, insecure, and immature dads, *you* can choose to love, to encourage, to connect with your son in ways that provide a positive example of what a father can be. You can be a much stronger influence for your sons than the characters they see on the screen. When you make time to be emotionally and spiritually present with them, when you listen to them, when you help them with their homework, when you go fishing or shoot baskets with them, wipe their noses, give hugs and kisses—when you do things like this, you are making a lifetime investment in your sons.

Most fathers measure themselves (and others) by the results they achieve, the status they attain, and the money they make; they look at the size of their homes and their ability to run faster, work longer, carry more, and push themselves harder. That's how *they* were raised. That's what they were taught it meant to be a man. They aren't paid, acknowledged, rewarded, or given raises because they are loving fathers.

But here's the catch—in a subconscious way, the yardstick fathers use to measure themselves is what their boys will use to measure *themselves*, both in how they think their dads see them and in how they see themselves and others.

When it comes to being a father, there are no experts. There are only guys who have studied, prayed, tried to do their best, and are willing to share their experiences. Even our friend Ken Canfield, president of the National Center for Fathering and one of the leading authorities on fathering, would tell you he isn't an expert. Like all dads, he is still learning and growing. Building and nurturing a father-child relationship requires the knowledge that it *can* be done, the commitment that it *will* be done, the persistence to keep on trying, the courage to do whatever is necessary to make sure it does get done, and the faith to believe that when and where we do fall short, our God will be faithful to his promises.

Build me a son, O Lord, who will be strong enough to know when he is weak and brave enough to face himself when he is afraid; one who will be proud and unbending in honest defeat, and humble and gentle in victory.

Build me a son whose wishes will not take the place of deeds; a son who will know Thee—and that to know himself is the foundation stone of knowledge.

Lead him, I pray, not in the path of ease and comfort, but under the stress and spur of difficulties and challenge. Here let him learn to stand up in the storm; here let him learn compassion for those who fail.

Build me a son whose heart will be clear, whose goals will be high; a son who will master himself before he seeks to master other men; one who will reach into the future, yet never forget the past.

And after all these things are his, add, I pray, enough of a sense of humor, so that he may always be serious, yet never take himself too seriously. Give him humility, so that he may always remember the simplicity of true greatness, the open mind of true wisdom, and the weakness of true strength.

Then I, his father, will dare to whisper, "I have not lived in vain."[17]

— GENERAL DOUGLAS MACARTHUR

SMALL BEGINNINGS

1. Think through your relationship with your father, both in the past and in the present if he is still living. What did he model for you? What did he do that was helpful? What do you wish he'd done differently? What are you modeling for your son?

2. Ask your son what he likes to do best with you—then do more of it. Another way to look at it is to ask, "If we could do anything that didn't cost more than $10, what would it be?"

3. During the time you spend with your son, are you mostly positive and encouraging? Are you looking for ways to build him up? Do you look for specific ways to compliment him? Once a day for the next seven days, tell your son *one thing* that you appreciate about him.

4. Read the following poem, spend a few moments thinking about it, and then take some time to seek God's guidance. Having done so, recommit yourself to being the kind of dad that God wants you to be, that you want to be, and that your son needs you to be.

> There are little eyes upon you,
> And they're watching night and day;
> There are little ears that quickly
> Take in every word you say;
> There are little lads all eager
> To do anything you do,
> And a little fellow who is dreaming
> Of the day he'll be like you.
> You are the little fellow's idol,
> You are the wisest of the wise,
> In his mind about you,
> No suspicions ever rise.
> He believes in you devoutly,

Holds that all you say and do,
He will say and do in his own way
When he's a grown-up like you.
There's a wide-eyed little fellow,
Who believes you are always right,
And his ears are always open,
And he watches you day and night.
You are setting an example
Every day in all you do,
For the little fellow who's watchin'
To grow up just like you.[18]

Chapter Eleven

WHAT BOYS NEED FROM THEIR MOM

UP FRONT *In this chapter ...*

◆ The most important things moms can do for their sons are to understand the distinct differences between boys and girls, to accept and value their maleness, and then to offer nurture that is in keeping with their sons' masculinity.

◆ Effective mothering includes understanding your son's need for activity, adventure, and risk taking; requiring responsibility from him; and respecting his personality type.

◆ Boys communicate differently than girls. Because boys express emotions through activity more than through talking, you will do well to grab those moments when your son has concluded an activity and may be more inclined to talk. Respecting your son's inner space will help him feel more comfortable talking with you when he feels ready to talk.

◆ An open and honest approach to discussing sex with your son can pay large dividends in helping him gain a healthy view of sexuality.

◆ Moms who can positively affirm their own individuality, who can listen empathetically, who can model emotional health, who can affirm their sons' maleness and their lust for life and adventure, and who can love their sons through thick and thin are in the strong position of providing their boys with the very things they need most from their mom.

Carrie's journey as a mother of sons began on July 25, 1982, when, after twenty-four hours of labor, our first boy was born—dark-haired and olive-skinned like his dad, and not much like Carrie in any way. We named him Nathan Jackson, packed our bags, and took him home, complete with high parenting hopes.

These hopes seemed to be at least somewhat well-founded. Besides her academic degree in elementary education and human development, Carrie had spent her pregnancy poring over every parenting book she could find. She waddled into that hospital confident she was prepared for motherhood. Within a week the truth became painfully clear.

She discovered in retrospect that all those books didn't give her the complete picture. In them there seemed to be an ideological battle between the secular and Christian world about how to discipline—for example, to spank or not to spank—but little was said about the differences between males and females. Carrie's life experience with males had been fairly limited—she had no brothers, though she played cowboys and Indians with her male cousins . . . then some dating in high school and college . . . then marriage to Gary for the span of only a year and half before *son number one* entered the world. Carrie's two best friends were of little help for son-raising advice—they were turning out girls as fast as we would turn out boys.

Carrie needed a bit of help understanding just who these strange creatures called *boys* were and what her role as mother should be. Her three angels could construct guns from anything. Running, climbing, jumping, karate chopping were their favorite pastimes. Matthew was up on his hands and knees at four and a half months—and crawling proficiently two weeks later. Carrie had to haul him off the backyard chain-link fence when he was fifteen months old. In that season (it seems so long ago!), she felt like she was spending endless months simply chasing down her boys to keep them from hurting themselves. While her friend was tying bows in her daughter's hair, Carrie was getting gum out of her son's hair for the third time that day. While her friend was decorating her daughter's room with floral pastels and frilly curtains, Carrie was washing Crayola off the wall. While her friend was off to dance lessons, Carrie was off to baseball practice. A mother with only sons longs for the feminine.

Yet along the way she grew to understand the blessing her sons were to her—gifts to be discovered, unwrapped, and treasured. To come to this point, of course, is a critical step, because what a son needs first from his mother is for her to accept his maleness.

SHAPING SONS

The nurture that mothers give their sons must be in tune with their male wiring. So, remembering that boys are active and adventurous risk takers, how do moms raise them and train them to become responsible children?

A Son Needs His Mother to Understand His Need for Activity

When our sons were little, they needed to let off steam through lots of running, jumping, and climbing. During the winter we'd spend hours in Burger King's indoor plastic playroom. In the summer we'd make daily trips to the park. Getting them out of the house and doing active things simply warded off frustration (and probably household destruction). Turning them loose on the playground, letting them climb the highest slide and jump off the three-meter diving board at the public pool helped foster their self-esteem and their identity as males.

Carrie was something of a risk taker as a child, so it wasn't particularly difficult for her to let the boys venture out. She still doesn't understand how other moms concentrate on protecting their sons from perceived danger rather than letting them work off their abundant energy. By all means, parents should protect their children from danger—but be sure you take into account your son's need for adventure and risk taking. Sons need their mothers to value their exuberance.

A Son Needs His Mother to Believe That He Can Be Responsible

Making beds, clearing dishes from the table, mowing lawns, shoveling snowy driveways, remembering homework—these are tasks of life moms can use to teach their boys responsibility. Otherwise our sons may grow up thinking, *I don't have to do anything*—and feeling they are entitled to everything.

Driving down our Denver street one winter morning, Carrie noticed a mom shoveling snow in her driveway—while in the windows of the house Carrie caught a glimpse of several males, including a dad. What was wrong with this picture? If a boy isn't sharing in these household chores as he grows up, it will be difficult for a mother to require it from him when he's a teenager. Moms are in the best position to teach and train their sons in family responsibilities during the boys' childhoods, then with time gradually increase responsibility and decrease monitoring.

With our two older sons, Carrie has been tenacious about requiring responsibility from them. Now fifteen and seventeen, the boys know their part as members of the family and are reasonably responsible about schoolwork, household tasks, and the like. The youngest son? Well, it took a candid (yet irritating at the time) conversation with a good friend to push Carrie out of her "mother-of-the-last-child" syndrome and require a little more responsibility of Andrew. Boys must be allowed to experience their mother's belief that they can take care of themselves and make positive contributions to the family system.

A Son Needs His Mother to Always Respect His Maleness

Carrie's philosophy of discipline has changed over time as she learned more about female-male differences and began to better understand the influence of personality types. Our sons share the characteristic of being male, but all three are unique in their personality. Carrie and our first son seemed to be constantly at war when he was young. What she now knows is that Nathan needed many more time-out sessions—he's an introvert, and much of his thinking and feeling processes are internal. At the time Carrie didn't understand this and instead demanded answers and obedience from him before he could give it. Thank goodness that kids are resilient. Nathan will always need to step away from a situation in order to think it out and feel it through—to first come to terms with problems on his own.

On the flip side, a mother who is dominated by her son does not respect his maleness either. When Nathan and Matt were thirteen and fourteen, riding in a car with them was as draining as during their toddler days—more so, in fact, because they had become more verbal and louder. Carrie certainly didn't scare them much anymore. We all remember one particularly infamous car trip to Nebraska, where Carrie was going to drop off the two older boys for a month's stay with Gary's mother. For four hundred miles Nathan and Matt were loud, argumentative, and disrespectful. Carrie dropped them off at their grandma's house, told them she loved them, and—relishing the prospect of quieter days with Andrew—drove back home again.

The weeks went by, and it was time for the boys to come home again. Carrie was in no mood to subject herself to the boys' bickering for another four hundred miles. After some creative thinking, we concocted a plan for them to take the bus back to Denver—and pay for their own fares. They didn't respond to the plan well, but Carrie continued to talk with them daily, listening and respecting them—and wishing them a very lovely bus ride home. It was a form of domination by her sons, pure and simple, that Carrie chose to escape.

INTIMACY THROUGH ACTIVITY, NOT TALKING

Much of Carrie's counseling practice is devoted to simply helping people become better, clearer, and more thorough communicators. Mothers learn early on that boys, like their fathers, communicate differently than females. In her book *You Just Don't Understand: Women and Men in Conversation,* sociologist Deborah Tannen explores research that clearly demonstrates that communication between males and females does not happen naturally. The good news, however, is that a mother is typically the first female a boy learns to communicate with—which means that if a mother can cultivate good communication skills in her son, she's giving him a big head start in communicating with women for the rest of his life.

A son needs direct, clear communication from his mother. Females tend to communicate in subtle ways that they expect the other person to understand, decipher, or otherwise figure out—despite the fact that their husbands and sons generally need direct, blatant language. Our adolescent sons do best when Carrie asks them directly to carry out tasks: "Next time I'm at work all day, could you please set the table and empty the dishwasher?" conveys an entirely different message than "All I do is work, and if you cared about me you'd notice what needs to be done and you'd do it." The first message communicates directly what Carrie needs from our son; the second communicates the frustration of coping with work and places guilt on our son for not meeting his mother's needs.

While females tend to be intimate by talking, males tend to experience intimacy through activity. Mothers who want to understand their sons emotionally should probably give up hoping that they'll accomplish this through long, leisurely hours of talking. Most moms need to meet their sons on the turf where the boys feel comfortable—riding in the car to or from an event is often a great time to connect with a son. Activity brings out emotions in males—so a son may be most emotionally aware after playing football or shooting baskets. He probably *isn't* very emotionally aware the first thing in the morning or when he's been sitting around watching television.

Don't push your son to talk about feelings. If you bring up the subject of his feelings and he doesn't respond, drop it. You can make your son comfortable with the subject by asking him if he wants to talk and by letting him know that it's okay if he *doesn't* want to talk about feelings at that particular time. A son needs to feel his mother's confidence that he can make decisions about his emotions—and that his private world is his own.

As our sons become adolescents, they have less of a need for us to solve their problems or draw out their emotions, but more of a need for us to listen. Listening to a son means we do not finish his sentences for him or become an authority on his world, but rather that we simply join him with our undivided attentiveness and let him clearly know that we believe in him—whatever the outcome of his issue.

Don't let being a mother stop you from being a woman. Our sons will go to almost any movie we want to see—even mushy flicks. When we all went to see *Stepmom,* Carrie really felt the pain of the ex-wife and began to cry a little. The boys didn't share Carrie's empathy with the Susan Sarandon character, and they even snickered now and then. On the way home they joked a bit about Carrie's weepiness, so Carrie simply told them exactly what she was feeling for the ex-wife—a woman who was coping with loneliness. Carrie didn't expect her boys to feel the same way she did, so she let them know why she was moved to the point of tears. And they listened.

Some mothers are inclined to stop being themselves when they have sons. To the contrary, a son needs his mother to be consistent with who God has created her to be. The goal is a balance of communicating in ways that are meaningful to him and allowing your individuality to flow through your communication.

LOVE, SEX, AND SONS

"There is a challenge of learning to help your son fall in love with the right woman, because you are the first woman he loves," said Goldie Hawn in an interview about her relationship with her son. "So you have to be darn good at being his first idealized mate, and then let him go. These are hard things to do."[1]

Letting Go

In some ways all of a mother's mothering points to this act of letting go. A healthy letting go begins early in a son's life, often accompanied by little love rituals. All our sons, for example, have always been comfortable saying, "I love you," often before we can say it to them. You'll hear "I love you" on the phone when they say good-bye, when they go out the door, and when they go to bed. The boys often give both of us a kiss along with the spoken "I love you." (For a while our youngest son wasn't into the kissing part, and we honored that. But he's now back to feeling comfortable with kissing and being kissed.)

We also set what we believe are healthy boundaries about bedrooms, nakedness, and the like—primarily because sons need their mothers to honor their privacy. In the morning rush of getting ready, or the evening preparation at bedtime, we try to cover up at least a little in front of the boys, and we expect the same sort of reasonable modesty from them. Nor did we foster the habit of letting our sons sleep in our bed with us when they were younger. Only rarely did a sleepy son wander into our room, and we usually let him sleep on the floor next to our bed. The goal was always to prevent confusion in a mom's relationship with her son—a confusion that can be difficult to avoid if she lets him sleep in the same bed with her.

We did not wait for the onset of puberty to talk to the boys about sex. We've always been candid about reproduction (whether animal or human), no matter what the boys' ages. Carrie learned early in motherhood that boys are just plain curious about sex. So whether the subject is new puppies or new brothers, we've been forthright with answers. As the boys have gotten older, they know our values regarding sexual behavior. Carrie recently attended our son's human sexuality class as a guest (he gets extra-credit points for bringing guests). Carrie didn't sit with him, but came in a little late (a strategic decision) and sat in the back. A pediatrician gave an explicit presentation on premarital sex and sexually transmitted diseases. When Nathan returned home, he talked candidly with his mom about the talk.

Sons need mothers as well as fathers to stay involved in household discussions of sexual behavior. Matt likes to joke around—even about sex. And Carrie is rarely shocked by his humor, but instead often turns it into an opportunity for deeper discussion. Given the intense pressure on teenagers to become sexually active, it's critical that mothers stay connected with their sons, that they keep relating to them on their terms and within their boundaries.

FROM MOTHER TO SON: A FEW FINAL THOUGHTS

Share who you are with your son. Demonstrate your individuality and femininity. Listen to his ideas, his goals, his dreams. Always be clear about your values, standards, and expectations. Model emotional health for him. Name your emotions and give them meaning. When he is able to share emotionally with you, be sure to listen, affirm, and then back off when he is done. Try to understand his individuality. Match consequences to his misbehavior. Do not meet your own caretaking needs at the expense of your son and his ability to learn to take care of himself. Affirm his maleness by affirming the other males in your life. If you are critical of males, he will read that as being critical of him. Don't expect your son to compensate you for an unsatisfying marriage. Encourage assertiveness, not aggressiveness. Join him in activity, and affirm his lust for life and adventure. Have abundant and delightful fun with your son—and remember always to tell him you love him.

SMALL BEGINNINGS

1. List the things you most enjoy about your son as a male.
2. Ask your son what activities he most enjoys doing. Venture out and join him in some of his interests wherever appropriate.
3. Assess your ability to set boundaries with your son. Begin to set boundaries around one or two areas where your son may be taking advantage of you.

Chapter Twelve

WHAT BOYS NEED FROM YOUR MARRIAGE

UP FRONT *In this chapter ...*

✦ Making your marriage a top priority is one of the most important things you can do for the present and future welfare of your boys.

✦ The health of your marriage relationship will depend in large measure on how well you understand and value the personality and gender differences between you and your spouse. The way you deal with these differences will be closely observed by your son and can provide a strong foundation for the way he in turn will function in his relationships.

✦ Your son learns much of what he knows about love and about the value of commitment from the way you demonstrate love and commitment in your marriage relationship.

✦ Expressing your emotions in healthy ways will make it easier for your son to understand the value of emotions—both pleasant and painful ones.

✦ Cultivating your friendship with your spouse is imperative for the health of your marriage relationship, as well as for building your son's trust in the strength of your relationship and providing a model for healthy opposite-sex relationships.

YOUR SONS WILL LOOK to your marriage to learn the value of relationships; what defines a good relationship; what it means to honor, to respect, to trust, to listen, and to forgive. What your children see in your marriage is what they will most likely reproduce in their own marriages. Your marriage can provide a sense of safety, stability, and security in your sons as they grow and mature. And it is a loving marriage that can reinforce your children's ability to enter into a loving and growing relationship with God. The picture of marriage you pass on to your sons may very well be your best legacy.

MARRIAGE—THE BEDROCK OF RAISING SONS

The Bible tells us that in the beginning God created marriage and the family. When he created humankind in his own image, he chose the family to serve as the cradle for personhood—the crucible in which the reality of the living God should be *taught* (through formal education) and *caught* (by the example of the parents' lives).

If God has, as we believe, intended all along for the family to be the foundation of society, then marriage is the cornerstone. If a family is to be healthy, it will make the marriage a priority. In *Because I Said So!* child-rearing and family life expert John Rosemond writes the following:

> If you put your children first, if you plan your life around them, the fabric of your relationship may not be able to endure the wear and tear of the parenting years. The marriage is the nucleus of the family. It creates, defines, and sustains the family. It transcends the identities of the two people who created it, and yet a healthy marriage not only preserves those identities but also brings them to full flower.[1]

As you cultivate your marriage, you cultivate your son. Your son's security is rooted to the security of the marriage. By the same token, the relationship with your son cannot upstage or interfere with your marriage. Such interference has been known to take many forms—letting a son sleep regularly in his parents' bed, letting him crowd out his parents' date night (or at least a childless night cuddling together on the couch). Especially as our own kids became teenagers, we really worked at balancing time with the boys with our own needs for *coupleness.*

Without boundaries, the responsibilities of parenting can completely take over a marriage relationship. Couples can drift apart and gradually become uncomfortable with coupleness itself. In these circumstances, the spouses become in essence merely "married singles"—and this kind of marriage does your children no favor. The strength you gather from being a *couple*—the friendship, emotional closeness, and sexual intimacy you keep alive with your spouse—is exactly what will sustain you in your parenting. Especially when your sons enter adolescence, they will be able to sense the security you share in your relationship with your spouse, and they in turn will feel secure themselves. Make your marriage a priority.

CELEBRATE YOUR DIFFERENCES

Widely respected relationship expert John Gottman has identified four behaviors as the strongest predictors of divorce: criticism, contempt, defensiveness, and stonewalling.[2] Behind each of these behaviors is the difficulty or inability to appreciate and work with individual differences. The health of a marriage relationship depends on participants who understand and value both gender and personality differences. If you do *not* understand these differences, you're likely to spend too much energy trying to change your spouse and your children.

Those differences very likely played a big part in attracting you to your partner in the first place. Over time, however—as you no longer appreciate the richness that a spouse who is so different from you can bring to your marriage—these very differences can irritate and frustrate. Working to *understand* these differences is the key to overcoming the temptation to criticize and demean your spouse. You can explore the results of personality type to help you understand some of the most important parts of a person's personality—which consists (as explored in chapter 6) of a combination of several inborn preferences or tendencies that strongly influence the kind of people we become.

When you don't realize that your spouse views the world quite differently than you do, conflict is imminent. In our case, for example, Gary is more introverted than Carrie is. He has more of an internal process, while Carrie prefers talking out problems and plans. Gary is an intuitive, future-oriented person who sees the big picture; Carrie, meanwhile, lives solidly in the present, with its details and duties. Carrie approaches the world with *feeling*, Gary with *logic*. We both are structured and organized, but Carrie leans a tad more to the spontaneous side.

Knowing what we know about each other, when we talk together now, we understand that we process our conversations in very different ways; consequently, we make a conscious effort to speak each other's language. Of course, the temptation is always there to want to *change* each other to fit our own personality. So we have to keep at it, always learning from the other's differentness, and adding some of our spouse's color to our own personality portrait.

As if personality differences weren't enough of a threat to marriage, along come gender differences. "Gender differences are puzzling, baffling, and one of the reasons for marital discord," writes marriage counselor Norm Wright in *How to Bring Out the Best in Your Spouse*. "We're attracted to a person of the opposite sex but have a difficult time understanding and accepting the differences between us. Many relationship problems would be resolved if our perceptions weren't colored by value judgments and criticism."[3] How we relate to each other's male-ness and femaleness directly affects our son's view of himself and of females. We may be *attracted* to the opposite sex, but have a difficult time understanding and accepting the differences between us.

So what raw materials are we working with? Here are common perceptions women have of men:

- Men don't share feelings or emotions.
- Men seem to go into a trance when they're watching sports or when certain subjects are brought up—like they can't handle more than one subject at a time.
- Men seem to think they can do things better, even when they can't.
- Men need more sensitivity, concern, compassion, and empathy.
- Men are so involved with their work and career—they want a family, but they don't get involved.
- Do they think about anything else but sex?

Men have their own set of common complaints about women:

- Women are too emotional—they need to be more logical.
- Women are too sensitive, always getting their feelings hurt.
- Women are so changeable—we wish they would make up their minds.
- Maybe women think we can read minds, but we can't.
- So what's wrong with the sex drive?
- Women think they have the spiritual gift of changing men.
- Women are so involved with other people and their problems.
- Women are moody and negative—you just can't satisfy them.

When a couple learns that such frustrations are normal responses to gender differences, they can then begin to accept each other rather than attempt to change each other. Earlier in the book we explored differences between the brains of men and women—in particular the findings that men tend to function on either the left *or* right side of the brain, while women are better able to function going back and forth *between* the right and left hemispheres. The implications? Women are usually able to multitask, while men do better staying on one task—which also means that women tend to communicate in indirect ways ... and that men generally need less conversation than women do ... and that women are generally more comfortable with emotion than men are. See the point? Many differences within a marriage have more to do with gender than they do with personality. A couple needs to understand that it is not always the case (in fact, it may very seldom be the case) that their spouse is out to get them—they're simply being who they are wired to be, a woman or a man.

Now, it is also true that *who they are* needs tending as well. Women typically have a need to be nourished and cherished. Carrie needs to know that her husband actually thinks about their relationship once in a while. Carrie needs Gary to spend time with her; she needs him to tell her that he loves her. Though he may judge anything beyond five minutes of conversation with Carrie to be "meaningless," she needs him to be willing to be attentive for as long as she needs to talk.

The fundamental need of men, on the other hand, is to be respected and honored. They enjoy it when their wives do things with them. Gary needs Carrie to sit with him at a movie and not talk or ask questions. He loves it when Carrie goes on a bike ride with him and when Carrie verbalizes her appreciation for all that he does for the family.

HOW TO MAKE MARITAL LOVE CLEAR TO YOUR SONS

How you love your spouse speaks volumes to your son about love. And the kind of love that speaks the most promise to him is *unconditional love*—the kind of love that is, by the way, a requirement for any experience of intimacy in marriage. As a mom and dad love each other unconditionally, they teach their children daily about what it means to love another person.

So what exactly does unconditional love look like?

Loving your spouse unconditionally means verbalizing your love. If you can't tell your wife that you love her, it won't be much easier telling your kids that you love them—especially when they enter adolescence. Carrie knows this feeling well; as a child she knew she was loved, but she didn't hear it verbalized much. And the silence left its mark on her.

I love you are words designed by God. He created in us the need for the expression of love. Carrie had to learn to say "I love you" without feeling strange. Our sons have been hearing it and expressing it since they were little, and it's becoming second nature for them now. *I love you* says to a person, "You are so worthwhile to me that even though sometimes it's difficult, I will still love you—and *tell* you that I love you." Life is short and, ultimately, filled with experiences of loss. So if our sons or our spouse were to go out the door in the morning, never to be seen by us again, we all want the words *I love you* to echo first and foremost in their minds.

Loving your spouse unconditionally means deliberately cultivating a servant attitude. Unless we back up our *I love yous* with acts of kindness and servanthood, the words ring hollow. Look each day for ways to give to each other. Gary brings morning coffee to Carrie (and even does refills), and he'll rub her back in the middle of the night if she's having trouble sleeping. One way Carrie shows her love for him is by filling his car with gas or getting it washed after she's used it. Sons need to see their fathers serving their mothers creatively. And if you don't know what actions and attitudes speak love to your spouse, just ask.

Loving your spouse unconditionally means cultivating commitment. Sooner or later a typical marriage experiences transition, suffering, pain, loss, joy, happiness, surprise, and boredom.

Commitment means we hang in there when our spouse is struggling. When your wife is depressed or anxious, do you support her and encourage her? Or do you wish she'd grow up and get her act together? The divorce rate in America suggests that cultivating commitment is a lost art—and the even higher divorce rate for second marriages seems to confirm that commitment gets no easier the second time around.

After twelve years of the security and stability of living in the same town, working at the same job, and attending the same church, God took us from a Denver suburb to the small town of Siloam Springs, Arkansas, where Gary joined the faculty of John Brown University to develop The Center for Marriage and Family Studies and to establish a graduate program in marriage and family counseling. It has proven to be a good move—yet no matter how good the place is where God moves a family of five, the dynamics of transition and change put stress on everyone.

This past year each one of us had our own problems coping with this major change. Carrie battled the blues and experienced bouts of loneliness—and when she feels this way, she may or may not want to talk. Gary could have felt alienated, but his commitment to Carrie gives her room to work her way through these episodes. Gary has been unusually busy laying the foundation of this new ministry. Carrie could have felt left out as he puts in long hours that deplete him of energy, but her commitment allows him the space to do what he needs to be able to do during this crucial first year without adding to the pressure he feels.

There hasn't been a time in our nineteen years of marriage that has been more stressful or difficult than this past year. But our boys have watched our commitment to each other minimize the potential for misunderstandings, arguments, and distancing ourselves from each other. We've tried to ask ourselves each morning, *What does it mean to be committed to each other?*—and then to be persistent in our commitment.

In order for our sons to trust our love for them, they must first witness our love for each other.

YOUR SONS ARE WATCHING YOUR EMOTIONS

God created us with emotions—all kinds of emotions that add zest to life. Remember that our basic premise is that emotions are not inherently good or bad—they simply are. It's *how we express our emotions* or *how we react to another's emotions* that becomes healthy or damaging. Our children learn a lot about their own emotions as they watch us deal with ours. Here are four common emotions your kids will assuredly see in you sooner or later:

Joy, or delight and happiness—do we even know what brings us delight? Do we express joy? Do your spouse and children ever hear you talk about being happy? When was the last time your spouse said to you, "I feel happy today"? Perhaps he or she said, "It was a good day"—yet to name the emotion you feel helps you understand yourself better. And when you understand yourself, you can more accurately communicate who you are to someone else.

Anger—a secondary emotion to the primary emotions of hurt, fear, and frustration—is most likely expressed through moods and attitudes rather than through putting a name to it ("I'm angry!"). Anger is the most common emotion expressed by males, who can signify it aggressively (yelling, physical abuse, foot stomping, and the like) or passively (in sarcasm, for example). Women, on the other hand, are typically less comfortable with expressing anger, preferring to internalize it. Unfortunately, internalized anger commonly manifests itself in anxiety and depression.

Yet anger can be expressed—and *ought* to be expressed—in productive and healthy ways. Instead of a spouse responding defensively when the other gets angry, we can break unproductive anger cycles by seeking to understand where the partner's anger is coming from. If Gary is angry, he needs to ask, "Am I hurt, fearful, or frustrated by something?" When Carrie gets angry, she needs to look beneath her anger for the primary emotion. We both must ask, "Do our children see us resolve anger, or do they see us blow up and never deal with what ignited the anger in the first place? Do they see us take responsibility for our anger, or do they see us blaming each other—or them—for our anger?"

So here's the goal with anger: Commit yourself to understanding the issues that lie beneath not just your anger but your mate's anger as well.

Depression is reported by more women than men; causes range from a rainy day to a chemical imbalance in the body. Depression can be a symptom of any one of a dozen things in you that need attention. Some of us may be overly stressed and in need of rest. Some may not be dealing with anger or grief, which may now be turning into depression. Some may have unhealthy eating habits that are contributing to depression. For others, change and transition in their lives may spur on depression. Bear in mind, however, that certain levels of depression are normal.

When a spouse is depressed, the couple will commonly experience conflict, distancing from each other, and very little social time together. What to do? A listening ear, support, and encouragement are helpful ways to deal with a spouse who is depressed. Educating yourself by reading about depression can help identify the point when the depressed spouse needs professional help. If you suspect your spouse is depressed, first try to talk about it together. Encourage him or her to begin doing something physical, even just walking regularly. Encourage healthy eating habits. A complete physical examination may be in order. You may need to encourage your spouse to see a counselor.

Guilt is an emotion that spares no couple. We feel guilty and we cause guilt; we put guilt on our kids and they put guilt on us. Despite the destructiveness of guilt, even this emotion can be constructive when it causes someone to change unhealthy behavior.

Guilt can alert us to a wrong thing we've done or said. Destructive guilt, on the other hand, focuses on ourselves, rarely motivates us to change our behavior, and *makes* us do things for others because we feel guilty, not because we love them and *want* to serve them.

It's important for our kids to see us handle the emotion of guilt in healthy ways—to model doing things for others out of love rather than out of guilt. Guilt-prone people don't empathize easily; they don't easily walk in another's shoes—they're too busy trying to deal with their own guilt.

Every day you can teach your sons a bit more about what it means to be made in God's image with a mind and a will—*and* a bunch of unruly emotions. The more open you are with your emotions—the more you name them and claim them and learn to resolve them in healthy ways—the more your son will feel safe and free to express his own emotions.

BUT DO YOU LIKE EACH OTHER?

Does your son see his parents enjoy their friendship together? Does he see them enjoy each other's company? Does he see you laugh together and cry together? Friendship with your spouse means enjoying life with a companion. You spent countless hours together during your dating days, you did the things that foster friendship—and then you went and got married, went to work, and had kids. And as the years slipped by, perhaps your friendship slipped away.

We've discovered that when couples finally *do* take time to be together and talk, they often end up talking about problems and issues instead of fun things. We also fell into this trap, and it took us a few years to figure out how to deal with it: We began to start the day with a chat time and prayer—*before* the boys awoke (this was before they were teenagers). Even Gary (not a champion chatterer) discovered that those morning talks were actually kind of fun for him too. And our chat times were not problem focused, but relationship focused.

Doing things together fosters friendship between partners. If you're not like those couples who seem to be in complete sync on everything—food, vacations, house décor, you name it— then you'll need to stretch your tastes a little and try new activities to keep the marital friendship alive. Gary loves to go to movies, and Carrie loves to eat dinner out leisurely—*not* thirty minutes before she's supposed to be at a movie. So we do our best to take turns—one week a quick burger and fries on the way to a movie, the next week a long, unrushed dinner with *nothing else that night* to have to show up at.

Stretching your tastes to occasionally accommodate your spouse took an exotic turn for Carrie a few years ago. Gary had jumped into scuba diving and completed his certification training. He desperately wanted Carrie to join him in diving, so— despite her utter disinterest in scuba diving, and even feelings of terror just thinking about it—she consented to try. To make a long story short, they've been diving together several times. Carrie isn't as enthusiastic about it as Gary is, but she has seen God's fascinating underwater creation up close and personal— something she would never have experienced if she hadn't agreed to go diving with her best friend. Just enthusiastically *trying* activities with your spouse speaks volumes about your love for him or her. If your marriage is suffering from a lack of friendship, it may be time to sign up for scuba classes or ballroom dance lessons or to head out for some weekend hiking. No matter what the activity, you would do well to begin discussing right now some new activities to participate in with your spouse.

Teaching your sons about the friendship between a husband and wife helps kids learn that healthy relationships take effort and attention; rarely do they come naturally.

We cannot emphasize enough the value of a healthy marriage and its effect on how your sons will approach their relationships in life. Begin to turn things around now. If you are a single parent, your son still needs to see you in relationship with other people. God did not design us to live as islands, but as individuals who *need* each other in order to be complete.

SMALL BEGINNINGS

1. Give some examples of how your marriage is a priority to you. Set two or three goals for the next thirty days that will help you make your marriage a bigger priority.
2. List some things your sons are learning about relationships from your marriage (be honest—list healthy *and* unhealthy things).
3. Take the "temperature" of the friendship factor in your marriage. Cultivate your friendship by discovering activities you both enjoy, and then doing them together regularly.

Chapter Thirteen

HELPING YOUR SON CULTIVATE A HEART FOR GOD

DISCIPLESHIP AND PARENTING

UP FRONT *In this chapter ...*

- ✦ Christian parents demonstrate a growing love relationship with Jesus unconsciously as well as consciously.
- ✦ Boys learn through both formal and informal instruction— from both the talk and the walk of their parents.
- ✦ Sons are more likely to listen to and trust parents who take the time to really know them. If they perceive that you think well of them, are quick to forgive them, believe in them, and love to be with them, they will listen to your teachings.
- ✦ Besides inoculating your son against cultural ills, the most important job you may ever have is helping to shape his character to reflect Jesus Christ.

GEPETTO WAS A KIND old watchmaker who lived with his cat, Figaro, and his goldfish, Cleo, in the back of his shop. One evening, after putting the finishing touches on a boylike puppet he had named Pinocchio, he mused, "Wouldn't it be nice if he were a real boy?" Then, as he glanced out his bedroom window at a beautiful starlit sky he saw a bright star and made a wish. "I wish my little Pinocchio might be a real boy."

Shortly after he had fallen asleep, a fairy appeared in the room, and her bright light woke up Jiminy Cricket. She walked over to the wooden puppet, touched its head with her wand, and said, "Little puppet of pine, wake—the gift of life is thine."

The strings fell off the puppet, and Pinocchio spoke: "I want," he said to the fairy, "to be a real boy."

"To become a real boy you must prove yourself brave, truthful, and unselfish. You must learn to choose between right and wrong."

"How will I know?"

"Your conscience will tell you."

"What is my conscience?"

"Your conscience is that still small voice people won't listen to."

Then she turned to Jiminy Cricket and told him he would serve as Pinocchio's conscience. She then gently lowered her wand onto Jiminy's head. "I dub thee the lord high keeper of the knowledge of right and wrong, counselor in moments of temptation, and guide along the straight and narrow path."

You know with what difficulty Pinocchio started out. He hung out with bad friends, learned bad habits, began to lie, and made a perilous excursion to Pleasure Island. But in the end he finally did the right thing, proving himself brave, truthful, and unselfish—and he became a real boy.

A PARENTING PRIMER

Your boy may be a *real* boy, but your parental job is to help him become a *whole* boy—one who grows up to be brave, truthful, and unselfish. Without your wise and loving parenting, your son will remain wooden, unaware of his own emotions and unable to connect intimately.

While there are many things God can use in the process of helping your son grow into a godly man, the most significant, the most powerful, and the most enduring influences are his mom and dad. From our research, observations, and interviews, we see *three basic patterns of parenting* that underlie the many different parenting styles:

Parenting by negation. Because these parents love their children, they want to protect them from the world's evil—and the best way to protect them, they've concluded, is to separate them from the evil, and the evil from them. Consequently, they may forbid their sons from watching television or movies, buying magazines that advertise cigarettes or alcohol, going to bowling alleys, and playing with playing cards (poker decks, that is— Rook decks and Uno decks are okay). This approach may seem extreme to some parents, but we've seen lots of parents who have adopted prohibitions and restrictions like these as their child-rearing standards.

Parenting by information. If we can just give our kids enough good information, these parents believe, if we can expose them to enough of the truth, then they will grow up to be good kids. In reality, while it is vitally important that we read the Bible together, memorize Bible verses, and listen to sermons, the plain fact is that biblical teaching isn't enough. As popular author and Bible teacher Chuck Swindoll once said on his radio show, biblical teaching doesn't work like nuclear fallout—exposure to it does not equal absorption of it. Good information is important, to be sure, but it isn't enough.

Parenting by demonstration, or lifestyle parenting. This approach combines the best of the previous two, but seems to us to be more consistent with Scripture. You may recall that Moses reminded the Israelites they were to love the Lord with all their heart, soul, and strength—and focus on the things of God, on the commandments of God. He instructed the parents to "impress them on your children. Talk about them when you sit at home and when you walk along the road, when you lie down and when you get up. Tie them as symbols on your hands and bind them on your foreheads. Write them on the doorframes of your houses and on your gates" (Deuteronomy 6:7–9).

This is informal, or lifestyle, instruction. It is *living* the truth in front of your son in the ordinariness of every day. Remember, we're not saying that formal instruction isn't important; yet our research and our experience bear out the words of Moses quoted above. The lifestyle your children see you model day in and day out is much more powerful than what people teach them in a classroom or even inside the walls of a church. Without question, classrooms and churches are important. But if we hope to raise boys who will grow up to become godly men, these boys must see a connection between the *talk* in homes and classrooms and churches—and the *walk* of their parents.

Boys grow up in a world of noise and busyness. Information and technology is increasing so fast that the utility poles have become a blur. Our sons have more sound, brighter images, better graphics, faster action—*and* are prone to more boredom, increased cynicism, greater despair, and higher levels of clinical depression. They're bombarded, bored, blinded, biased, and bankrupt.

Our boys need moms and dads who live before them in ways that speak truth, who shine in their lives as beacons of hope.

If it's true that some things are better caught than taught, then just what is it that our kids are catching? What do our kids see when they look at us? A mom and dad who delight in the Lord? Decisions consistently made on the basis of seeking *God's* direction? Parents praying on our own—and *with* them and *for* them? Do they see us spending time in the Word because we actually want to learn more about Jesus and about how to live for him?

As Gary was preparing for a talk some years ago, he noticed a detail in Scripture he had missed the hundreds of times he had read it before. The apostle John wrote that the good shepherd cares for his sheep:

> The sheep listen to his voice. He calls his own sheep by name and leads them out. When he has brought out all his own, he goes on ahead of them, and his sheep follow him because they know his voice. But they will never follow a stranger; in fact, they will run away from him because they do not recognize a stranger's voice. . . .
>
> I am the good shepherd. The good shepherd lays down his life for the sheep. The hired hand is not the shepherd who owns the sheep. So when he sees the wolf coming, he abandons the sheep and runs away . . . because he is a hired hand and cares nothing for the sheep.
>
> I am the good shepherd; I know my sheep and my sheep know me—just as the Father knows me and I know the Father—and I lay down my life for the sheep. . . .
>
> My sheep listen to my voice; I know them, and they follow me.
>
> —JOHN 10:3–5, 11–15, 27

We've never herded sheep, but from what we've read, sheep are *not* likely to follow a voice they don't know. His sheep hear his voice, Jesus said, and they *know* his voice. And that afternoon, as Gary read this verse afresh, he heard a voice inside him asking, "Do your boys know your voice, or have you become a stranger to them? Do they know that, like their heavenly Father, you are a good shepherd who knows them, understands them, and truly cares for them?"

ADVICE FROM PARENTS WHO'VE DONE IT RIGHT

Here are some simple, practical suggestions that come not just out of our own experience, but also out of the experiences of parents we've interviewed who have done parenting right—parents with all kinds of styles and all kinds of sons:

Love God's Son

This is the starting point. If we want spiritually healthy kids who love Jesus, reflect his character, and want to spend time with him, then we must cultivate those same characteristics in ourselves first. We can't give our kids what we don't have; we can't take our sons where we haven't been. If we aren't willing to let God parent our hearts—if we're not willing to trust God to be a good shepherd for us—then why should our children be willing to let God parent their hearts? It's only as our kids observe *us* becoming more like Christ that they want to become more like him.

Are you prepared to set yourself apart for and open yourself up to the work of the Holy Spirit in you so that you can become a good shepherd to your son? Do you really want to become more like Jesus? Are you willing to allow God's Spirit to work in your life in ways that lead your boy to see more of Christ in you?

Love Your Son

Here's the environment you want to create for your son: a strong, consistent, Christ-centered, love-based relationship in which he knows he is loved, accepted, and understood. This also happens to be the essence of the gospel—and it really is best *caught,* not taught. An environment like this can spell the difference between kids who follow Jesus Christ as adults and those who don't.

Parenting expert John Gottman shares what he sees as the secret to success as a parent:

The key to successful parenting is not found in complex theories, elaborate family rules, or convoluted for-
mulas for behavior. It is based on your deepest feelings
of love and affection for your child, and is demonstrated simply through empathy and understanding.
Good parenting begins in your heart, and then continues on a moment-to-moment basis by engaging your
children when feelings run high, when they are sad,
angry, or scared. The heart of parenting is being there
in a particular way when it really counts.[1]

Our boys need more than guidelines, guardrails, and a handbook of what not to do. They need shepherds who understand
the times and who understand their hearts. Counselor and popular author Larry Crabb spoke directly to the issue when he
made this profound observation:

The deepest urge in every human heart is to be in relationship with someone who absolutely delights in us,
someone with resources we lack who has no greater joy
than giving to us, someone who respects us enough to
require us to use everything we receive for the good of
others, and because he has given it to us, knows we
have something to give.[2]

Share the Difficult Times with Your Sons

Several years ago a rapidly growing cancer was found in Gary,
and he was immediately scheduled for surgery. After we called
our closest friends and asked them to pray for us, we sat down
as a couple and talked about how much to tell our boys.

After a lot of prayer we decided to tell the boys everything.
I'll never forget their questions: "Are you gonna die? How long
do you have to live?" and dozens more. And the more questions
they asked, the more opportunity Gary had to share the reality

of his fear, his anxiety, his uncertainty—as well as the power of his faith.

We prayed together that day, and our sons became an active part of Gary's prayer support team. Throughout the surgery and the months of healing, they prayed, and they became aware of the power of their prayers. They commented about the many people who called and wrote to let us know they were standing with us.

What Satan had intended for evil, God used for good.

Give Your Sons Role Models

Boys need heroes they can respect and admire. Widen their options by nurturing close relationships with other adults. Make sure your boy is around men and women who model honesty and intimacy in relationships, who are committed to Jesus Christ and put him first.

For six years we were in a covenant group of adults that met monthly (not counting the other times the men met by themselves). For six years we were in each other's homes and sharing each other's lives. It was no secret to our boys that three men in our group were praying for them, by name, every day. And every once in a while one of the guys would give Nathan or Matt or Andrew a call just to check in and see how he was doing, and to let him know that he was praying for him. We can't overstate the impact these men had on our sons.

Guiding your sons toward inspiring biographies can be a powerful tool as well. Franklin Graham's *Rebel with a Cause* is excellent for boys. We've also watched a video version of the story of missionary Jim Elliot and his 1956 martyrdom at the hands of Ecuador's Auca Indians.

Pray with Your Sons and for Them

We don't want to belabor the point—but it deserves repeating yet again: *Every couple* we interviewed who raised boys who now live for Jesus believed that prayer was the key to their parenting success.

Better than passing on *instruction* in prayer is simply *being* a man or woman of prayer, a couple who prays daily, and a parent who prays with your son. Almost every night we go into our boys' rooms to chat with them—and before we leave, we offer a prayer of thanksgiving for the day and a prayer of petition for the next day. We get together in the morning for a brief time of prayer before school, a time when each of our boys prays with us.

We don't have to beg them or force them to pray. Depending on how awake they are, the prayer may be long or short—but over the years it has become a routine part of our family life and a part of the legacy we hope to pass on to our boys.

Let Your Sons See How You Integrate Biblical Values in Difficult Situations

During their almost twenty years of marriage, our friends, Greg and Erin, have twice gone through the experience of having a new home built. Even though they'd heard a myriad of horror stories about building a new home, they decided to give it a try. One project turned out great, and one turned into a nightmare. One home they moved into with joy, and the other they moved into with sighs of relief.

It was the *character* of the builders that made the difference.

Both builders promised, but only one delivered. Both had good intentions, but only one followed through. Both said they could be trusted, but only one proved trustworthy. Both started well, but only one finished well. One was anxious to make sure the job was done right, but the other took weeks to return phone calls and months to complete what could have and should have been done in a day.

As our friends' sons saw all this unfold, they saw their parents' disillusionment, disbelief, and disappointment turn into frustration and, at times, anger. The sons too experienced their own anger and amazement at the irresponsibility of an *adult* no less, and they told their parents what they thought they should do. While their solutions were tempting, in the end it would have involved compromising their parents' values. Greg and Erin listened carefully to their boys and then gently reminded them that revenge was not an option. Instead they eventually steered the conversation to the question "What would Jesus do?" They prayed and talked about it and decided the best thing to do was to assume only the best, continue to speak the truth in love, and take one decision at a time.

This response didn't solve the problem, and it certainly didn't give Greg and Erin the temporary satisfaction of getting even—but it did give them a way to transform a thorny, expensive, real-life dilemma into an opportunity to model biblical principles.

Let Your Sons See the Joy

"Lord, if you can't make me a better boy, don't worry about it," a youngster was overheard praying. "I'm having a real good time like I am." When boys grow up into men, some still pray the same prayer, convinced that if they turn their lives over to God, they won't have any more fun.

Yet nothing could be further from the truth. "I have told you this," Jesus said to his disciples, "so that my joy may be in you and that your joy may be complete" (John 15:11)—and Jesus spoke those words in the knowledge that his crucifixion was just a few hours away. In the midst of the most painful thing the Son of God would ever experience, he talked about joy.

The difficulties of life give parents a unique opportunity to model the wonderful paradox of joy. If in the midst of the most trying time of Jesus' life, the darkest time he would ever experience, humanly speaking—if even then he could experience joy, so can we. In the middle of health problems, financial problems, job problems, or family problems, we have an unparalleled opportunity to model an attitude of joy and peace for our son that transcends the world's understanding.

During some of the difficult times we have faced, the words of Hebrews 12:2 have come to mind: "Let us fix our eyes on Jesus, the author and perfecter of our faith, *who for the joy* set before him endured the cross, scorning its shame, and sat down at the right hand of the throne of God" (italics added). Our boys need to see us model this kind of joy, even as we're enduring crosses and scorning whatever shame comes our way. After all, it isn't all fun and games. But there is great comfort in knowing that *joy* can exist in the middle of all kinds of trials and turmoil. When your son walks through his own dark valleys, he will remember how you walked through yours.[3]

SMALL BEGINNINGS

1. Identify specific ways to cultivate your own relationship with the Lord. Is there meaningful prayer, praise, worship, and Bible study in your life? Does your son see that an intimate relationship with the Lord is a priority in your life? For more on cultivating your own heart for God as well as helping your son do so, see the book *Raising Kids to Love Jesus* by H. Norman Wright and Gary J. Oliver.

2. Pray with your son on a regular basis—short prayers as he leaves for school, short prayers during the day for specific concerns, short prayers when he goes to bed.

3. Take your son to one spiritually focused event each year— such as a family conference, a spiritual life meeting, or a Promise Keepers event. On the way home talk about what each of you learned and what each of you will apply to your own lives.

4. Make a few photocopies of the spiritual traits inventory on pages 233–34 *(don't write directly in the book because you may want to complete this inventory more than once);* take this

inventory based on where you see your son's spiritual development right now.

Take the inventory once for each of your sons (or record the development of all your sons on one copy by putting their respective initials next to their circled numbers). If you are married, ask your spouse to take this inventory too—then compare your results and average your scores.

Then as you note your son's three highest ratings, stop what you're doing and thank God for these strengths. Does your son know these are his strengths? When was the last time you complimented him on these particular areas of his life? Now look at his three weakest areas—when was the last time you prayed for these needy areas of his life? How could you encourage him here?

Depending on the relationship you have with your son, you might ask him to take the inventory for himself.

INVENTORY

What Spiritual Traits Are Being Developed in Your Son?

Son's name:_____

Son's age :_____

Circle the number that best represents your son's current developmental level in each category (1 = no development; 5 = average development; 10 = the highest development you can imagine for a boy his age).

1. A *godly* young man who loves the Lord and has a desire for spiritual things.

   1   2   3   4   5   6   7   8   9   10

2. A *compassionate* young man who can rejoice with those who rejoice and weep with those who weep.

   1   2   3   4   5   6   7   8   9   10

3. A *careful* young man who has learned how to achieve balances in his life—who values and appropriately expresses both his aggressiveness or anger and his vulnerability or fear—one who controls these without hiding or exploding them.

   1   2   3   4   5   6   7   8   9   10

4. A *responsible* young man who is responsible, trustworthy, and does the best he can.

   1   2   3   4   5   6   7   8   9   10

5. A *wise* young man who knows how to learn from his own and others' experiences and who applies such learning to new situations.

   1   2   3   4   5   6   7   8   9   10

6. A *creative* young man who values his God-given talents and uses them for his own joy and the betterment of others.

   1   2   3   4   5   6   7   8   9   10

7. A *courageous* young man who will take appropriate risks but not those that needlessly may hurt anyone.

   1   2   3   4   5   6   7   8   9   10

8. A *secure* young man who knows how to lose as well as how to win.

   1   2   3   4   5   6   7   8   9   10

9. A *prayerful* young man who knows the importance of daily time talking to his Lord.

   1   2   3   4   5   6   7   8   9   10

10. A *reverent* young man who values life as a gift from God and who protects that life through proper care and knowledge.

    1   2   3   4   5   6   7   8   9   10

11. A *flexible* young man who can adapt to necessary changes when they are not damaging, but who holds to principles that dare not change.

    1   2   3   4   5   6   7   8   9   10

Adapted from Grace H. Ketterman and Herbert L. Ketterman, *The Complete Book of Baby and Child Care for Christian Parents* (Old Tappan, N.J.: Revell, 1982), 359–60.

Chapter Fourteen

HELPING YOUR SON MOVE FROM ADOLESCENCE TO ADULTHOOD

Early Adolescence (Ages 13–15)

UP FRONT *In this chapter...*

- ✦ Sharing the house with a boy who is entering adolescence isn't a job but an adventure as you witness the many strengths the teenager is developing—loyalty, humor, energy, responsibility, and a sense of fairness, to name just a few.
- ✦ Parents feel their own set of emotions as their son moves into adolescence—fear, helplessness, inadequacy, frustration, anger, loss, and excitement.
- ✦ If parents recognize the signs of growing pains and understand the physical changes that accompany early adolescence—irritability, clumsiness, fatigue—they may be able to avoid becoming stressed-out.
- ✦ Early-adolescent boys tend to think in the present, in sequence, with a focus on personal experience—and they are just learning to think abstractly.
- ✦ Young teens begin to shift relationships away from home to peers—which means they will soon be spending more time with friends, outside of your sphere of influence.

◆ Your son may pull away from you emotionally, but he is still counting on you for support. Communicate genuine interest in him when he talks to you about life in general.

◆ It may seem like you are losing your son, but you're really just saying good-bye to the little child. Help him begin to make the transition from childhood into adulthood by expressing delight in the changes he's beginning to experience.

WE HAVE ENJOYED WATCHING our three sons grow—from the day they came home from the hospital, to their first steps, to watching them get on the bus for that first day of school, right on down to the present day. Our bookshelves are lined with photo albums and numerous videos packed with warm memories from those precious days gone by—soccer games, graduations, holidays, family events, good times with friends, and so much more. Each new year has brought us new challenges and new joys.

We had just started to think we were getting this parenting thing down when adolescence appeared on the scene. This is the time in a parent's life our well-intentioned friends (not to mention our own parents) warned us about—"You'll see, just wait until they're teenagers!" To listen to common wisdom, the teenage years are often perceived as a hurricane in the sea of life, marked by rebellion and defiance that cut a path of damage through the lives of parents who desperately seek ways to take shelter and wait for the storm to pass.

Unfortunately, the bashing of teenagers is common. "Teenagers are young people who get too much of everything," noted one youth pastor, "including criticism." Pointing out their faults and their immaturity is easy. But our experience has led us to agree on this: So far we have thoroughly enjoyed our sons' teenage years! In fact, in many ways this stage of life has felt more rewarding than any other. Not that it's always been smooth sailing. The period of adolescence is filled with changes and challenges—most of them enjoyable, but some of them painful. But for us it has more often been like an adventure—an exhilarating ride on a roller coaster—than a disease to be treated.

Many parents also realize that teenagers have many wonderful strengths. They can have a zest for life that is powered by boundless energy. Their sense of humor is often witty, and they can be fiercely loyal. They are generally *more* responsible than less, and their sense of fairness can bring strong reactions to injustice wherever it is encountered.

SEASONS OF CHALLENGE

Before adolescence can be embraced as an adventure, one must accept the plain fact of the violence, disease, and trauma that can infiltrate this period of life. The rapids of adolescence has its share of killer currents:

- Adolescent boys are significantly more likely than adolescent girls to die before the age of eighteen, not just from violent causes but also from accidental death and disease.
- Adolescent boys are significantly more likely than adolescent girls to die at the hands of their caregivers. Two out of three juveniles killed at the hands of their parents or stepparents are male.
- Adolescent boys are fifteen times as likely as peer females to be victims of violent crime.
- One-third of adolescent male students nationwide carry a gun or some other weapon to school.
- Gunshot wounds are now the second leading cause of accidental death among ten- to fourteen-year-old males.

- Adolescent boys are four times more likely than adolescent girls to be diagnosed as emotionally disturbed.
- The majority of juvenile mental patients nationwide are male. Depending on the state, most often between two-thirds and three-fourths of patients at juvenile mental facilities are male.
- Most of the deadliest and longest-lasting mental problems experienced by children are experienced by adolescent males. For example, there are six male adolescent schizophrenics for every one female. Adolescent autistic males outnumber females two to one.
- Adolescent males significantly outnumber females in diagnoses of most conduct disorders, thought disorders, and brain disorders.
- Adolescent males are four times more likely than adolescent females to commit suicide. Suicide success statistics (that is, cases in which death actually occurs) for adolescent males are rising; suicide success statistics for adolescent females are not rising.
- Adolescent males seem to have much more trouble than their female peers in reaching out for help when they are in deep trouble.
- Attention Deficit Hyperactivity Disorder (ADHD), like so many other brain disorders, is almost exclusively a male malady. Only one out of six adolescents diagnosed with ADHD is female.
- One out of five males has been sexually abused by the age of eighteen. Most sexual offenders are heterosexual males who have been physically and/or sexually abused as boys themselves.[1]

Our two teenage sons were shocked when they read these statistics. "It sounds to me like the deck is stacked against boys," said Nathan. Matt asked simply, "Why is this happening?"

That comment and that question are on the lips of experts too. But the alarming statistics don't stop there. Educator and therapist Michael Gurian has looked at research that details the challenges boys face specifically in the educational arena. He observes that, in addition to the fact that boys are the primary victims of violence in schools, they comprise the majority of mentally ill and substance-abusing adolescents in the schools; furthermore, boys exhibit the majority of academic problems as well:

- Adolescent boys are twice as likely as adolescent girls to be diagnosed with learning disabilities. Two-thirds of high school special-education students are male.
- Adolescent males drop out of high school at four times the rate of adolescent females (this includes females who drop out to have babies).
- Ninety percent of adolescent discipline problems in schools are attributed to males, as are most of the expulsions and suspensions.
- Adolescent males are significantly more likely than adolescent females to repeat a grade.
- Adolescent males on average get worse grades than adolescent females. The majority of salutatorians and valedictorians now are female.
- Adolescent females now dominate school clubs, yearbook staffs, and student government groups.
- More college students are female (fifty-five percent) than male (forty-five percent). More graduate students are female (fifty-nine percent) than male (forty-one percent).
- According to the National Center for Educational Statistics of the United States Department of Education, fewer boys than girls now study advanced algebra and geometry, about the same number study trigonometry and calculus, and more girls than boys study chemistry.

- Adolescent males are outscored by adolescent females by twelve points in reading and seventeen points in writing. The United States Department of Education recently pointed out that this gender gap in reading/writing is equivalent to about one and a half years of school.

In fact, statistics tell us that there is only one area of healthy activity where males outperform females: sports.[2]

SEASONS OF CHANGE

Saying good-bye to childhood can be difficult, especially for parents. When your son reaches the age of eleven, be prepared to do just that. While he may still look, talk, think, and act like a young boy, rest assured it won't last much longer. The changes that come with the teenage years are many, and they cut across every area of your son's life—physical, mental, emotional, and social. In fact, the only stage of life where change and growth are more rapid than in adolescence is in the first two years of life.

Learning about the physical, mental, and social changes that come with the onset of the teenage years can help us better understand and relate to our sons. And leading the charge into all these changes is the mixed blessing called *puberty*. Because many parents don't really understand adolescent male development, it may be difficult to give our adolescent males the kind of love they need in order to become fully responsible, loving, and godly men. Many would say that today's generation of adolescent boys are arguably our least understood and most under-nurtured population.

"A VERY BIOLOGICAL TIME": PHYSICAL CHANGES

Author Michael Gurian describes adolescence as a very "biological" time for boys.[3] Some friends told us that early in their son's puberty, they visited his sixth-grade teacher. The conversation got around to the developmental changes that begin to take place in early adolescence. "Many parents don't really see it coming," the teacher began, "so take your family pictures this year, because by next year they won't look like kids anymore." Our friends heeded the advice and took their family picture that year—and just like the teacher said, within a year or two the sixth-grader-turned-eighth-grader had lost every childhood trait.

Puberty affects every dimension of your young adolescent's existence. His body seems to change shape overnight—actually, he experiences a truly rapid rate of growth that requires a great deal of energy, so getting adequate sleep (around nine hours a night) is very important for his sustained emotional well-being each day. This rapid rate of growth in stature (sometimes four to five inches in a few months) can even be physically painful. His legs and joints may ache, and sporadic growth can create awkward moments of clumsiness—which can be frustrating for your son. While these changes are inevitable for all teens, the impact they have is strongly tied to the timing of when they occur.

EARLY PUBERTY

The powerful effects of this process have been demonstrated in the research on early versus late puberty. The onset of puberty, especially if your son is an early or a late maturer, has been shown to influence his body image, moods, and emotions; his relationships with parents; and his relationships with peers.

In general, an early onset of puberty makes the experience more positive for boys than a late puberty. The full impact of early maturation is felt most in seventh and eighth grades, as physical changes collide head-on with social changes. The advantages of developing early include—

- Greater satisfaction with how he looks and with life in general
- An increase in size and muscle—a welcome change that can predict athleticism and strength

- More positive feelings about himself and higher levels of self-confidence
- Greater popularity with peers
- An advantage in gaining leadership positions, both in formal settings (athletic teams, school offices) and in informal ones (position within the peer group)

The only real disadvantage of developing early for a boy seems to be that he may have trouble living up to the expectations of his parents or other adults, that is, parents and teachers may expect him to act his appearance, not his age.

LATE PUBERTY

On the other hand, late puberty can expose boys to a number of disadvantages. Boys who mature late are at the tail end of their peer group. In general, girls begin puberty before most boys, and early-maturing boys come next. So while the rest of their peers are now looking more adultlike, late-maturing boys are still relatively small and boyish-looking. Their behavior is often a reflection of their looks—they can *act* more childish than their maturing peers. They long for the day when they will change in appearance. As a result, they often find themselves having to live with—

- Lower self-esteem
- Higher levels of insecurity
- Feelings of inferiority and rejection
- Being the target of name-calling and teasing (*squirt, wimp,* or worse)

Researchers have found that many of the negative effects of puberty, especially for these boys who mature late, can be softened by strong, supportive relationships with family and friends. Bear in mind that the effects of puberty can be felt for a long time, so it's important that we give steady, ongoing support to our sons.

"My worst time was seventh to ninth grade," recalled a twelfth-grade boy. "I had a lot of growing up to do, and I still have a lot more to do. High school was not the 'sweet-sixteen' time everyone said it would be. What would have helped me is more emotional support in grades seven through nine."

Puberty is just plain powerful. So don't assume your son is in complete control of all his emotions and reactions. Hormones speak loudly—and maybe you can't change when and how they speak in your son, but you can help your son understand what those hormones are saying.

HERE AND NOW AS ULTIMATE REALITY: CHANGES IN THINKING

In addition to the physical changes that come with puberty, the way your son thinks is also changing. What goes on in the mind of a boy on the brink of adolescence? How does he look at his world and the people in it? How does he think about God and the Christian life? How does he see his family? No doubt his beliefs, attitudes, and values—those things that are important to him—are being shaped.

Research suggests that the typical mental framework of children in this age range includes an emphasis on here-and-now experience, a focus on personal experience as reality, a tendency toward thinking in sequence, and a willingness to accept things at face value. Let's consider how each of these four areas affects the thinking of the early adolescent.

Emphasis on Here-and-Now Experience

The most important day in the life of an early adolescent is *today*. Little thought is given to what has already happened, and not much more thought is given to what is going to happen. Adults often spend time longing for the past or living for the future; young adolescent boys do not. While they do remember the past and look forward to things in the future, they live in the present.

Focus on Personal Experience

The thinking of early-adolescent boys is still rather childlike, in spite of a growing exposure to a complex world. A boy during early adolescence has not yet acquired the ability to think in the abstract. (By age thirteen he is just beginning to think abstractly.) His thinking and problem solving involve objects, relationships, or situations with which he can identify personally. He has gained the ability to recognize the reality that a person can be many things simultaneously. He has gained experience as he has come to see his parents in various roles and as he has come to understand that being one thing does not mean you cannot be something else.

Thinking in Sequence

Life for a young adolescent consists of a series of events. If you ask a son at this age to think about the big picture of his experiences and to describe for you the lessons to be learned from them, expect a blank stare and a mumbled "I don't know." His thinking is less analytical, more sequential.

Think of a movie film on a reel-to-reel projector. Early adolescents think about their life and relationships as though the film were rolling, frame by frame. As each frame is viewed separately and sequentially, they eventually blend together to tell a story. In contrast, older teens have gained the ability to take the film off the reel and turn it sideways. This gives them the opportunity to look at many frames at the same time in order to discover the overall themes and lessons. Young adolescent boys have a difficult time turning the film. *Patience* becomes an invaluable virtue and an essential personality trait for successful parents at this stage of their son's life.

Accepting Things at Face Value

For the most part, early-adolescent boys still accept what their parents say as being truth. They have not yet reached the point where parental wisdom is something to be questioned—at least not very loudly. If you don't know it yet, Dad and Mom, this is your last major opportunity to give your son instruction that will be accepted in childlike innocence. As your son progresses through this stage, you will notice an increasing reluctance to accept something just because you say it.

THE WONDER YEARS: SOCIAL CHANGES

Fans of the late 1980s TV show *The Wonder Years* followed Kevin Arnold through "the wonder years" of junior high—years marked by a huge increase in the significance of friends. Kevin had two—Paul and Winnie. The show's theme music was the Beatles' "With a Little Help from My Friends." Kevin's triumphs and setbacks with his friends were chronicled weekly, as viewers were shown how the world of a young teen boy is often full of fresh, new possibilities and perspectives. Girls take on a whole new meaning for boys, achievement in activities becomes more significant, and friends become emotionally preeminent.

During his own "wonder years," your son will develop new friendships, and gradually he will spend more and more time away with friends than at home with you. Sure, parents wonder about the influence of those friends. Yet the good news is that the quality of friends your son selects generally is not much of a problem in early adolescence. Your cooperation is still needed for those get-togethers with friends who do not live in the neighborhood (although you can quickly start to feel like a chauffeur). Interactions with friends can still be controlled and regulated by parents as they see fit.

As your son approaches middle adolescence, however, be aware that controlling his interactions will become more difficult.

You will be forced to trust your son because you have no other choice. What he does with the time he spends with friends away from your home will be *his* choice and *his* responsibility. You hope and pray that the training you have given him and the values you have tried to instill in him, combined with his ability to listen to the gentle whisper of the Holy Spirit, will see him through.

SHIFTING ROLES: CHANGES AT HOME

While boys vary in how they handle all the changes that come with puberty, one thing is certain: Your son will never be your little boy again. The feelings of affection that can be so strong in childhood can at this stage in life be more shaky. Parents and sons both report that these warm feelings for each other decline from the sixth to the eighth grade. It is encouraging, however, that the decline is usually from *very positive* to *less positive* (rather than all the way down to *negative*).

Studies have found some interesting differences in how young teens view their parents. Boys tend to rate mothers and fathers equally well as companions, but fathers are routinely viewed as the enforcer of family rules and values. A child begins to feel that he may be able to get away with more when dealing with Mom than with Dad. As he moves closer to puberty, a boy may even start to get mouthy with his mom in a way that he wouldn't dare try with his dad. But overall, the decline in parental power is pretty minimal in the early stages of adolescence—at least compared to middle and late adolescence.

When teens are asked about whom they can count on for emotional and social support, moms win. Dads are seen as providing significantly less support than moms (though dads come out better than teachers). At the same time, boys see dads as being not only more willing but also more excited about letting them grow up. Moms seem generally less willing to let their little boys set out on their journey to manhood. Nevertheless, this stage of life is precisely the time when moms can give up their boys and look forward to them developing into manhood—all of which will require major changes in expectations, kinds of interaction, and amount of time spent together. Our friend Twyla often used to play with her sons in the yard or on the floor in the living room. As they entered early adolescence, she began going out on "dates" with them—to the batting cage, the movie theater, Chuck E. Cheese's, the miniature golf course, or whatever.

Early adolescents are generally still open to instruction and to accept that what parents have to say is the way things are—they still assume we know what we're talking about. (So make the most of it while you can!) Seize this prime opportunity for parental teaching, and be sure to address situations *as they occur* and avoid the temptation of waiting for a more convenient time.

If your boys are at all like ours, they love to talk about things when it's time for bed. For years we wondered if this was just a ruse to stay up later. (When they were toddlers, it surely was!) But we decided that, even if it is somewhat of a con, we will go for it. If our sons are willing to talk about what's going on in their life, what they're thinking and feeling, some of the emotions they're struggling with, what their friends are thinking, where they are in their relationship with the Lord, we'll stay up for that any time!

One of the best ways to know whether your son is learning what you want him to learn is to ask for feedback. As you talk with him about life, relationships, or the Christian faith, ask open-ended questions to find out what he already knows. These questions can be asked in a way that communicates genuine interest and curiosity—and not in what he could be anticipating as "an interrogation." Listen for the way he looks at these issues. When you believe you understand what he is thinking, get into the habit of asking at least one more clarifying question.

Then, as you try to instruct him by sharing new information and perspectives, ask him to tell you what he thinks you are saying. Think of examples he can identify with, and keep at it until you're sure he understands. Don't just assume he knows what you mean. It's well worth the time and effort.

PARENTS HAVE FEELINGS TOO

Your son is not the only one who is changing. Most parents begin to have similar feelings as their sons change and move into adolescence. Understanding those emotions in yourself are just as important as understanding what your son is feeling. In fact, as parents we need to admit we don't always have our act together and we experience times when our emotions get the best of us.

Author and psychologist Bruce Baldwin has identified six emotions most parents of adolescents will experience.[4] To a degree we have already experienced each of these emotions prior to this stage in our son's life. Not all of these emotions will arrive during early-adolescent growth, but chances are good that each will surface at some point during adolescence, so be prepared.

Pure fear. While the social world of the early adolescent is rather small at first, it gradually expands to include relating to more people and spending more time away from home. The world is a more dangerous place today than it was a generation ago, and parents often fear for the physical and emotional safety of their growing child. And truly there are plenty of things to be afraid of today: violence, drugs, drunk drivers, peer pressure, immoral media influences—the list could go on and on. It does not help that our sons' movement into this more dangerous world happens at about the same time they become more private about what is going on in their lives. No big surprise that the fear factor kicks into action!

A sense of helplessness. Helplessness is a difficult feeling for most of us to handle, because we want to be able to control life. But there will be times when, as a parent, you can do nothing but stand back and watch the pain and turmoil your young son will experience at certain points in his life. Even when you try to offer support, your son's own suspicion of your motives or his budding need for independence may cause him to push you away and shut you out.

We cannot always rush in and rescue our son from the cruelties of other teens or the consequences of his own actions. Life can be a hard teacher—but you *can* continue to love your son unconditionally and encourage him unwaveringly.

Inadequacy. It would be good if we always knew what we are doing as a parent. We don't. Living with a teenager will, at least occasionally, highlight that fact, and feelings of inadequacy are sure to follow. When those feelings come, it is important to remember it's okay to feel inadequate. We can learn from our mistakes and press on in our attempt to be the best parents we can be.

Frustration and anger. It is inevitable that some of the behaviors that are part of the growing-up process will frustrate us and trigger our anger. Our sons' push for independence will show up in resistance to our advice, the testing of limits, and relatively wild emotional swings. Frustration and anger will be normal, and perhaps frequent, reactions. For the sake of our sons, we need to learn to resolve our anger in appropriate ways. As parents we need to be a calming influence as our sons face the tumultuous challenges of growing up.

A growing awareness of loss. We don't always like to admit it, but our sons are growing up. We already feel some sense of loss as they become more and more involved in a life outside of the home. We are forced to realize that in just a few short years they will be going out into the "real world" and lost to our families forever (at least in a formative, growing kind of way). The positive side of this awareness is that it motivates us to be an active part of their lives *now*, before we lose the chance. Making the most of today's moments prevents regrets in the future.

Excitement. Negative emotions are a natural part of parenting a growing teen. But in healthy families there are many positive emotions as well. As much as we may not be looking forward to the day when our boys will live outside the home, we also get excited about their growth toward manhood. Healthy parent-son relationships will have these moments of excitement, not because we are anxious to see them go, but because we look forward to seeing them become their own person.

HOW CAN I HELP MY EARLY-ADOLESCENT SON?

Focus on Being a Godly Parent, Not Just on Raising a Godly Son

As parents, we need to recognize what we control and what we don't. We *can* control our own behavior and our responses to our son. We *don't* control his reactions. There are really very few things a parent can *make* a teenager do if he chooses not to. It is important to gain his cooperation—to win your son over, rather than trying to win over your son. It's a subtle, but at the same time a very significant, distinction.

God does not make us choose a certain way. He doesn't get in a power struggle with us. He provides us with the truth and with the opportunity to be godly. But ultimately he leaves it up to us to choose what we will do with that opportunity, and then he loves us enough to allow us to experience the logical consequences of a bad decision. In the same way, we can work and pray to be the best possible parents for our son, but he will make his own choices and be responsible for who he becomes in the end. In short, there are no guarantees. But do understand this: As his parents, you are the greatest influencer in terms of what he will choose.

Lay a Relational Foundation in Childhood

The best predictor of how you and your teenage son will relate to each other is found in the relationship you build with him when he is a young boy. Those early patterns of interaction set the stage for what your relationship with your son will look like during this period of his life. If those patterns have been healthy, you can probably expect the healthy relationship to continue. Young adolescent boys still feel close to their parents and need them as a major source of support, even if they don't always act like it. While they enjoy spending time with friends, their family relationships are still the most important relationships in their lives.

Research suggests that one indicator of a satisfying parent-teen relationship is that both the parents and sons *say* they have a warm relationship. The term *warm relationship* may sound like a nebulous indicator, but it has been proven time and again to be the single most important predictor of relational satisfaction and intimacy. The flip side is that if either a son or a parent perceives that the other person is cold with respect to how he relates to him, there will be a significant block in their communication and intimacy. So if your son is still small, invest the time and energy that will pay off not only now but also in the future. While it is never too late to begin building a warm, loving relationship, creating a solid foundation is always easier than repairing a damaged one.

Spend Ample Time with Your Son

Relationships are forged in the context of time. It is impossible to build a strong relationship without spending *quantity* time together, not just quality time. It's a principle, by the way, that holds for most relationships—with God, with spouses, with friends, as well as with our children.

As our sons move into their teenage years, spending time with them becomes more of a challenge. In fact, with our three sons we've discovered that just *finding* them becomes a challenge. So make the most of your opportunities to do things together with your son. Plant in his mind warm memories of special times together that will deepen the relational root system that will grow into a rich relationship for many years to come.

Trust Your Son

"We'll trust you when you prove you can be trusted," some parents tell their adolescent boys, which can make adolescents bitter and frustrated about the guilt they're made to feel, and about the necessity of having to prove their innocence. Like many other parents, we decided early on that we would communicate a different message to our boys: "We'll trust you until you prove you can't be trusted," we told them, "and then we'll deal with the problem." With few exceptions, they have rewarded our trust. And when they do make mistakes, they work to quickly rebuild that trust.

Most parents view this as a one-way proposition, but healthy relationships are characterized by *two-way* trust. The trust between you and your son should be mutual, and it should be something you evaluate from time to time. Here are several questions you can ask yourself to measure the trust level of your relationship: Can your son trust you to listen to him when circumstances look bad? Can he trust you to take him at his word, even when you really don't want to? Does your son trust that you care more about him than how well he achieves in sports and other activities, or even what kinds of grades he gets? Does he believe that you like him *as he is*, and that he can open himself up to you without fear of condemnation or ridicule?

Support Your Son's Involvement in Activities by Your Attendance

Go to your son's concerts, his games, his school plays, his science fairs. Your support will give him a sense of security and an affirmation of competence. While he may not *express* his thanks to you, you can be sure he will remember your tangible expressions of love and support well into his adult life. In Denver our boys were active in a variety of sports, but when we moved to Siloam Springs, they were new kids in a new system—which translated into more time on the bench than what they were used to. From our perspective it became more important than ever that we show up for as many games as we could.

Due to an early-season injury and being the new kid on the block, our son Matt spent all but a few minutes of the basketball season on the bench. On occasion he talked of quitting, but we encouraged him to stay with it. Our encouragement came in the form of supportive conversations *and* our presence at the games. He would tell us that because he wasn't likely to play anyway, there really wasn't any need for us to come to his games. Our response? "You are probably one of the best benchwarmers on the team and, besides, we wouldn't want to miss the history-making event when you get to play." His laugh and his smile let us know he appreciated us being there.

Be Less of an Enforcer and More of an Encourager

The fact that many early-adolescent boys see their moms as the clear winner when it comes to providing emotional support presents a powerful challenge for dads. Many dads make the mistake of paying the most attention to their sons when they fail to toe the mark, and their conversations quickly zero in on house rules—how the boy has flaunted them and how the dad must enforce them. Instead we should cultivate the example of Barnabas—a New Testament missionary whose name meant "Son of Encouragement" (Acts 4:36). Christian parents need to spend more time trying to become *moms and dads of encouragement.*

Unfortunately, despite our good intentions, our sons are likely to interpret our efforts as indicators that they are not measuring up to our expectations, that they have let us down, that we are disappointed in them, and that they aren't good enough. Our correction or criticism will be accepted more graciously if it is sprinkled rather than poured. What needs to be poured is the message that our sons are loved and accepted unconditionally and that we will stand by them through their struggles as a steady source of security, no matter what.

As Much as Possible, Treat Your Son Like an Adult

Teens would love to be treated like the adults they will become. In our efforts to remind them that they have certainly not arrived yet, we can be tempted to treat them like children.

Indeed, if truth be told, that is exactly how they sometimes act. But we would all rather be seen in terms of our potential, not our lapses into immature attitudes and behaviors.

One of the most helpful concepts we have used is to see adolescence as the "toddler stage" of adulthood. Remember the days when your little guy was learning to walk—and the excitement you felt? As a dad, you knelt about ten feet away, encouraging your young bundle of determination to make that long journey into your waiting arms. As his eyes grew wide and he stumbled forward, you were there to encourage him and to help him up when he fell. And there was no way for him to learn to walk without falling. Bumped noses and bruised knees were badges of effort, and eventually he gained confidence and learned to walk skillfully. Feelings of joy filled your heart as you thought, *That's my boy!* You would never have dreamed of trying to hold him back and keep him confined to his crib.

In a very real sense our teenage sons are "adults in training." Our sons' initial attempts at adulthood are pretty wobbly at first, and they often fall and bump their emotional and social noses. But with praise and encouragement from us, they keep on trying. If we hang in there with them, if we offer help and encouragement instead of put-downs and criticism, they eventually gain confidence and become more skilled in adultlike attitudes and behavior. Our job is to guide them as they learn to walk as godly young men.

Connect Privilege and Responsibility

Part of being treated like an adult is to make the connection between privilege and responsibility. On the one hand, our teenage boys often want all the privileges of being treated like an adult, but they *don't* want the responsibilities that come with it. Parents, on the other hand, often want their growing children to be responsible in the same way that adults are, but they hesitate to give them corresponding privileges. But these are in reality two sides of the same coin. Healthy development will include increasing amounts of both—and parents can and should negotiate increased responsibilities *and* privileges with their son as he gets older.

Talk with Your Son About the Future

While your son is still wide-open to your instruction, talk with him about the changes he can expect when puberty arrives. Talk with him about your hopes and dreams for his teenage years; talk about the joys and challenges of relationships with friends and with girls. Just *talk* with him!

The mother or father who can help a son think strategically and critically when making decisions, who knows how to listen and interact, who can communicate feelings as well as convictions, who can teach a son to bear in mind the consequences when making choices—these parents are well on the road to helping their son become a healthy man of God. Remember, talking about the future doesn't necessarily have an *immediate* impact, but as your son begins to *experience* some of the things you've talked about, he may very well be more open to discussions in the future.

Pray

This sincere piece of advice is by no means intended to be some nugget of trite spirituality tossed in for good measure. As Christian parents, we need to recognize the awesome power of prayer. God loves our son and has a plan for his life. The resources we have available in Christ will help us guide our son through his adolescence and will help him discover that plan. Pray for wisdom. Pray for patience and clear understanding. Pray that your son will discover his identity in Christ and build a relationship with him that will carry him through all his years as an adult.

A WHOLE NEW WORLD

For your son, early adolescence is a time of letting go of the safe and comfortable role of a child and striking out into the world on his own. He is in search of his identity as a man and as a follower of Jesus Christ. His choices often reflect his attempts to test the waters of autonomy, to tell the world that, right or wrong, the time has come to start living his own life.

Appearances to the contrary, you are *not* losing your son. But when adolescence comes, you *will* need to say good-bye to your little boy—the same little guy who squealed with delight when you tossed him in the air, who drooled all over your clean clothes and filled his diaper as soon as Mom left to run an errand. This is the cute toddler who loved to crawl up into your lap, just to cuddle. You taught him how to ride a bike, throw a baseball, and bait a hook.

He needed you then, and he needs you now—but in a different way.

He needs you to be his friend, his coach, his confidant. The next stage of being a parent can be every bit as precious, rewarding, and fun as the previous stages. It is time to celebrate this special phase in the journey that will take your son to what God has designed him to become . . . a strong young man. Just as God is our anchor in times of turmoil and uncertainty, we as parents need to be his anchor in what can be a confusing season of life. Our sons need to see us as dependable, consistent, safe, and secure. They need us to not only seek to understand what they are going through, but to help them in making the transition meaningful in their lives.

SMALL BEGINNINGS

1. Reread chapter 12 on making your marriage a priority—you will undoubtedly refer back to this chapter frequently during your son's adolescent years.

2. Keep attuned to what your son is interested in—the music he listens to, the movies he wants to see, the friends he hangs around with. As you talk with your son about these matters, be careful not to dominate the conversation, and whenever possible avoid heavy-handed rule giving, but rather cultivate (it doesn't come naturally) the ability to discuss boundaries and guidelines with him.
3. Learn more about your son's world and the stresses and pressures he faces by talking with other parents and with his teachers.
4. The next time you and your son have a conflict, apply this practical and powerful bit of advice: When in doubt, remember that you can't go wrong by giving support and encouragement. If you are tempted to overreact, take a time-out to pray, to reflect, and to collect your thoughts. Try to be even more gentle in your conversation. Intentionally lower your voice and speak more slowly.

Chapter Fifteen

HELPING YOUR SON MOVE FROM ADOLESCENCE TO ADULTHOOD

Late Adolescence (Ages 16–19)

UP FRONT *In this chapter ...*

- ✦ Late adolescence is the ideal time to let your son experience both success and failure in the safe environment of your home, and thus to practice becoming the man God has created him to be.
- ✦ Although older teens exhibit increasing analytical skills, parents should not expect consistency in the use of these skills.
- ✦ During this time of late adolescence as your son is determining who he is, how you relate to him influences how he handles questions of identity. So be sure to give him lots of loving acceptance and let him know you assume he can think for himself.
- ✦ Give your teenager room to examine his faith through questioning and doubting what he has been taught. Celebrate his independence and personal faith journey.
- ✦ Most older teens say they prefer to be with friends rather than with family, yet they spend much of their time at home. They are becoming more secure in what they like and don't

like in a friend, and at the same time they are growing less susceptible to peer pressure.

✦ The media bombard a late adolescent with sexual images. Add in his growing preoccupation with girls, and you have one big temptation!

✦ Working outside the home can bring the benefits of responsibility and financial independence to a teenager, but it can also cut into family and school time. Set guidelines with your son for part-time jobs.

✦ Parents must make the transition from wielding power over their son to giving him more freedom. Negotiating solutions to problems with your son will build his self-confidence and increase his maturity.

OUR FRIENDS STEVE AND Twyla Lee shared with us their emotions at the transition of their sons from adolescence into young adulthood:

It seems like only a few months ago that we were setting our boys in our laps and reading stories to them at bedtime. Time speeds by quickly, and days turn into years in a matter of moments. Our oldest son is now gone to college, never to return and live with us in the same way he did while growing up. He is grown. Our youngest son starts his last year of high school next fall. Then he will be gone. Time flies.

As we reflect on the last years of their adolescence, we are struck by the wonder of watching boys turn into men. We have participated in the excitement and challenges of that transformation. We have made mistakes, but that is part of being a parent. We hope we have learned from those mistakes. One thing is for sure—we and our sons agree that we have wonderfully warm, loving relationships. We also know that they love the Lord and are discovering his will for their lives. We are blessed![1]

Although this child of yours will *always* be your son, the years of late adolescence (ages sixteen to nineteen) are the final years you have to significantly influence and mold him as he becomes a man. In most cases, once he leaves home for college, a job, or military service, the work of parenting as you have known it for the past eighteen years is over. To be sure, you may still have some leverage in his decision making, but for the most part, he will be on his own. So while the period of late adolescence carries with it the budding hope of adulthood, your son is on the verge, but not yet there.

So what should be the goal of this closing season of adolescence? At the very least, we believe it should be to encourage your son to practice being a man while you're still providing the safety net of home and family—with all the security it brings. Cherish these last years he will be in your home, as you guide him along in his quest to become the man God wants him to be.

GETTING A "SENSE OF THE GAME": CHANGES IN THINKING

Rational, sensible parents would never consider handing over the family car keys to a teenager who has not had the required hours of formal training behind the wheel. The parent who wants to help prepare a son for adulthood can think of late adolescence as the time for a "thinker's permit." You can provide your son with intentional opportunities to get behind the wheel of his mind and practice adultlike thinking and decision making. Teens who become godly decision makers have generally had plenty of training and experience in learning how to make godly decisions.

The changes that can take place in your son's thinking patterns allow him to move much closer to being a mature adult. We say *can take place* because these changes are not automatic. Exercising his mental "muscles" is similar to an athlete exercising his physical muscles. If your son is getting a mental workout, gaining in the mental strength that will help him think responsibly and make mature, adultlike decisions, you can expect to see the following changes in how he thinks about and looks at his world.

Your Son Shows an Increasing Ability to Think in the Abstract

For teens who have been encouraged to practice the mental abilities they began to develop as middle adolescents, they should be getting better at analyzing situations and making responsible decisions. You can encourage your son to think of different alternatives rather than simply tell him what to do. Not all teens are encouraged to do so, and their lack of practice is often reflected in immature behaviors and poor decision-making skills.

A word of caution is in order: Although your son is making his way past that wobbly "adult toddler" stage, he does still make mistakes. Studies have shown that teens (and adults, for that matter) apply increasingly mature thinking skills to some areas, but not others. For instance, your son may show real maturity in thinking about what he wants to do after high school graduation. He may systematically evaluate the advantages and disadvantages of going to college versus going to work, or he may do exhaustive research on why he should go to one college over another. Yet, at the same time, you may see him making childish decisions about what to do with his friends on a Friday night. If those decisions end up getting him in trouble, you may hear, "Sorry, Dad and Mom, I just wasn't thinking." And he'll be right! You can encourage your sons to use their growing ability to think responsibly, but don't expect maturity and well-thought-out decisions in every issue that faces them.

Your Son Will Be Less Self-Conscious and Less Concerned About an Imaginary Audience

A middle adolescent is preoccupied with how others see him, concerned that other people are seeing and judging everything he does. As a late adolescent, your son still cares about what others think, but these opinions exert far less pressure and cause less anxiety at this stage than they did during middle adolescence.

In short, late adolescents are gaining in what child development expert John Flavell calls a "sense of the game."[2] In order to play the "game" of life well, a man needs to learn how to "read" other people, evaluate alternatives, anticipate and solve problems, and relate to others in effective ways. Their growing mental skills allow boys ages sixteen or older to do a better job of distinguishing between those whose opinion is important and those whose opinion is not. As a result, older teens tend to be more comfortable with who they are, and they tend to possess a more stable sense of self-esteem.

Your Son's Thinking Broadens to a Wider Range of Topics

The world of a junior high, or middle school, student is pretty narrow—typically confined to things like hanging out with friends, finding out who likes who, dealing with the pressures and activities of school, and planning what to do on the weekend. Middle adolescents begin to apply their newfound ability to think abstractly to these and certain other areas, but their concerns are generally limited to what is affecting their life at that particular moment. Late adolescents may be equally concerned with some of the above issues, but they also often become more aware of and interested in things that are outside of their own personal world.

Famine in Africa, abortion protests, political events in Washington, and questions of theology may capture the attention of late adolescents more quickly than when they were younger. *You're living in a dream world,* you may be thinking as you read this. After all, the high school teens you know are nothing but a bunch of selfish, immature kids who only care about getting what *they* want and having a good time, right? To be sure, there are times when that's exactly what late adolescents are like—but there are other times when they may surprise you with their maturity. Taking the time to gently nudge them toward reflection on the big questions of life will often pay off in productive thinking and unselfish behavior.

Don't underestimate the importance of giving late adolescents opportunities to think and make decisions about life, themselves, and their relationships. If truth be told, it will not be long before they will *have* to do that as full-fledged adults.

WHO AM I?—DEFINING YOUR SON'S IDENTITY

The changes in thinking that take place in late adolescence will prompt a teen to confront a number of identity issues. At various times an older teen will ask himself, "Who am I?" and healthy development requires that he examine several areas, such as:

- What are my strengths and weaknesses?
- What are my sexual values?
- What qualities are important to me in my friendships?
- What do I believe about God?
- Am I happy with how I'm doing in school?
- What kind of work do I want to do as an adult?

All of these questions, together with many more, help our son define his identity. Most researchers and theorists believe that adolescence, especially late adolescence, is the time in life when we begin to wrestle with these crucial questions in a deeply meaningful way.

Different teens approach these questions in different ways. Some tackle them in a serious way, while others simply ignore them. Researchers have discovered that how a teen deals with identity issues is related to the way his family functions—that is, how your son deals with questions of identity will be determined in part by how you relate to him. So what are the different ways your son might approach these questions, and what role do you play in helping him choose the way he will go?

Let's examine the profiles of four eighteen-year-old boys who are in the process of becoming men; each has taken a different approach in answering the question "Who am I?" Each reflects a type, a particular style, of thinking about one's personal identity.

The Avoiding Type

Jim is concerned almost exclusively about today and about doing things with his friends; as a result he isn't inclined to think about who he is or what he wants to do with his life. He figures he'll just "go with the flow" and eventually fall into something he likes. He calls his meetings with his high school counselor to discuss postgraduation plans "a real drag." He says he has no goals—except to live for what he can get out of *today*.

Teens like Jim, who *avoid* dealing with questions of identity, often possess low self-esteem and exhibit irresponsible behavior. Their thinking is more childlike than adultlike. They tend to live solely for themselves, and all pleas to "grow up" are met with indifference.

Avoiding teens tend to come from families characterized by distant or rejecting relationships. The home front typically is a negative atmosphere, and fathers of *avoiding* teens are often critical of their children, or they are often emotionally absent. The lack of healthy family relationships seems to lead to an *I don't really care* attitude about life and about setting goals.

The Settled Type

Casey seems to have all the answers when it comes to questions of identity. He knows what he believes, what he wants to do with his life, and what his values are. The problem with Casey is that he's *always* known these things. You see, Casey has always been told what to believe and who he should be—and that's just the way it is. He has never considered being anything else.

Teens like Casey have virtually no struggle when it comes to identity formation. They tend to constantly seek the approval of others, especially parents. In a sense, they let other people do their thinking for them. They seem to have all the questions answered, but they can get defensive when asked why they believe what they do. They are generally happy and have high self-esteem, although they are not very adaptable. Their relationship with parents is usually warm and loving, while at the same time the parents tend to find both direct and indirect ways to pressure them into accepting family values and beliefs.

The Searching Type

Joe has been struggling as he thinks about his future. There are so many options to consider, and he's just not sure what direction he wants to take in life. Every time he thinks he has figured out who he is and what he wants to do, he talks himself out of it.

Joe grew up in the church, and he admires the strong Christian commitment his parents have. He accepted Christ as Savior and Lord during his fourth-grade year, and his faith is important to him. Lately, though, he's had some doubts about his faith—doubts that are leading him to seek answers to his questions. He's beginning to meld his thoughts and beliefs into something that can support him in the transition from adolescence to adulthood, but it hasn't been easy.

Teens like Joe are *searching*. They wrestle with questions of identity, and they don't settle for easy answers. They generally possess a healthy level of self-esteem, and their relationships with parents seem to be positive and nourishing. They tend to belong to families that encourage children to take responsibility for their lives and to think for themselves. While these parents want their children to adopt their values and lifestyle, they do not want to spoon-feed them the "answers" to life.

The Achieved Type

Terry is a confident, happy eighteen-year-old who knows who he is and what he believes. Not long ago he was searching for answers, just like Joe. Terry spent a lot of time thinking about himself and about God's plan for his life. Discussions with his father, his pastor, and a close adult friend of the family helped him sort out answers to his questions.

Teens like Terry have succeeded in developing a mature outlook on identity issues. They have invested a lot of thought into the important issues in their life. After considering all the possibilities, they have made choices to which they are now committed. They are well equipped to handle the situations that life brings their way.

Terry and others like him are settled and comfortable in their identity. Like the searching types, they tend to come from families where love and care are blended with encouragement to be one's self—to be the persons God intends them to be.

Which of the four types do you want your son to be? We'd like nothing better than that you opt for the *achieved* type. Late-adolescent boys (and girls) who become *achieved* types seem to be best prepared to handle the ups and downs that adulthood brings. They know who they are, and they know why. And *you* are a key player in helping them get to that point. As our children leave home to take their place in the world, we want them to go with a strong sense of identity that will help them stand as committed men and women who know what it means to love and serve their God.

WHAT ABOUT GOD?

Thinking through and learning to "own" their faith in God is another crucial mental area in which late teens develop. Sixteen-year-old Shane has found himself bothered by doubts about his Christian faith. His active witness in school is prompting several guys to ask him questions—questions he has a hard time answering. "How do you know the Bible is from God? If God is so loving, why is there so much suffering and evil in the world? Wasn't Jesus just a great teacher? How do you know Jesus was God and that he died on a cross and rose from the dead?" These and other questions have been getting to Shane, making him wonder why he believes what he does.

The more Shane thought about it, the more he realized that he *didn't* know why he believed what he did. He had grown up with answers that had worked for him, but those same answers were not satisfying his skeptical friends. At first he tried to submerge his doubts, but they kept surfacing: "What if I'm wrong? What if my parents and my church are wrong? How do I know that Christianity is the only way to heaven?" He needed to find out.

Shane was afraid to approach his dad. He considered Dad so sure of himself—so strong, committed, faithful—and Shane had no clue what to say to him. But Shane desperately wanted to be strong in his faith as well, and eventually those nagging doubts drove him to seek advice from his father. Unfortunately, Dad responded to Shane's questions and doubts with anger and a defensive attitude. Instead of discussing the questions with his son, Dad told him to just have more faith and to resist Satan's attempts to get him to doubt. No discussion and no answers left Shane feeling nothing but guilt for his doubts and questions.

Parents can underestimate the importance of helping their teenagers carefully think through and test their faith. Our sons need to *own* their faith for themselves, and coming to grips with the doubts and the questions is a necessary step to that ownership. Neither indoctrination nor spoon-feeding will give your sons what they need to cope with questions and doubts. If we tell them what to believe, it is *our* beliefs they hold, not theirs. We must help them discover faith for *themselves*, not for us.

Giving our sons the freedom to explore questions of faith can be scary, to be sure; after all, they may not end up where we want them to go. The truth is, however, that we cannot force our sons to believe what we want them to believe. Spiritual guidance in late adolescence is best handled by helping them think about their faith, not by trying to limit or eliminate their questions. "In my interviews with faith dropouts," writes Tom Bisset in *Why Christian Kids Leave the Faith*, "nothing evoked stronger reactions than the simple question, 'Did you feel free to make important decisions about your faith at home and in church?'"[3]

The questions our sons ask need to be celebrated, not feared. They are thinking about vital questions, as they should, in order to learn to be independent and, in the case of spiritual matters, to be assured about their faith. As we work *with* our sons rather than against them to answer those questions, their faith grows and roots itself deeper in their souls.

Talk with your son. Discuss questions of faith; debate issues with him. Help him to think, but don't think *for* him. In giving him the freedom to think for himself, you increase the likelihood that he will invite you to share in that process with him. As you think together with him, call him to a knowledge of the Scriptures. Encourage him to search out God's Word for answers to his doubts and questions; the answers are there for him to discover.[4]

The journey to an *achieved* identity grounded in a solid faith relationship with Jesus Christ is an individual one that must be traveled by our sons. We cannot travel it for them, but we can walk alongside them as they seek to develop a mature faith that is their very own, a faith that can sustain them as they enter adulthood.

LOTS OF TIME WITH PEERS: SOCIAL CHANGES

In the busy lives of active teenagers, it may seem as though they are never home. But the reality is that late adolescents are home more often than it seems. A clever experiment by Mihaly Csikszentmihalyi and Reed Larson has provided some insight into how high school students spend their time and who they spend it with.[5]

In the study, seventy-five students were given beepers to carry with them wherever they went. The beepers would sound approximately every two hours during their waking hours. The students were asked to record where they were, what they were doing, and who they were with when the beeper sounded.

The study revealed that *home* is where teens spend much of their time—but when it comes to who they hang out with, their peer group rose to the top. More than half of their waking time is spent with other teenagers, while only twenty percent of their time is spent actually being *with* their family (and very little of that time with parents only). Clearly much of their time at home is spent either sleeping or eating (any surprises there?!) and a much lesser amount of time interacting with family members.

The teens in this study reported they were happiest when they were with their friends, and being with their family ranked second. The reason, at least in part, is that they *have more fun* with friends than family. Joking, laughing, and just goofing off are more common with friends than with family. Builds a pretty strong case for family fun, huh?

As the above study confirms, being with friends is an important part of late adolescence, to be sure. At the same time the intense needs to conform and to be accepted by the entire peer group lessen to some extent. Generally late adolescents have less concern about being liked by *everyone* they have anything to do with; this concern now seems to extend only to one's immediate circle of friends. Middle adolescents are intensely concerned with asking the question, "Do you like me?" while late adolescents are more likely to ask the question, "Do I like you?" Fears and insecurities are still present, without a doubt, but late adolescents have reached a point where they possess a much better sense of identity. They have begun to discover who they are and who they want their friends to be.

In the context of this important circle of friends, there *is* one thing that captures a lot of your son's attention. No, it's not homework, or helping out at home, or scraping the bubblegum off the bottom of desks as a volunteer service project! Yes, you guessed it—it's girls. It's an interest that started shortly after puberty, and it now occupies a prominent place in his thinking—and sometimes in his behavior.

BOYS AND GIRLS IN LOVE

While preteen boys may not have been very interested in girls, by middle adolescence their hormone-driven interest spurs a sharply focused awareness that girls are designed differently—and they like that difference. Those wonderful curves that God in his infinite wisdom created for women do not escape the notice of your son. Thinking about girls is a frequent subject in your son's mind—more frequent than you might imagine.

And then you add in the influence of television and other forms of the media. A recent study found that an American teen watches 14,000 sexual encounters a year on television alone. Most adolescents spend one second learning the *positive* discipline of intimacy for every one hundred hours they spend absorbing *distorted* images of intimacy from the media. Three-quarters of today's boys are reported to have sex by the time they graduate from high school; the figures are somewhat less for girls (one-half of today's girls). In fact, the median age for first intercourse is 16.6 years for boys and 17.4 years for girls.

According to the "Sex and America's Teenagers" study (conducted by The Alan Guttmacher Institute in 1994), the following proportions of age-specific groups of students have engaged in sex:

- Nine percent of twelve-year-olds
- Sixteen percent of thirteen-year-olds
- Twenty-three percent of fourteen-year-olds
- Thirty percent of fifteen-year-olds
- Forty-two percent of sixteen-year-olds
- Sixty-nine percent of seventeen-year-olds
- Seventy-one percent of eighteen-year-olds[6]

As with all the other developmental milestones, adolescents are brand-new at this opposite-sex "stuff." Their earliest experiences involve making trial-and-error forays into the world of dating. Even though they fall on their relational noses at times, they gradually become more skilled at opposite-sex interactions. Their early efforts can be cute, and sometimes amusing, to those of us who have long ago learned to "walk" and have put those days behind us. They are interested in establishing relationships, but they are often naive about how to go about doing it.

The TV series *The Wonder Years,* which followed Kevin Arnold from ages eleven to seventeen, would often spotlight the ups and downs of adolescent romance. In one episode, after an especially confusing exchange with his girlfriend, Winnie, Kevin commented, "That's when I discovered that love was going to be a lot more complicated than I had imagined." No kidding!

Most teens are still trying to master the challenges of intimacy, and they are prone to romanticizing boy-girl relationships and seeing relationships as easier and less complicated than they really are. Tune into a teen radio station at night and listen to young teens call in their dedications to girlfriends and would-be girlfriends. Love songs abound. Such is young love—romance without real relationship.

As boys move through the early stages of adolescence and on toward adulthood, dating tends to become much more couple-oriented. Relationships become more serious, and they also find a foundation in a stronger level of maturity than do junior high, or middle school, romances. Make no mistake, however, there is still *a lot* to be learned.

These excursions into the world of "love" are a normal experience for young teenage boys and girls. How you react to these experiences will affect not only your ongoing relationship with your son, but also his sense of who he is as a male. Putting him down, making sarcastic comments, or telling him he is too young to understand real love only put distance between you and him. We made a decision early on that we would support our sons in their relationships as long as they were healthy ones. We wanted our sons to feel we were on their side, because we knew there would be much that they could only learn through experience.

While dating can be an important part of our son's development, we still need to encourage him to keep his social world large enough to include many friends. When teens lock themselves into an exclusive relationship that consumes all of their time, they cheat themselves out of a rich, satisfying social life. Furthermore, a narrow relationship can turn his world too isolated and "me" or "us" focused. A couple who becomes isolated from a wide base of friends increases the risk of giving in to a powerful adolescent force—sexuality.

A preoccupation with girls can result in a great deal of sexual temptation for your son, either mentally or behaviorally. Teenage boys today are bombarded by sexual messages that fly in the face of God's standards. Movies, television sitcoms, songs, MTV videos, and magazines all send the message that it's "normal" to be sexually active as a teenager. Even sex education experts have adopted this standard. Abstinence may be given lip service, but the real sex education message is clear: Do what you want to do—just be safe.

A small Christian college recently held a discussion on sexuality at which a young man made the following comment: "I don't want to seem like a prude or anything, but the Bible clearly teaches that sex before marriage is sin." The pressure to live a godly lifestyle without appearing "uncool" is real, and it can be relentless. Even at a Christian college he felt compelled to not look like "a prude" to fellow Christians. Every teen is hearing a message that there's nothing wrong with sex before marriage—as long as you love each other and take the proper precautions. And many teens, including Christian teens, are surrendering to that message.

Research has been rather clear that, at least in terms of their behavior, Christian youth are not all that far behind non-Christian youth in their level of sexual activity. Youth pastors and others who work with teens are well aware of the rampant sexual involvement, and they often tell sad stories at national youth conferences of Christian teens snared by sexual struggles. According to Josh McDowell, a popular Christian author and speaker, "Statistics show the figure [of sexually active teens] to be between 65 and 80 percent depending on the statistics one chooses. Surprisingly, Christian teenagers are generally only ten percentage points or so behind the overall figure."[7]

So what does all of this mean for your growing son? For one thing, he is not immune to the pressures and the cultural messages that push kids into early sexual behavior. You also should realize that the values he holds are no guarantee that he will not find himself trapped in ways he knows are wrong.

Helping your son deal with his sexuality is important, and many good resources are available to guide you along the way.[8] You can let your son know that everyone else is *not* doing it, in spite of what teens often think or hear from some friends. In addition to our verbal instructions, our sons need to know that we love them no matter what, and that they can bring to us their questions and concerns about anything—including dating and sexuality (and then we must *really* listen to them).

Moms take on a critical role as a safe source of information regarding the female perspective. As our oldest son, Nathan, has become involved in a valued and important relationship with a young woman, he increasingly comes to Carrie to ask for the female perspective—because he realizes that his girlfriend sees and responds to some things very differently than he does. The open lines of communication have certainly brought Carrie's relationship with him to a point of closeness that was absent during his earlier adolescent years. Just remember to distinguish between *helping* him understand and *telling* him what to do. If you stumble into the latter territory, you'll shut down the lines of communication fast.

NOT EVERY BOY DATES

A significant number of adolescent boys have little desire to go through traditional dating, at least during high school.

One Sunday after church one of our son's fifteen-year-old friends asked him if there was anything wrong with him because he doesn't have a girlfriend and doesn't really want one. "No way," Matt said. "There is plenty of time for girls. Just enjoy doing what you like and someday when you are not even looking or expecting it, a special girl will show up in your life." Not bad insight for a fifteen-year-old, wouldn't you agree?!

There are often very healthy reasons for not developing romantic relationships. A boy may feel that pursuing a girl can negatively affect his studies at school; he may have lots of extracurricular activities, such as participating on sports teams or school clubs; he may judge that it requires a lot of money he doesn't have; or he may work part time and not have much free time.

And, of course, there may be fear of rejection. Boys at this stage are still forming their own sense of identity, and dating can be frightening for some. Love your son just as he is, and for most boys this experience called *dating* will take care of itself in its proper time and place.

GOOD-BYE FAMILY, HELLO MINIMUM WAGE: ENTERING THE WORKPLACE

A new social world opens to the late adolescent: the world of work. Late adolescence is a time when many teens get their first *real* job. The attraction of earning their own money—and more of it than Dad or Mom is usually willing to give—can be a powerful motivator. The novelty of the experience, the lessons that can be learned, and even the fun that comes with doing something like cooking food, or actually using the words *sir* or *ma'am* in a sentence, make employment look like a great idea.

Recognize that should your son enter the workplace as a part-time worker, he will receive a number of benefits but he also will encounter some drawbacks. He will learn responsibility, for sure. Whether it is working in a fast-food restaurant, doing landscaping for a lawn service, bagging groceries, or any number of other jobs, he will learn about being on time for work, how to follow the instructions of an employer, and how to work with other employees as part of a team. And to top it off, along with learning all these valuable character traits, he gets paid for it!

There are drawbacks to working, however. Many teens who work part time are less involved in family and school activities; they may have less time for schoolwork, and their grades often suffer. Those who work more than fifteen hours per week are especially prone to the problems connected with working.

These results suggest two things. First, adding a part-time job to the busy life of a teenager will reduce what is an already small amount of time spent with the family. Second, developing character traits such as being punctual and being a team player can be accomplished in many ways besides holding a job. Many students gain similar qualities through participating in extracurricular activities at school, holding leadership positions in their church youth group, or joining in other organized activities. Speech, music, drama, athletics, clubs, and other opportunities can all teach responsibility and can aid in character development.

Whether or not your son should take a part-time job, especially during the school year, is a decision you should talk about together. It may help to take a brief look at how two particular families handled this issue.

Mark and his son, Josh, sat down to talk after supper one evening. Mark listened as Josh talked about why he wanted a job. Though Josh did talk about the skills he would learn, his major motivation was money. Josh was thrilled with the prospect of earning enough money to buy new clothes and make payments on a car.

"You'd have to give up some things," his father answered. "Time with friends, time with family, activities at school, free Saturdays. Have you thought much about that?"

"Well, I guess so. I really don't want to give up those things. But I don't see any other way. I mean, I need to earn some money, Dad."

As Josh and his dad continued to talk, they came up with a solution that made both of them happy. Mark decided to become Josh's employer. In addition to his regular chores around the house, Josh was now hired to do more significant tasks. For example, Josh was given the responsibility of painting the house. Mark worked alongside him, which gave him the opportunity to teach Josh some valuable skills. Josh was able to earn the money he wanted, and he got to spend some special times with his dad. As Josh would finish each job, they would negotiate for a new one. They both got what they wanted, and their relationship benefited as well.

Paul and his son, Joe, took a different approach. Paul listened carefully to Joe, then discussed the matter with his wife. After carefully thinking and praying about it, they concluded that it could be a good experience for Joe. Their consent was not without some strings attached, though. Joe sat down with his parents, and soon they had negotiated some guidelines.

Like Paul, if you decide to move ahead toward investigating a part-time job for your son, you would do well to work out some guidelines for as long as your son is in school and living at home. Here are some to consider:

- Before saying yes, be sure you and your wife agree. If not, discuss your concerns together.
- The job cannot interfere with his ability to complete his homework and maintain an acceptable grade point average.
- Agree on a maximum number of hours per week.
- The job cannot interfere on a regular basis with church and youth group activities.
- His work cannot become a source of family tension or conflict.
- A portion of his income needs to be set aside for tithing and for saving.
- Agree on a trial period (three months, for example), after which time you can review how things are going.

Whatever way you choose to negotiate this area of your son's life, one thing is important—do *not* simply hand your son money to satisfy his financial wants. He has reached a point where he is becoming a man, and the connection between income and responsibility is a vitally important and necessary lesson to learn as he approaches adulthood.

LETTING GO: CHANGES AT HOME

A while back our friends Steve and Twyla told us about the time their soon-to-be seventeen-year-old son was anticipating a spring break trip with a few friends. They were planning to travel about five hundred miles to the east coast with the family van and spend a week exploring.

"When he first approached us with his idea," the boy's dad told us, "he had done a great job of planning an itinerary, building in regular phone calls to update the parents, and generally taking care of a lot of details that were designed to put our questions to rest. It helped to know they would be staying with his girlfriend's family, so they wouldn't be entirely on their own.

"He was surprised when we thought it was a good idea. It's not that we were without concerns. Part of me wanted to say no, but past experience taught us to believe that they can handle it. We saw this trip as an opportunity to tell our son that he was becoming a young man, and that we were confident in his abilities to be responsible and trustworthy. Letting go of our sons as they approach adulthood will always involve calculated risk, but that is life."

The dad paused. "In just a little over a year from now, he will be striking out on his own, completely free of having to ask for our permission to go places or do things. We wanted to give him practice for doing that well while we still could guide him."

Whether your son is dealing with the details of everyday life (such as getting to places on time, managing money, or getting enough sleep), handling his sexual drive, dealing with social relationships, or going on a trip out east like Steve and Twyla's son, now is *not* the time to clamp down. It's the time to *let go*, with the assurance that you will be by his side when he needs you. It's too early to give him total freedom from authority, of course, but it's also too late to try to run his life.

This is the key to the late-adolescent stage of development—instilling in your son the confidence that he is capable of responsibility and trust. You are preparing him to believe that he is able to handle even the unexpected and difficult situations that responsibility brings and to help him feel worthy of trust. We hope you have been giving your son lots of opportunities to learn that. He is coming into the homestretch, and the open door of adulthood is not far away.

Remember, our sons are marching down the road toward independence. We need to encourage them to walk that road and we need to be willing to walk alongside them. Late adolescents who are able to achieve a solid sense of autonomy are more self-confident and mature than those who do not.

Some teens see their parents as roadblocks to independence. They believe that the primary task they have as a teenager is to break free from their parents. It does not have to be that way, but the result depends on the parents.

Parents of a well-adjusted teen gradually give him more and more freedom to run his own life and to make his own decisions. It's appropriate to treat your son as he would like to be treated—as someone who's becoming a responsible and respected adult. It is a good thing to move from parental power toward shared power. Discussion and negotiation, not heavy-handed commands, are the tools for resolving problems and conflicts.

The family conflicts of middle adolescence tend to decrease as teens gain in maturity and in decision-making prowess. They have been practicing being an adult for some time now, so at least the plan is for these conflicts to diminish!

Now, are we saying that parents have no veto power? Not at all. While there should be an ever-increasing reduction in parental power as children grow to adulthood, parents are never without influence. At no stage do teens in healthy families perceive power to be equal, and, surprisingly, they don't think it should be either. God has given us responsibility for the godly training of our children, and even our children recognize that.

Responsible, godly parents do not throw out guidelines and standards; they do not abandon their teens. Some standards are not negotiable—the prohibition of drugs, premarital sex, smoking, lying, cheating, and so on. But even in those cases, we cannot force our teens to obey. We must be clear about our values and expectations, but we are more likely to positively influence our teenage children and gain their cooperation when we participate in discussions rather than hand down commands to them.

Author and speaker Carol Kuykendall has summarized this time of life for us as parents:

> As our children conquer each milestone of independence, they tell us we are doing our job. What better reward do we need? Give your children roots and wings. . . . Roots go deep and help our children grow strong. They ground them against the assaults of the world and stabilize them. Roots come from bonding, loving, communicating, making memories, and observing traditions. Wings lift children upward and inspire them. They help them soar freely, strongly, and close to God. They come from letting go, cutting ties, pushing off, and stirring up the nest. Children need both. Roots I can handle; wings are my challenge.[9]

Giving them wings, letting them go—that is our goal as parents. How can you help your son step into adulthood as a godly young man? You need to—

- Move from parent control to self-control as your son grows.
- Encourage your son's growing independence by adding both privileges and responsibilities each year.
- Teach your son *how* to think, not *what* to think; allow him to make decisions and to fail.
- Avoid doing things for your son on a regular basis that he is capable of doing for himself.
- Keep your goals in mind. Raise your son to leave you. Your responsibility is to equip and to prepare him for life without you.

Much of what we have written in these chapters on adolescence accent the typical changes and challenges that come with this time in the life of your son. Regrettably, there are far too many families that must endure significant problems and crises with their teen. Delinquency, addictions, physical or emotional rebellion, sexual activity—the list goes on and on. Dealing with these severe issues is well beyond the scope of this book. If the problems you are experiencing with your teenage son are extreme, we encourage you to get solid Christian counsel. One thing is certain, however. As parents we *must* act in the best interest of our child and continue to work at creating a loving relationship, being willing to carry out whatever actions and accountability that calls for.

We have tried to paint a positive picture of adolescence. Unfortunately, much of what we hear about this time of life is negative and sarcastic. It's easy to take potshots at teenagers—but that's part of the problem, of course. We would never dream of criticizing and discouraging a young child who is learning to walk, but that's exactly what we can so easily end up doing with adolescents who are learning to "walk" as adults.

We must remember that our sons are not *our* possessions, they are *God's*. He has loaned them to us for a time as a gift so that we might prepare them for life and to serve his kingdom. It is up to us to work our way out of a job. We *want* our sons to shift their dependency from us to God. Love your son and help him become the man God wants him to be. Then let him go. You will not lose your son, no, you will only lose your *child*.

SMALL BEGINNINGS

1. If letting go has been a problem for you, begin to view successful parenting as *helping your son go out on his own*. Consider ways you can give him more freedom and bless him as he completes the task that adolescence was designed to help him accomplish.
2. Look for opportunities (few and far between though they may be) to talk with your son about his concerns and

struggles with sexuality and about his commitment to purity, and then together establish guidelines for healthy dating.

3. Your son is not going to be around much longer. Enjoy him, enjoy his friends, laugh with him, play with him, pray with him.

CONCLUSION
CARING IS NOT ENOUGH

IF

RUDYARD KIPLING

If you can keep your head when all about you
Are losing theirs and blaming it on you;
If you can trust yourself when all men doubt you,
But make allowance for their doubting too;
If you can wait and not be tired by waiting,
Or being lied about, don't deal in lies,
Or being hated, don't give way to hating,
And yet don't look too good, nor talk too wise;

If you can dream—and not make dreams your master;
If you can think—and not make thoughts your aim;
If you can meet with Triumph and Disaster
And treat those two impostors just the same;
If you can bear to hear the truth you've spoken
Twisted by knaves to make a trap for fools,
Or watch the things you gave your life to, broken,
And stoop and build 'em up with worn-out tools;

If you can make one heap of all your winnings
And risk it on one turn of pitch-and-toss,
And lose, and start again at your beginnings
And never breathe a word about your loss;
If you can force your heart and nerve and sinew
To serve your turn long after they are gone,
And so hold on when there is nothing in you
Except the Will which says to them: "Hold on!"

If you can talk with crowds and keep your virtue,
Or walk with Kings—nor lose the common touch;
If neither foes nor loving friends can hurt you;
If all men count with you, but none too much;
If you can fill the unforgiving minute
With sixty seconds' worth of distance run—
Yours is the Earth and everything that's in it,
And—which is more—you'll be a Man, my son![1]

Kipling said so well what we all pray our sons will become. In our surveys and interviews of hundreds of parents about what they hope most for their sons, not one of them listed a fine job—but rather things like character and integrity. It's one thing to get into this or that career—it's much more difficult to prepare a son to become a godly young man.

Not that your sons will always appreciate your efforts. But don't give in to the tendency of trying to earn their approval of how you are doing. If you let your own children be the chief evaluators of how you're doing at parenting, you'll be in trouble (and depressed to boot!). Yes, there will be days your kids will tell you that actually you're a pretty good mom or dad, and they truly appreciate your consistent and loving discipline. But then there are the other 362 days of the year.

On the other hand, when you do blow it, let your kids know you blew it. There's such a thing as sharing your mistakes and weaknesses with your children—and also letting them know what God is teaching you through them. You *will* make mistakes, to be sure—the only questions are how often and how big, and are you willing to learn from them? Will you let God help you become a better parent because of them?

MAKING YOUR REGRETS CONSTRUCTIVE ONES

Because you'll inevitably make mistakes, you'll inevitably have regrets. The key is to make them *solution-focused* regrets, not *problem-focused* regrets. Problem-focused regrets are all about loathing yourself for what you did wrong, how stupid and selfish you were, what an incredible failure you are, how your boys will probably never recover from having such a loser as a mother or father. Problem-focused regrets keep you declaring *If only . . .* and asking *What if . . . ?* Parents are capable of spending so much time wallowing in their parental failures that they never see God's loving hand in helping them learn from their failures, grow through them, and become better parents because of them.

Solution-focused regrets, on the other hand, acknowledge problems but don't stay stuck on them. A solution-focused regret asks, *What can I learn from this? How can I grow? What can I do differently next time?* Parents with solution-focused regrets aren't proud of their mistakes, but they're pleased with what they learned from them and how God can use those lessons in them and in their kids. They have learned that God can do more with a parent who walks with a limp than with a perpetual strut.

One of Gary's regrets has been how easy it is for him to let frustration turn into anger, into becoming negative, then overflowing with hypercriticism on to the boys. He used to beat himself up after every failure, but finally with God's help and Carrie's encouragement, he started focusing on the times he handled his frustration in a healthy way. And Gary discovered that there were things he could do to catch that damaging emotion before it took control—instead of raising his voice, choosing to speak a little bit softer; instead of talking faster, speaking deliberately; instead of instantly being critical, choosing to precede his comment with a compliment or some kind of encouragement. Gary discovered that when he asked Carrie and the boys to pray for him and freely remind him of his commitment, they were more than happy to do so. Actually, the boys took something of a fiendish delight in such reminding! But it has worked out okay, and Gary's solution-focused regret has led to improvement and growth.

Psychologist Larry Crabb reminds us that God's primary task isn't to fix us, pressure us, or manipulate us—but to reveal himself to us. At times his work will include probing deeply into our messy hearts or insisting we do something we really don't want to do. But the core purpose is always the same—not to repair or exhort us, but to draw us into a fuller appreciation of his beauty, to dazzle us with the sunrises of his nature, to awe us with the Grand Canyons of his character, to entice us with the endless fields of fragrant flowers blooming in his heart.[2]

Similarly, we believe that a core purpose in parenting is to be a tool in God's hands to draw our sons into a fuller appreciation of God's beauty, to dazzle them with the sunrises of his nature, to awe them with the Grand Canyons of his character, and to entice them with the endless fields of fragrant flowers blooming in his heart.

Jesus didn't simply enroll his disciples in a discipleship course. He didn't give them a notebook with fill-in-the-blank statements. He lived with them. He loved them. He showed them the Father. It isn't primarily *what* we say and teach that will transform our sons, but *who we are* and *what we do*. It is in the degree to which our boys, before their very eyes, watch Mom and Dad become "conformed to the likeness of [God's] Son" (Romans 8:29). "It is by living the Christ-life that we prove that we love it, that we have it," writes Andrew Murray, "and thus will influence the young mind to love it and to have it, too."[3]

In *Happiness Is an Inside Job,* lecturer and teacher John Powell writes about the importance of learning to be what he calls "goodfinders"[4]—the kind of person exemplified by the New Testament's Barnabas, "Son of Encouragement" (Acts 4:36). Parents need to be "goodfinders," not faultfinders—individuals who know the power of praise and the energy that comes from consistent encouragement.

Christian trends researcher George Barna lists what American adolescents need most today—and it's *not* more money or improved health care or better education or more free time. The number-one need of adolescents today is *unconditional love* from their parents. Barna reminds us that baby boomer parents are overachievers who have projected and transferred that mind-set and behavior on to their children: You are a great kid if you're the best on your soccer team, if you get straight As, if you keep your bedroom clean and organized, if you study and drive and work and obey perfectly.

For ourselves, we know we simply need to spend more time loving our boys for who they are, for who God created them to be—not for how perfectly they can live up to our expectations. To acknowledge Nathan for his quiet approach to life even when the occasion might call for him to be more proactive . . . to laugh with Matt about his rowdy antics on those nights we actually wish he would just curl up in his bedroom and read a book . . . to thank Andrew for his sparkle, knowing that if he weren't such a people pleaser, he wouldn't get his feelings hurt so easily at school. But it's too easy to get caught up in questioning or affirming their *performance*—Have you cleaned your room? How did you do at basketball practice? What's that C doing on your report card? "Goodfinders" reach down inside a person and seek to bring out and affirm who God created them uniquely to be.

KEEP PLAYING!

You may have heard the story of a mother who, hoping to encourage her young son's progress on the piano, took her boy to a Paderewski concert. After they were seated, the mother spotted a friend in the audience and walked down the aisle to greet her. Seizing the opportunity to explore the wonders of the concert hall, the little boy rose and eventually explored his way through a door marked NO ADMITTANCE.

It was only when the houselights dimmed that the mother, upon returning to her seat, discovered that her child was missing. When the curtains parted and the spotlights focused on the grand Steinway onstage, the mother saw, to her horror, her little boy sitting at the keyboard, innocently plunking out "Twinkle, Twinkle Little Star."

The piano master made his entrance, moving quickly to the piano, and whispered into the boy's ear, "Don't quit. Keep playing." Then leaning over the boy with his left hand, Paderewski began filling in a bass part. A few bars later his right arm reached around to the other side of the child as he added a running obbligato. Together, the old master and the young novice transformed a scandalous situation into a creative and wonderful experience. The audience was mesmerized.

God calls parents to be a Paderewski to their sons. Rather than scold, shame, and criticize, we need to be there to say, "That's okay, honey, don't quit, keep playing"—which is, after all, what God tells us: *Don't worry, but seek my kingdom first* (see Matthew 6:33) ... *Don't worry, I won't let anything come your way you and I can't handle together* (see 1 Corinthians 10:13) ... *Don't worry, I'm working all things together for your good* (see Romans 8:28) ... *I began a good work in you, and I'm bound to finish it* (see Philippians 1:6).

The lives of healthy and mature young men are characterized by openness, honesty, self-awareness, vulnerability, consistency, integrity, and faith—the marks of men who know God. If we are helping our sons become godly men, we will see them become man enough to—

- Acknowledge their need of God.
- Take an honest look at themselves from God's perspective (mind, will, emotions).
- Have their lives characterized by the fruit of the Spirit.
- Say, "I was wrong ... I'm sorry. Will you forgive me?"
- Face and deal with their own issues and allow God to heal their wounds.

- Become accountable to some other men.
- Love and accept those who are different than they are. They can learn how to disagree with what a person does and still see him or her as having infinite worth and value.
- Risk becoming passionate men who aren't afraid to love.
- Risk being tender as well as tough, willing to acknowledge that there is nothing as strong as gentleness and nothing as gentle as real strength.
- Model the fact that sometimes we stand tallest when we are on our knees.
- Have the courage to care, commit, make a promise . . . and keep it!

Healthy parenting has not been tried and found wanting. It has been found difficult and left untried.

Andrew came home from his second-grade class one day and found Gary in the kitchen.

"Dad," he said, barely suppressing a huge smile, "would you rather have one dollar a week for fifty-two years—or one penny, doubled each week for fifty-two weeks?"

I took the bait. "Well, anyone knows that all those years' worth of dollars have to amount to more than messing around with pennies for just one year."

His smile finally burst forth as Andrew showed me how wrong I was: A buck a week for fifty-two years earns $2,704. A penny doubled each week renders a trillion dollars in under a year.

Parenting is about multiplication—about how investing in our sons' lives today will multiply good in their future. Yet our culture offers us so many other options to invest in—like the hoard of incompetent, amoral, and uninvolved parent models on television. A *USA Today Weekend* reporter made this observation:

> How wonderful it must be to be young in this golden age of childhood, when children rule the roost and parents defer to their kids' superior intellects. . . .

Teenagers, of course, have always thought they were smarter than their parents—the crucial TV difference now is that the parents apparently agree. . . . On one program the mother doesn't think she should interfere with her fifteen-year-old son's planned sexual escapade because she believes that it would be a breach of his "privacy." On another program the dad is too preoccupied to object when his teenage son brings his sleepover girlfriend down for breakfast, and Mom must apologize when she even dares to suggest that it might be good for her daughter to go to college.[5]

Raising sons is a great honor and a tremendous responsibility. We hope that God will use this book to help you multiply your influence in the lives of your sons, and that your confidence as parents will be increased by the power of the Holy Spirit. May your relationship with your children deepen, and may God bless you richly as the parents of sons.

RECOMMENDED READING

In our extensive review of the literature we discovered that there is an abundance of books available on raising teenagers. Here are the ones that we (and many other parents we've talked with) have found to be the most helpful. They are practical, relevant, and biblically based, and we are convinced you will enjoy reading them.

Arp, David, and Claudia Arp. *Suddenly They're 13: Or the Art of Hugging a Cactus*. Grand Rapids: Zondervan, 1999.

Clark, Chap, and Steve Lee. *Boys to Men: How Fathers Can Help Build Character in Their Sons*. Chicago: Moody Press, 1990.

Cline, Foster, and Jim Fay. *Parenting Teens with Love and Logic: Preparing Adolescents for Responsible Adulthood*. Colorado Springs: NavPress, 1993.

Habermas, Ronald T. *Raising Teens While They're Still in Preschool*. Joplin, Mo.: College Press, 1998.

Habermas, Ronald T., and David Olshine. *How to Have Real Conversation with Your Teen: Tips from Veteran Youth Workers— With Teens of Their Own*. Cincinnati, Ohio: Standard, 1998.

Rainey, Dennis, and Barbara Rainey. *Parenting Today's Adolescent: Helping Your Child Avoid the Traps of the Preteen and Teen Years*. Nashville: Nelson, 1998.

Smalley, Gary, and Greg Smalley. *Bound by Honor: Fostering a Great Relationship with Your Teen*. Wheaton, Ill.: Tyndale, 1998.

Tripp, Paul David. *Age of Opportunity: A Biblical Guide to Parenting Teens*. Phillipsburg, N.J.: P & R Publishing, 1997.

NOTES

INTRODUCTION: *The Masculine Crisis*

1. Ken Gire, *The Reflective Life* (Colorado Springs: Chariot Victor, 1998), 17–18.

CHAPTER ONE: *The Unique Challenge of Raising Boys*

1. Items in this list are gleaned from the following: Herb Goldberg, *The New Male: From Self-Destruction to Self-Care* (New York: Morrow, 1979), 20–21, 44, 218; Aaron Kipnis, *Knights Without Armor* (New York: Putnam, 1992), 11–34, 47, 57, 159; Daniel Evan Weiss, *The Great Divide: How Females and Males Really Differ* (New York: Poseidon, 1991).
2. Kipnis, *Knights Without Armor*, 65–66.
3. Barbara Kantrowitz and Claudia Kalb, "Boys Will Be Boys," *Newsweek* (May 11, 1998), 54.
4. Adapted from Claude W. Olney, *Where There's a Will There's an A: How to Get Better Grades in Grade School* (Paoli, Pa.: Chesterbrook, 1983), 21. Used by permission of Olney Seminars, P.O. Box 686, Scottsdale, AZ 85252.

CHAPTER TWO: *Why Boys Act the Way They Do*

1. Donna Shalala, Secretary of Health and Human Services— "Raising the Children of the Millennium." Speech given at Bryn Mawr Presbyterian Church, Bryn Mawr, Pennsylvania (April 27, 1998).
2. Statistics gleaned from Children's Defense Fund report in Neil Howe, William Strauss, and Ian Williams, *13th Gen* (New York: Vintage, 1993), and from a special report, "Struggling to Save Our Kids," *Fortune* (August 10, 1992), 38–39.
3. Betsy Borns, *Parenting*, vol. 9, issue 2, 1995, n.p.

4. Quoted by Donna Shalala, "Raising the Children of the Millennium."

5. Richard A. Swenson, *Margin: Restoring Emotional, Physical, Financial, and Time Reserves to Overloaded Lives* (Colorado Springs: NavPress, 1992), 30.

6. Swenson, *Margin,* 62.

7. The Carnegie Council on Adolescent Development, *Great Transitions: Preparing Adolescents for a New Century* (Washington, D.C.: Carnegie Corporation, 1996), chap. 1.

8. David Elkind, *All Grown Up and No Place to Go: Teenagers in Crisis* (Reading, Mass.: Addison-Wesley, 1984), 100.

9. Elkind, *All Grown Up and No Place to Go,* 3–4.

10. Ronald Koteskey, *Understanding Adolescence* (Wheaton, Ill.: Victor, 1984), 29–30.

11. Frank Pittman, "The Masculine Mystique," *Networker* (May/June 1990), 42.

12. Noted by J. H. Gagnon, "Physical Strength, Once of Significance," in D. S. David and R. Brannon, eds., *The Forty-Nine Percent Majority: The Male Sex Role* (Reading, Mass.: Addison-Wesley, 1976), n.p.

13. Mark Rosin, Interview with Alvin Toffler, "The Family of the Future," *Parents* (March 1982), 67.

14. Personal communication from Dr. Steve Lee.

CHAPTER THREE: *Are Boys Really That Different?*

1. Excerpted from the October 1996 edition of Family News from Dr. James Dobson. Copyright © 1996 Focus on the Family. All rights reserved. International copyright secured. Reproduced with permission from Elizabeth Christine Hays, author of the list.

2. Robin Gur study quoted in Michael Gurian, *The Wonder of Boys: What Parents, Mentors, and Educators Can Do to Shape Boys into Exceptional Men* (New York: Tarcher/Putnam, 1996), 14–15.

3. Excerpted with permission from the January 1997 edition of Family News from Dr. James Dobson. Copyright © 2000 Focus on the Family. All rights reserved. International copyright secured.

4. Noted in Gurian, *The Wonder of Boys*.

5. Quoted in Michael Gurian, *A Fine Young Man: What Parents, Mentors, and Educators Can Do to Shape Adolescent Boys into Exceptional Men* (New York: Tarcher/Putnam, 1998), 210–11.

6. Gurian, *A Fine Young Man*, 221.

7. Gurian, *A Fine Young Man*, 223.

8. Quoted in *Time*, vol. 153, no. 18 (May 10, 1999), 59.

9. Anne Moir and David Jessel, *Brain Sex: The Real Difference Between Men and Women* (New York: Carol Publishing, 1991), 24.

10. Moir and Jessel, *Brain Sex*, 27.

11. Noted in Gurian, *The Wonder of Boys*, 9.

12. William Pollack, *Real Boys: Rescuing Our Sons from the Myths of Boyhood* (New York: Random House, 1998), 55–56.

13. Gurian, *The Wonder of Boys*, 11.

CHAPTER FOUR: *Made in God's Image: Balancing Mind, Will, and Emotions*

1. William T. Kirwan, *Biblical Concepts for Christian Counseling* (Grand Rapids: Baker, 1983), 46ff.

2. Gleaned from V. Waters, "Therapies for Children: Rational-Emotive Therapy," in C. R. Reynolds and T. B. Gutkin, eds., *Handbook of School Psychology* (New York: Wiley, 1982), 572.

3. Adapted from Michael E. Bernard and Marie R. Joyce, *Rational-Emotive Therapy with Children and Adolescents* (New York: Wiley, 1984), 128.

4. Archibald D. Hart, *Feeling Free* (Old Tappan, N.J.: Revell, 1979), 20.

CHAPTER FIVE: *Cultivating the Emotions of Your Son*

1. Pollack, *Real Boys*, 138.
2. Daniel Goleman, *Emotional Intelligence: Why It Can Matter More Than IQ* (New York: Bantam, 1995), 33ff.
3. Gleaned from Gurian, *A Fine Young Man*, 36ff.
4. Deborah Tannen, *You Just Don't Understand: Women and Men in Conversation* (New York: Ballantine, 1991).
5. Dorothy C. Finkelhor, *How to Make Your Emotions Work for You* (New York: Berkley Publishing, 1973), 23–24.
6. Quoted in Henry Dreher, "Do You Have a Type-C (cancer-prone) Personality?" *Redbook* (May, 1988), n.p.
7. For more information on alexithymia, see Henry Krystal, *Integration and Self-Healing: Affect, Trauma, Alexithymia* (Hillsdale, N.J.: Analytic Press, 1988).
8. Summary of conclusions drawn by Ronald F. Levant, "Toward the Reconstruction of Masculinity," *Journal of Family Psychology*, vol. 5, nos. 3 & 4 (March/June 1992), 388–89.
9. Quoted in A. J. Hostetler, "Feeling Happy, Thinking Clearly," American Psychological Association, *The Monitor* (April 1988), 6–7.

CHAPTER SIX: *What Type of Son Do You Have?*

1. David Keirsey and Marilyn Bates, *Please Understand Me* (Del Mar, Calif.: Prometheus, 1978), 1. Used by permission.
2. Adapted from Arnold H. Buss and Robert Plomin, *A Temperament Theory of Personality Development* (New York: Wiley, 1975), 237.
3. This list and the three similar lists that follow it are adapted from Earle C. Page, *Looking at Type* (Gainesville, Fla.: Center for Applications of Psychological Type, 1983).
4. These questions are taken from LaVonne Neff, *One of a Kind* (Portland, Ore.: Multnomah, 1988). This wonderful

little book unfortunately is out of print. If you come across a copy in a used bookstore, grab it.

5. For more about the value of understanding personality type, read Charles Meisgeier, Elizabeth Murphy, and Constance Meisgeier, *A Teacher's Guide to Type: A New Perspective on Individual Differences in the Classroom* (Palo Alto, Calif.: Consulting Psychologists Press, 1989).

6. We strongly urge you to read more about personality type. You may want to begin with the book *Raising Kids to Love Jesus* by H. Norman Wright and Gary J. Oliver (Ventura, Calif.: Regal, 1999), which contains four chapters on understanding and applying the insights of personality type to parenting, as well as providing practical illustrations for using these insights in your particular family setting.

CHAPTER SEVEN: *Anger: Understanding the Fundamental Male Emotion*

1. Harriet Lerner, *The Dance of Anger* (New York: Harper & Row, 1985), 1.

2. Nancy Samalin, *Love and Anger: The Parental Dilemma* (New York: Viking, 1991), 5.

3. Adapted from Gary J. Oliver and H. Norman Wright, *When Anger Hits Home* (Chicago: Moody Press, 1992), 248–49.

CHAPTER EIGHT: *Helping Your Son Cultivate Healthy Anger*

1. Archibald D. Hart, *Stress and Your Child* (Dallas: Word, 1992), 110–11. All rights reserved. Used by permission.

2. Adapted from Carol Tavris, *Anger: The Misunderstood Emotion* (New York: Simon & Schuster, 1982), 136–37.

3. Willard Gaylin, *The Male Ego* (New York: Viking, 1992), 251.

CHAPTER NINE: *Responding to the Emotions Your Son Evokes from You*

1. The biblical Barnabas (whose name means "Son of Encouragement"—see Acts 4:36) was known to have a knack for recognizing and encouraging others' potential (see Acts 9:27; 11:22–26; 15:37–39).

CHAPTER TEN: *What Boys Need from Their Dad*

1. Adapted from comments by Richard Levak in foreword of Will Glennon, *Fathering: Strengthening Connection with Your Children No Matter Where You Are* (Berkeley, Calif.: Conari Press, 1995), xiii–xiv.
2. These thoughts are adapted from Aaron Hass, *The Gift of Fatherhood: How Men's Lives Are Transformed by Their Children* (New York: Simon & Schuster, 1994), 9–10.
3. Glennon, *Fathering*, 32.
4. Quoted in Gurian, *The Wonder of Boys*, 111.
5. Three times this decade—in 1992, 1996, and 1999—the National Center for Fathering (10200 W. 75th Street, Suite 267, Shawnee Mission, KS 66204; phone 913-384-4661; fax 913-384-4665) polled Americans to determine their opinions about the status, behaviors, and attitudes of fathers in America. These statistics come from the 1999 poll.
6. Gleaned from Ken Canfield, *The 7 Secrets of Effective Fathers* (Wheaton, Ill.: Tyndale, 1995); David Blankenhorn, *Fatherless America* (New York: Basic Books, 1995); and Gurian, *The Wonder of Boys*.
7. Noted in Samuel Osherson, *Finding Our Fathers: The Unfinished Business of Manhood* (New York: Free Press, 1986).
8. David Mains, *Healing the Dysfunctional Church Family* (Wheaton, Ill.: Victor, 1992), 123.
9. Insights gleaned from John Piper, *A Hunger for God: Desiring God Through Fasting and Prayer* (Wheaton, Ill.: Crossway, 1997).

10. Glennon, *Fathering,* 154–55.

11. Story quoted in Glennon, *Fathering,* 157.

12. Quoted in Glennon, *Fathering,* 4–5.

13. Quoted in Glennon, *Fathering,* 5.

14. Quoted in Wayne Rickerson, *Family Fun and Togetherness* (Ventura, Calif.: Gospel Light, 1979), n.p.

15. White House Conference on Children (April 17, 1997).

16. Glennon, *Fathering,* 121.

17. Quoted in Gurian, *The Wonder of Boys,* 126.

18. Quoted in Joe White, *Faith Training: Raising Kids Who Love the Lord* (Colorado Springs: Focus on the Family, 1996), 39.

CHAPTER ELEVEN: *What Boys Need from Their Mom*

1. Quoted in "A Heart of Goldie," *Good Housekeeping,* vol. 228, no. 4 (April 1999), 200.

CHAPTER TWELVE: *What Boys Need from Your Marriage*

1. John Rosemond, *Because I Said So!: A Collection of 366 Insightful and Thought-Provoking Reflections on Parenting and Family Life* (Kansas City, Mo.: Andrews McMeel, 1996), n.p.

2. Discussed in John M. Gottman, *The Heart of Parenting* (New York: Simon & Schuster, 1997).

3. H. Norman Wright and Gary Oliver, *How to Bring Out the Best in Your Spouse* (Ann Arbor, Mich.: Servant, 1996), 59.

CHAPTER THIRTEEN: *Helping Your Son Cultivate a Heart for God: Discipleship and Parenting*

1. Gottman, *The Heart of Parenting,* 18.

2. Larry Crabb, *Connecting: Healing for Ourselves and Our Relationships* (Nashville: Word, 1997), 45.

3. The book *Desiring God* by John Piper (Portland, Ore.: Multnomah, 1996) has challenged and transformed our ideas about joy. Piper's thorough study on what God has to say about joy seems to consistently surprise many Christians.

CHAPTER FOURTEEN: *Helping Your Son Move from*
Adolescence to Adulthood: Early Adolescence (Ages 13–15)

1. Gleaned from Gurian, *A Fine Young Man,* xix–xxiv, 15; and
   Pollack, *Real Boys,* 11–26.
2. Statistics gleaned from Gurian, *A Fine Young Man,* 14ff.
3. Gurian, *A Fine Young Man,* 5.
4. Gleaned from Bruce Baldwin, "Puberty and Parents," in
   Human Development 91/92, eds. Larry and Judith Fenson
   (Guilford, Conn.: Dushkin, 1991), 183–87.

CHAPTER FIFTEEN: *Helping Your Son Move from*
Adolescence to Adulthood: Late Adolescence (Ages 16–19)

1. Personal correspondence from Steve and Twyla Lee.
2. John H. Flavell, *Cognitive Development* (Englewood Cliffs,
   N.J.: Prentice Hall, 1977), 125.
3. Tom Bisset, *Why Christian Kids Leave the Faith* (Nashville:
   Nelson, 1992), 103.
4. There are several helpful books you might want to read
   and share with your son: Paul Little's, *Know Why You Believe,*
   Updated and Expanded Edition (Colorado Springs: Chariot
   Victor, 1999); Josh McDowell's, *The New Evidence That*
   Demands a Verdict (Nashville: Nelson, 1999); and Lee
   Strobel's, *The Case for Christ* (Grand Rapids: Zondervan,
   1998) just to name a few.
5. Mihaly Csikszentmihalyi and Reed Larson, *Being Adolescent:*
   Growth and Conflict in the Teenage Years (New York: Basic
   Books, 1984), 9.
6. Quoted in Gurian, *The Wonder of Boys,* 222.
7. Josh McDowell and Dick Day, *Why Wait?* (San Bernadino,
   Calif.: Here's Life Publishers, 1987), 99.
8. See such resources as Richard Durfield and Reneé
   Durfield, *Raising Them Chaste: A Practical Strategy for Helping*
   Your Teen Wait Till Marriage (Minneapolis: Bethany House,
   1991); Stanton Jones and Brenna Jones, *How and When to*

Tell Your Kids About Sex: A Lifelong Approach to Shaping Your Child's Sexual Character (Colorado Springs: NavPress, 1993); Mark Laaser, *Talking to Your Kids About Sex* (Colorado Springs: WaterBrook, 1999); and the True Love Waits web site at www.truelovewaits.com.
9. Carol Kuykendall, *Learning to Let Go* (Grand Rapids: Zondervan, 1985), 15.

CONCLUSION: *Caring Is Not Enough*

1. Quoted in James Dalton Morrison, ed., *Masterpieces of Religious Verse* (New York: Harper & Brothers, 1948), 279–80.
2. Adapted from Crabb, *Connecting*, 10.
3. Andrew Murray, *How to Raise Your Children for Christ* (Minneapolis: Bethany House, 1975), 12.
4. John Powell, *Happiness Is an Inside Job* (Allen, Tex.: Tabor, 1989), 89.
5. Robert Blanco, "The World According to TV," *USA Today* (August 6, 1999), E1–2.